COUNTER-BLASTING CANADA

COUNTER-BLASTING CANADA

MARSHALL McLuhan

WYNDHAM Lewis

WILFRED Watson AND SHEILA Watson

EDITED BY

Gregory Betts, Paul Hjartarson, and Kristine Smitka

THE UNIVERSITY
of ALBERTA PRESS

Published by

The University of Alberta Press
Ring House 2
Edmonton, Alberta, Canada   T6G 2E1
www.uap.ualberta.ca

Copyright © 2016 Gregory Betts,
Paul Hjartarson, and Kristine Smitka

**Library and Archives Canada
Cataloguing in Publication**

Counterblasting Canada :
Marshall McLuhan, Wyndham Lewis, Wilfred
Watson, and Sheila Watson /
edited by Gregory Betts,Paul Hjartarson,
and Kristine Smitka.

Includes bibliographical references and index.
Issued in print and electronic formats.
ISBN 978-1-77212-037-0 (paperback).
—ISBN 978-1-77212-149-0 (epub).
—ISBN 978-1-77212-150-6 (mobi).
—ISBN 978-1-77212-151-3 (pdf)

1. McLuhan, Marshall, 1911–1980.
2. Lewis, Wyndham, 1882–1957. 3. Watson,
Wilfred, 1911–1998. 4. Watson, Sheila, 1909–
1998. 5. Canadian literature (English)—20th
century—History and criticism. 6. Vorticism—
Canada. 7. Art and literature—Canada.
8. Modernism (Literature)—Canada.
9. Canada—Intellectual life—20th century.
I. Betts, Gregory, 1975–, author,
editor II. Hjartarson, Paul Ivar, editor
III. Smitka, Kristine, 1982–, editor

PS8117.C69 2016   C810.9'0054
C2016-901204-2   C2016-901205-0

First edition, first printing, 2016.
Printed and bound in Canada by
Friesens, Altona, Manitoba.
Copyediting and proofreading
by Joanne Muzak.
Indexing by Adrian Mather.

The University of Alberta Press is committed
to protecting our natural environment. As
part of our efforts, this book is printed on
Enviro Paper: it contains 100% post-consumer
recycled fibres and is acid- and chlorine-free.

The University of Alberta Press gratefully
acknowledges the support received for its
publishing program from the Government
of Canada, the Canada Council for the
Arts, and the Government of Alberta
through the Alberta Media Fund.

This book has been published with the help of
a grant from the Canadian Federation for the
Humanities and Social Sciences, through the
Awards to Scholarly Publications Program,
using funds provided by the Social Sciences
and Humanities Research Council of Canada.

Government of Canada   Gouvernement du Canada

Canada Council for the Arts   Conseil des Arts du Canada

Alberta Government

re maelström and vortex

Wilfred Watson

the ezra 1 pound
vortex 2 is
a 3 structure
　　　　　　　　of 4 energies
the percy 5 wyndham lewis
　　　　　vortex 6 is
a 7 structure
　　　　　　　　of 8 enmity
9 by

which 1 the
artist 2 holds
up 3 the
　　　　dead 4 world
to 5 its
　　　　living 6 shame—
the 7 mcluhan
　　　　vortex, 8 as
9 beautiful

with 1 concupiscence
of 2 ergo-sum
as 3 the
　　　parabola 4 descartes
fell 5 in
　　　love 6 with,
writes 7 an
　　　equation 8 for
9 the

maelström 1 versus

the 2 maelström...

yet 3 still

the 4 maelström

hurls 5 stars

against 6 men,

men 7 against

stars... 8 It

9 is

the 1 summer

solstice 2 and

as 3 this

long-drawn-out 4 summery

day 5 drains

light 6 out

of 7 the

lagoon, 8 I

9 think

of 1 edith

sitwell's 2 "still

falls 3 the

rain" 4 and

of 5 F.T. Prince's

"soldiers 6 bathing"...

Still 7 falls

blind 8 as

9 our

loss 1 the

hammer 2 of

the 3 developer

upon 4 man's

body 5 nailed

to 6 the

god 7 upon

the 8 cross...

9 Xt's

```
         blood   1   splashes
          the    2   firmament
          but    3   in    .
                              despite   4   of
         this    5   and
                                 of   6   the
        terror   7   of
                              god's   8   peace
9   still

         still   1   rides
          the    2   bronco
        buster   3   the
                         chain-saw   4   maelström
           to    5   a
                      phantasmagoric   6   success
       without   7   any
                          substance   8   or
9   duration,

          his    1   hands
       reaching  2   towards
          the    3   bird-
                           mocking   4   sky
          an     5   arm's
                            length   6   or
         less,   7   and
                           howling   8   his
9   name

          out    1   at
        oblivion, 2   yesterday's
         soft    3   cunt,
                            which   4   like
      tomorrow's 5   sun
                           forgets  6   today
         what    7   tonight's
                             moon   8   has
9   done...
```

Contents

III Art and Anti-Environment

Prolepsis

Acknowledgements

THE FRENCH POET Isidore Ducasse (the Comte de
Lautréamont) said that "poetry must be made by all." That may
be so, but it is certainly the case that all books are made by many
people. Indeed, many hands were involved in the creation of this
book and all deserve our sincere gratitude. We are especially
grateful to the estate of Wilfred Watson for permission to include
"re maelström and vortex" as the epigraph to *Counterblasting
Canada*. The editors would also like to thank Raymond Frogner and
James Frank, University of Alberta Archives; Gabrielle Earnshaw
and Kathryn Van Dusyn, Special Collections and Archives, John
M. Kelly Library; EMiC UA research group members, particularly
Kristin Fast, who helped organize the Watsons-McLuhan panels for
the 2011 Media Ecology Association conference where this project
was first conceived, and Harvey Quaman, whose support proved
invaluable; Sophie Tellier and Martin Lanthier, Library and Archives
Canada; Geoffrey Harder and his staff in the Digital Initiatives
Centre at the University of Alberta; Marco Adria who, as director of
the Communications and Technology program at the University of
Alberta, was instrumental in bringing the Media Ecology Association
to Edmonton in 2011 to celebrate the centenary of Marshall
McLuhan's birth; Wayne DeFehr for his contributions to the
Watsons-McLuhan panels in 2011; Elena Lamberti for her sugges-
tion of the title for this book; Michael McLuhan, Shirley Neuman,
Fred Flahiff, and Diane Bessai; the Social Sciences and Humanities
Research Council of Canada; Awards to Scholarly Publications
Program; and especially all of the contributors to this project.

Introduction
Gregory Betts, Paul Hjartarson, and Kristine Smitka

> The vortex is the point of maximum energy.
>> It represents, in mechanics, the greatest efficiency.
>> We use the words "greatest efficiency" in the precise
> sense—as they would be used in a text book of MECHANICS.
>> You may think of man as that toward which perception
> moves. You may think of him as the TOY of circumstance,
> as the plastic substance. RECEIVING impressions.
>> OR you may think of him as DIRECTING a certain
> fluid force against circumstance, as CONCEIVING
> instead of merely observing and reflecting.
>
> —Ezra Pound, "Vortex"

I

IN 1914, Wyndham Lewis, Ezra Pound, and a
handful of experimental artists launched England's first prototypical
avant-garde movement. The group called themselves "vorticists"
and provocatively named their magazine *Blast: Review of the Great
English Vortex*. The first issue appeared in England with a spectac-
ular fuchsia cover and began with the brazen declaration, "Long Live
the Vortex! Long live the great art vortex sprung up in the centre of
this town" ("Long" 7). The opening manifesto of this already existent
vortex declared the movement for the "Reality of the Present—not
for the sentimental Future, or the sacripant Past." A movement,
then, grasping the vitality of the moment, including the "stupidity,
animalism and dreams" of humanity. Their embrace of the "crude
energy" of life includes a commitment to violence, harsh angles,
and ugliness. The work that follows in the magazine is strikingly
jarring, blatantly aggressive, and deliberately obnoxious. This is,

indeed, the origin of the famous cult of ugliness that became an important catchphrase of twentieth-century modernism. No longer would art bend to prettify itself, to make its language ornamental, to flatter or mollify its readership, no longer was it bogged down and beholden to the past. Art and literature were breaking free of those shackles and consciously inciting anger and anxiety; as Ezra Pound wrote in the first issue, "Come my cantilations, / Let us dump our hatreds into one bunch and be done with them" ("Come" 45).

Led by what Hugh Kenner calls the "savagely energetic intelligence" of Wyndham Lewis (xiv), the vorticists were initially an outgrowth of the radical expressionism championed by Marinetti and the Italian Futurists. They borrowed the violent rejection of the past (renouncing museums, for instance), but broke with the Italians over the utopian future and Marinetti's notion of art's relationship to time. Lest they be confused with the Futurists' "savage worship" of the automobile or with their hypocritical pedantry, Lewis paused in the second issue of *Blast* (July 1915) to clarify the difference ("A Review" 42): unlike the Active-Man model of the Futurists, he explained, the best art is produced outside the "troubled world" to synthesize and represent that same world more precisely. Accordingly, vorticists sought to remove personality from art to attain the greatest level of abstraction. In defiance of possible futures and self-promoting personalities, vorticism set about producing an unprecedented analysis of the present, including its technologies, media, politics, and architecture.

The machinic present the vorticists were discovering, however, acted against them and interrupted their progress: the movement was truncated by the descent of the continent into war, an interruption from which it never quite recovered. In all, the vorticists published two issues of *Blast*, held one art exhibition, and organized a small number of public lectures and showings at their home in the Rebel Arts Centre in London. While the movement died on the vine, its influence lingered in the work of Lewis and Pound, and it continues to capture international attention in the form of travelling exhibitions, anniversaries, and numerous books and volumes. The vorticists never intended that the movement be confined to the British Isles and, as a testament to their accomplishments, it continues to circulate in transnational contexts today.

Counterblasting Canada examines a rich network of Canadian intersections with, and extrapolations of, the vorticist narrative. Without question, Lewis was the most Canadian of the so-called titans of modernism. Born in Canada, Lewis also served with the Canadian army in the First World War, took refuge from the Second in Windsor and Toronto, and maintained a Canadian passport until his death. As has been documented in Sheila Watson's special issue of *artscanada* on Wyndham Lewis in Canada (1967), George Woodcock's edited *Wyndham Lewis in Canada* (1971), Catharine Mastin, Robert Stacey, and Thomas Dilworth's *"The Talented Intruder": Wyndham Lewis in Canada, 1939–1945* (1993), and Gregory Betts's chapter on vorticism in Canada in *Avant-Garde Canadian Literature: The Early Manifestations* (2013), Lewis had numerous Canadian family connections and produced a great deal of work here. While Lewis was not specifically responsive to the Canadian literary milieu, his connections to this country are not insignificant. This book, finally, tracks his involvement in and influence on Canadian letters.

During his time in Windsor, for instance, Lewis delivered a series of lectures at Assumption College in 1943 on the importance of North American cultural energy. These lectures were eventually collected into *America and Cosmic Man*, a volume that, as Adam Hammond argues in this collection, "demonstrates a passionate enthusiasm for North American society and politics." In attendance at the lectures was a young Canadian scholar then working in St. Louis, Marshall McLuhan. McLuhan was deeply impressed by the lectures and initiated a correspondence with Lewis that would eventually lead Lewis to briefly relocate to St. Louis. Amongst other important ideas, Lewis's Windsor lecture introduced McLuhan to the idea that technology helps fashion a global village by externalizing and projecting the private imagination into the public realm. With the advancement of globe-spanning mass media, people were suddenly imaginatively and emotionally involved with others around the entire planet. Lewis's residence in America was truncated by money and visa complications, however, and he returned to Windsor. Lewis, in turn, lured McLuhan back to Canada with the promise of starting a magazine together—a revival of *Blast*, no less—but he whisked back to England shortly after McLuhan had quit his job in St. Louis and relocated to Toronto, where he would stay for the rest of his life.

McLuhan's intersections with Lewis did not end with that disappointment. In 1947, McLuhan developed some of the ideas he gleaned from Lewis's Windsor lectures into an entire (as yet unpublished) book on the "New American Vortex" that he hoped could be initiated. In 1951, McLuhan published *The Mechanical Bride*, a book he freely admitted was largely inspired by Lewis's *Time and Western Man* (1927). Although McLuhan's career branched out from this vorticist origin in various directions, he never lost his interest in Lewis; on the contrary, he attracted colleagues and students, many of whom had independently found their way to Lewis and vorticism; together, they began an assessment of his work. McLuhan's students at the University of Toronto became some of the world's principal scholars of Wyndham Lewis and vorticism. Hugh Kenner, for instance, who in an acclaimed study of the London "vortex" coined the phrase "titans of modernism" used above, produced the first book-length study of Lewis's works in 1954. A decade later, the author Sheila Watson, who rediscovered Lewis's work while spending a year in Paris with her husband, Wilfred Watson, completed an important dissertation on the overarching aesthetics of Lewis's career (supervised by McLuhan), as well as the special Lewis issue of *artscanada*. She was the first to link both his literature and visual art to a central, coherent expressionist philosophy. Others interested in Lewis and vorticism, such as Wilfred Watson, John Reid, and Edward Carpenter, congregated around McLuhan, who, in turn, self-published *Counterblast*, a lovely tribute to the fortieth anniversary of *Blast* that highlighted the ongoing need for another blast, especially in Canada. The 1954 chapbook was designed and typeset by Harley Parker, another important figure in the growing network of Canadian vorticists. Parker and McLuhan would carry on to collaborate on a number of projects, including an expanded book-length edition of *Counterblast* in 1969.

Before Sheila Watson's dissertation on Lewis, when she was still teaching at Moulton Ladies' College in Toronto, she conceived of and began writing *The Double Hook*, the novel that was quickly registered as one of the landmark works of Canadian modernism when it was published in 1959. According to Betts, Glenn Willmott, and others, the composition of *The Double Hook* was greatly influenced by Lewis and McLuhan in both its experimental form and content. In *Counterblasting Canada*, Linda Morra advances these arguments by noting that "there is no better place…to observe the ideological affinities between McLuhan and Watson than in the characterization of the artist figure, Felix," (215) in Watson's novel *The Double Hook*. Nevertheless, these affinities were peppered with points of departure, as highlighted throughout the collection. Dean Irvine, accordingly, suggests that we need to recognize *The Double Hook*'s inherent dialogism; in particular, he draws attention to Watson's consistent, career-length use of self-conscious satire (which he describes as "metasatire") to comment on the role of art in society. It is through Watson's metasatire, Irvine argues, that her art is able to imagine counter-environments that might allow a society to see itself. Indeed, McLuhan argued that exactly such a role was particular to art and its essential contribution to society. Watson's fictions, meanwhile, depict the devastating impact of a lack of art on a community and thus represent counter-environments in their subsequent collapse into either violence or mythology. Irvine tracks both McLuhan's and Watson's work in this vein back to Lewis's writings in *Men Without Art* (1934) where he first proposed the fundamental equation of art and satire, and dependency of "civilized behaviour" on art and ritual.

Wilfred Watson, too, became deeply invested in art's role in moderating human violence. When Watson began his career as a poet, he was steeped in English modernism, and thoroughly conversant with the works and criticism of T.S. Eliot. Eliot had, in fact, published Watson's first poetry collection *Friday's Child* (1955), which went on to win both the Governor General's award for poetry and the British Arts Council Poetry Prize that year. According to Paul Hjartarson and Shirley Neuman, "Watson entered the 1960s having heeded criticisms that poems in *Friday's Child* were derivative of the Modernists and that he had not found his own voice; his journals through the late 1950s include several assessments of what he had achieved or failed to achieve with that collection" (86). Years later, reflecting on this period in his development, Watson would claim, "I consciously attempted to follow Ezra Pound & unlearn what I'd learned from the poets of the Roberts Faber Book of Modern Verse, which started with an anachronistic inclusion of G.M. Hopkins and end[ed] with one or two lyrics by Dylan Thomas" (86). Some of Watson's "unlearning" was "enabled by his systematic reading of the works of Wyndham Lewis beginning in late 1955 and intensified after Sheila Watson began her Ph.D. research on that writer" (86). According to Watson, he first met McLuhan in 1947; their relationship as writers, however, did not begin to develop until 1961 when they heard one another give papers at an Humanities Association of Canada meeting in Montreal. The turn to Lewis and McLuhan provoked a significant shift in his poetics. For instance, the calm, meditative lyricism predicated on a stable subject position navigating a troubled world disappeared, gradually replaced by ever more aggressive experiments with multimedia, polyvocal experimentation, total theatre, and radical politics. Paul Tiessen argues that McLuhan valued Watson as the embodiment of the avant-garde artist, capable of waking the somnambulant public; simultaneously, Watson probed McLuhan's theorization of technology and art when crafting his stage productions. Taken together, as Betts argues, with their innovative teaching, creative writing, and academic writing, McLuhan, Wilfred Watson, and Sheila Watson actively attempted to create an immersive maelstrom, ultimately a counter-environment, through which to finally regard the psychological and cultural impact of media.

In *Counterblasting Canada*, eleven leading scholars offer a new context in which to situate the writings of Wyndham Lewis, Marshall McLuhan, Sheila Watson, and Wilfred Watson, and in a series of radical new readings and interpretations of their work, demonstrate the importance of the intellectual concerns that link these key figures of twentieth-century Canadian culture. They represent the core of a group unified by a shared intellectual pursuit that followed in the wake of the initial vorticist blast. Although these writers are distinguished by their distinct interests, aesthetics, and philosophical orientations, taken together they constitute a group we discuss cumulatively as Canadian vorticism. As this moniker implies, this avant-garde network is both embedded in a national context and, as the inclusion of Lewis insists, extends beyond the nation into broader international artistic networks. We are not attempting to erase Lewis's more significant role in English modernism; his Canadianness is not the central question or concern of this project. Rather, *Counterblasting Canada* looks backwards to the intellectual inheritance of the Canadian vorticists from their English avant-garde progenitors, particularly from Lewis, and situates them in a diverse and multidisciplinary Canadian assemblage of authors and artists.

The "Analepsis" and "Prolepsis" sections of *Counterblasting Canada* focus on the special institutional role played by McLuhan, and consider various developments from his career-length work critiquing and even remaking the institutions of cultural analysis. Indeed, McLuhan can be distinguished from the other Canadian vorticists by the extent of his involvement in remapping the institutions that facilitate academic literary studies to include mass media, popular culture, and other forms of analysis of the effects of technology. He began in the English department but was ultimately pushed out of that space because of his unorthodox approach to his discipline. On October 24, 1963, McLuhan received the official approval from Claude Bissell, president of the University of Toronto, to open the Centre for Culture and Technology, a space designed specifically to create a new forum for this broader media studies. The centre was an obvious extension of his interdisciplinary study of media in all its aspects, but it also facilitated his experiments with radical pedagogy—that is, teaching methods intended specifically to disrupt student consciousness of their media-saturated environments. Between the open door policy that allowed anybody to drop in for a class or session, and the various celebrities who did (including John Lennon and Yoko Ono), his work there certainly shattered the normal habits of academia. It is widely acknowledged that the field of communication studies emerged out of McLuhan's concerted, interdisciplinary study of mass media and popular culture in his books and at the centre. While this collection of essays approach Canadian vorticism from a primarily literary studies orientation, in the "Analepsis" and "Prolepsis" sections, Leon Surette and Darren Wershler consider the importance of McLuhan's engagements with the institutions of higher learning and the consequences of his entanglements with disciplinary boundaries. The final essay also suggests the possibility of revisiting all the subjects of *Counterblasting Canada* from a communication studies perspective, discourse, and methodology. In this way, Wershler's essay provides a projective bridge between this and future interdisciplinary scholarly projects.

II

Marshall McLuhan gained international fame as a public intellectual for his theories on the importance of media and technology to society and its individuals, but, of course, this is not all that he did during his lifetime. Recent scholarly re-evaluations by the likes of Elena Lamberti, Richard Cavell, Jeffrey Schnapp, and Adam Michaels—not to mention Douglas Coupland's popular market biography of McLuhan—have begun to draw attention to McLuhan as a humanities professor, as a pioneer in book publishing, and even as an artist. *Counterblasting Canada* extends these recent efforts by situating him within a Canadian social and intellectual milieu of like-minded thinkers and artists.

There are two common ways to describe the history of McLuhan's reception. One interprets the current fascination with

McLuhan—a fascination that was not ignited by but that certainly fueled his centenary in 2011—as a renewal of interest. This narrative of "rebirth" (Lamberti 5) or "resurfac[ing]" (Grosswiler xi) traces the rise of McLuhan's star status in the 1960s, its diminishment in the 1970s and 1980s, and a resurgence that begins in the 1990s in response to technological developments that seemed to be transforming the world into the very global village McLuhan had foretold. The second school of thought argues that the decline in McLuhan's reputation "during the 1970s...was largely limited to North America, where he was almost exclusively read as a communications critic" to the detriment of his reputation; instead, Richard Cavell asserts the importance of McLuhan's work to the theories of "Eco, Lefebvre, Baudrillard, Kittler, Deleuze and Guattari, Barthes, and Derrida" and to "a wide range of artists" and to "media production in general" (Cavell, *McLuhan in Space* xvi). This second position attests to the interdisciplinary nature of McLuhan's writing, the ways in which he has inspired both critics and artists on an international scale.

Critical engagement with Marshall McLuhan has been extensive, and new orientations for critical analysis of his work continue to surface. Cavell, for instance, in his 2002 book *McLuhan in Space: A Cultural Geography*, argues that space, rather than technology, is the unifying concept of his oeuvre. McLuhan has been repositioned both within modernity (Judith Stamps) and within modernist and postmodern contexts (Glenn Willmott), a move that aligns him with cultural studies and all of its material preoccupations (Paul Grosswiler). He has been resituated not only in literary contexts, most recently via a formalist analysis of his mosaic compositional strategies (Elena Lamberti), but also in relation to the Toronto School of Communication Theory, and specifically in dialogue with the work of Harold Innis that resulted in the delineation of communications as a discrete field of inquiry (Rita Watson and Menahem Blondheim). In debates concerning a tradition of Canadian writing on technological development—the triad of McLuhan, Innis, and Grant (Arthur Kroker)—McLuhan's contribution continues to be examined. Marshall McLuhan is most frequently, and most famously, celebrated—or denigrated—as a media guru who prophesied the world in which we now live. The characterization of McLuhan as media guru was at the forefront of Douglas Coupland's biography of McLuhan in the Extraordinary Canadians series; but, regrettably, Coupland perpetuates the repeatedly debunked myth that McLuhan was a solitary genius. He describes McLuhan's acumen as biologically determined by the double arteries that fed his brain, then places this medical evidence in a pastiche of other determining factors (most frequently his relationship with his mother) to attest to the singularity of McLuhan's brilliance. In so doing, Coupland perpetuates McLuhan's star status, founded on his ability to foretell the future; his importance is not only historical, Coupland argues, but also pressingly relevant: we should look back at him to "find out what's coming next" (15). Add to this list the critical guides, W. Terrence Gordon's *McLuhan: A Guide for the Perplexed* (2010) being a chief example, and you will find a plethora of approaches that attest to McLuhan's interdisciplinary engagements and contemporary relevance.

This collection differs from the existing wave of new scholarship on McLuhan by situating him within a Canadian assemblage of creative writers, visual artists, and academics. To situate him in this way is to shift the focus from McLuhan as solitary genius to the network of artists and intellectuals with whom he was in regular conversation and to reconsider debates among members of the group. This intellectual and social network was not motivated by nationalist ambitions but by shared interests in technology and in the role of the artist. Although it was formed at a particularly galvanizing moment in the history of Canadian nationalism, and although the writers, artists, and academics often spoke to (and frequently against) that wider *Weltanschauung*, this Canadian assemblage was distinctly international in its imaginative scope. The core dialogue investigated in this collection is the web of interconnections shared by Sheila Watson, Wilfred Watson, and Marshall McLuhan stemming from their interests in and interactions with Wyndham Lewis. These dialogues are documented in notebooks and correspondence, and in their published work, both individual and co-authored. This core network bifurcated into the specific locales of Toronto and Edmonton, and then cross-pollinated in a rhizomatic pattern with other artistic producers, including Jack Shadbolt, Harley Parker, and General Idea, which expanded the network into diverse geographical locales.

If we imagine this conversation as a series of concentric circles, there is the Watson, Watson, McLuhan dialogue at the centre of the vortex; expanding outward, we see a core collective of thinkers grappling with Lewis and McLuhan's work, and challenging both with insights of their own. Of course, these concentric circles, much like radio waves, do not stop at national borders, but in fact radiate outward into ever expanding geographical patterns. To situate McLuhan in this environment is to speak back to the narrative that he emerged from isolation and lived and operated singularity, instead situating him in a transnational network of thinkers. Furthermore, scholars—and especially scholars in *Counterblasting Canada*—are only beginning to trace the extent of his involvement in and contributions to Canadian literature. The very depiction of McLuhan as a solitary genius is itself perplexing, given that he thrived on collaborative engagements, especially with Canadian writers, even if his collaborators sometimes felt silenced or overwhelmed in the process.

In an intriguing synchronicity, while McLuhan scholars are becoming increasingly attuned to the fact that he was not just an abstract theorist or pop culture spectacle, scholars of Canadian literature have become increasingly attuned to his significance and contributions to literary networks here, especially via his relationships to both Watsons. *Counterblasting Canada* builds from this recent confluence of scholarly attention on McLuhan from both directions by attending to a close network of his Canadian friends and colleagues that we have taken to calling the Canadian vorticists. Indeed, our attention shifts to the vibrant network of like-minded fellow travellers, primarily the novelist Sheila Watson and her husband, the poet and playwright, Wilfred Watson, by exploring the grounds and implications of their shared intellectual inheritance from the British avant-garde school of vorticism and its related modernisms. It has been our task not just to map out the networks linking these principal figures, but also to advance scholarship on each of them through the connections we have discovered.

III

Recent public release of archival documents has allowed contributors to *Counterblasting Canada* to investigate hitherto unacknowledged interconnections among the Canadian vorticists. In fact, the Sheila Watson fonds at St. Michael's College, University of Toronto only opened to the public in 2009. When letters by Wilfred Watson and Marshall McLuhan in that collection are added to their counterparts by Sheila Watson in the Marshall McLuhan fonds at Library and Archives Canada and in the Wilfred Watson fonds at the University of Alberta, there are more than two thousand extant letters among these three writers alone. Those letters, along with the writers' notebooks, journals, and manuscripts, illuminate their rich and sustained conversation about technology and the role of the artist in the modern world. *Counterblasting Canada* represents the first endeavour to engage critically with the implications of these conversations and uses archival evidence to contextualize the publications of each author within the context of their ongoing dialogue. In this way, our project strives to unearth a dialogue, while remaining cautious of any assumptions that the archive can provide evidence free of ideology. As Derrida has warned us, the desire to unveil the truth through the archival (re)turn remains an impossibility. For the archive, as the prosthesis of memory, remains incomplete and deeply embedded in (and reflective of) ideological conflict. For this reason, the archive cannot hold the final word, but rather opens to future conversations.

To introduce readers to emerging lines of scholarly inquiry concerning Canadian vorticism, we have divided *Counterblasting Canada* into three sections: "The Art of Being Read," "The Antennae of the Race," and "Art and Anti-Environment."

These three sections are framed by an "Analepsis," consisting of Leon Surette's essay, "Remembering McLuhan," which we have placed at the outset of *Counterblasting Canada*, and a "Prolepsis," Darren Wershler's "Marshall McLuhan as Vanishing Mediator," which we have made the final essay. Once we have discussed the first three sections, we will explain our rationale for framing the collection with these essays.

The first section, "The Art of Being Read," which includes essays by Gregory Betts, Elena Lamberti, and Adam Hammond, examines how Marshall McLuhan, Sheila Watson, and Wilfred Watson read Wyndham Lewis, particularly his later, "North American" texts. How these writers understood and responded to Lewis's argument in *America and Cosmic Man* (1948) that "a new kind of 'Cosmic Man'…was being forged in the cultural turmoil of the American nation" (Betts 21) is of particular interest. Through theories of the avant-garde (Betts), cosmopolitanism (Lamberti), and global modernism (Hammond), this section resists—as do the other sections—a diachronic argument of influence, instead illuminating late modernism's departures from its earlier iterations.

"Approaching McLuhan's scholarship as the expression of an avant-garde initiative," Gregory Betts argues in "The New Canadian Vortex: Marshall McLuhan and the Avant-Garde Function of Counter-Environments," "helps to unravel a central paradox of his scholarly production: how a rather conservative mid-century English professor of somewhat obscure literary texts at a famously conservative institution became the spokesman for the emerging contemporary technological age" (20). Betts locates McLuhan's unique conception of the avant-garde in his response to Lewis's Windsor lectures: after hearing Lewis deliver those lectures, subsequently published under the title *America and Cosmic Man* (1948), McLuhan wrote his first, still unpublished, book, *The New American Vortex*. In the opening pages of that text, McLuhan declares, "After Joyce, Eliot, Pound and Lewis it is for us in America to form the new vortex in which a totally new assimilation of human traditions must occur" (qtd. in Betts 21).

Like Betts, Elena Lamberti approaches McLuhan's writing through Lewis's. In her essay, "Watson, McLuhan (& Lewis): Conscious (Modernist) Solitudes, Challenging Canadians," however, the key text is not *American and Cosmic Man* but *Self Condemned*. For Lamberti, 1954, the year in which Lewis published *Self Condemned*, is a key date, for in that year Marshall McLuhan published *Counterblast*, his manifesto for a North American vorticist movement, and Sheila Watson, Lamberti argues, began final revisions to *The Double Hook*. McLuhan, in his Introduction to the 1954 edition of *Counterblast*, in fact cites both *America and Cosmic Man* and *Self Condemned*:

> In 1954 Wyndham Lewis blasted Toronto in the novel SELF-CONDEMNED. His René (reborn) seeking his true spiritual self selects Toronto, Momaco: (Mom & Co.) as a colonial cyclotron in which to annihilate his human ego. He succeeds.
>
> In AMERICA AND COSMIC MAN Lewis saw North America as a benign rock crusher in which all remnants of European nationalism and individualism were happily reduced to cosmic baby powder. The new media are blowing a lot of this baby powder around the pendant cradle of the New Man Today. The dust gets in our eyes.
>
> COUNTERBLAST 1954 blows aside this dust for a few moments and offers a view of the cradle, the bough, and the direction of the winds of the new media in these latitudes. (n. pag.)

In her essay, Lamberti draws a parallel between McLuhan's work on the 1954 edition of *Counterblast* and Watson's revisions to *The Double Hook*: in these works, she argues, both writers "started to elaborate their original forms of writing, embarking on a lifelong search, which often took the works of Wyndham Lewis as a point of reference" (50).

In "Excellent Internationalists: How Sheila Watson and Marshall McLuhan Made Wyndham Lewis Influential," Adam Hammond resists a linear trajectory that would outline Lewis's influence on Canadian writers. Hammond divides his essay into two parts: in the first, he examines "Lewis's political conversion to internationalism during his North American years" and how that conversion transformed his prose style; in the second, he argues that McLuhan and Watson, "reshaped and transformed Lewis, taking what was best in his North American internationalist thought and synthesizing it with his earlier modernist style."

> By adapting his ideas to meet the needs and realities of an increasingly multicultural post–Second World War Canada, they made Lewis *useful* to the cultural life of the nation, giving him a powerful, if indirect, role in shaping Canada's multicultural identity. Watson and McLuhan were not simply influenced be Lewis; they turned him into an influence. (61)

For Hammond, *America and Cosmic Man* is the key text because it marks not only Lewis's conversion to internationalism, "a genuine and dramatic shift from his political thought of the 1930s," but also his abandonment of "dialogic modernist complexity" in writing for an "increasingly straightforward" prose style. In the second half of "Excellent Internationalists," Hammond contrasts what he terms McLuhan's "Lewisian bricolage" with Watson's more nuanced use of "elements of Lewisian modernist style to enact a genuine internationalism in which the local is interweaved with the global, but with all its strangeness and specificity intact" (81).

The second section of *Counterblasting Canada*, "The Antennae of the Race," focuses on art as an "early warning system," which Ezra Pound's "bullet-headed" people ignore at their own peril. Writing at the outset of the Cold War, Marshall McLuhan conceived art as a form of radar not unlike the DEW Line, a Distant Early Warning system of radar bases constructed across the Canadian Arctic by NORAD, the North American Aerospace Defense Command, to provide advance warning of a Soviet nuclear strike. As Adam Welch points out, in *Understanding Media* McLuhan "had invoked... 'art, at its most significant, as a DEW line, a Distant Early Warning system that can always be relied on to tell the old culture what is beginning to happen to it'" (91). This section of *Counterblasting Canada*, which includes essays by Welch, Paul Tiessen, and Philip Monk, examines McLuhan's understanding of the role of art in the modern world, his relation to artists, including Wilfred and Sheila Watson, and the response of contemporary artists to his writing.

In "Dispatches from the DEW Line: McLuhan, Anti-Environments, and Visual Art across the Canada–US Border, 1966–1973," Welch argues that McLuhan developed his 1967 Marfleet lectures out of the "conjunction of two seemingly disparate ideas": artists as the makers of counter-environments; and Canada as a counter-environment to the United States, a conjunction that led McLuhan to conceive Canada itself as an artist figure (88). In the chapter, Welch explores how McLuhan's thinking about Canada as "Borderline Case," the title of McLuhan's first Marfleet lecture, informed contemporary art initiatives, from General Idea's Border Research Request to Bill Vazan's various projects to the Image Bank's "Image Request Directory." "McLuhan's reading of the country as an artist-figure in his lecture and elsewhere in his writing," Welch argues, "resonates strongly with the interaction and occasional interrogation of the United States carried out by artists in Canada during the period" (103).

While McLuhan was developing the ideas he would articulate in his Marfleet lectures, he was also collaborating with poet and playwright Wilfred Watson on *From Cliché to Archetype*. In "Wilfred Watson, Playwright: Writing (to) McLuhan," Paul Tiessen examines Watson's correspondence with McLuhan during this period. Tiessen's chapter builds on his study of the extant papers of both writers (and of Sheila Watson's as well). Whereas in an earlier essay, "'Shall I Say, It Is Necessary to Restore the Dialogue?': Wilfred Watson's Encounter with Marshall McLuhan, 1957–1988," Tiessen had examined that relationship through the lens provided by Watson's notebooks and journals, in this chapter his primary focus is on the letters the two men exchanged while collaborating on *From Cliché to Archetype* and, within that correspondence, on "a single thread running here and there through those letters: references to Watson's plays, to the writing, the production, and the reception of his scripts" (109). According to Tiessen,

> It was Watson, of course, who made his theatre work a recurring topic. Thereby he held McLuhan as audience of some of his day-to-day experimental concerns. The theatre trope provided him with a demonstrable means of asserting his separate identity. It marked off a terrain where he felt himself flourishing within a community of artists. It let him reveal to McLuhan that as artist—indeed, avant-garde artist—he thrived within a collaborative working environment such as he hoped he and McLuhan were forging. (109)

As Tiessen details, Watson did not thrive in collaboration with McLuhan as he had in theatrical productions with members of the Studio Theatre troupe, and *From Cliché to Archetype* proved a major disappointment for both men.

Like Tiessen's chapter, Philip Monk's "Marshall McLuhan, General Idea, and Me!" can be considered a companion to Welch's: each is a case study. Whereas Tiessen focuses on Watson's collaboration with McLuhan, his probing via poetic and theatrical experimentation of McLuhan's understanding of media, Monk examines the extent to which McLuhan's media theory informed the artist collective General Idea (1969–1994), particularly in the group's early years. Monk's examination, however, comes with a caveat: "Not limited in their media analysis to McLuhan, General Idea were incredibly syncretic in amalgamating various influences within their fictional system. And being *mediumistic*, these influences extended, as well, to the Kabala and Mme. Blavatsky" (153). With that caveat, Monk argues,

General Idea's enterprise was a system of myth produced by the cut-up method. McLuhan's own method was collage-like—and his books were image banks of "what's happening." McLuhan called *The Medium is the Message* "a collide-oscope of interfaced situations" (Medium, 10), which is a perfect description of what General Idea were writing about. Even an academic book such as *Gutenberg Galaxy* McLuhan called a collage event: "Thus the galaxy or constellation of events upon which the present study concentrates is itself a mosaic of perpetually interacting forms that have undergone kaleidoscopic transformation" (Gutenberg ii). This perfectly describes what the whole correspondence art movement was all about...Belying their symbol of stability (that of a bank), image banks were systems of signs in motion composing varied cosmologies.... As image banks, not only *FILE*, but *The 1984 Miss General Idea Pavillion* itself were such precarious constructions. (159–60)

Moreover, Monk argues, General Idea shared its "major operative concept," the "borderline (really, an interface)" with McLuhan.

The third section of *Counterblasting Canada*, "Art and Anti-Environment," includes essays by Dean Irvine, Linda Morra, and Kristine Smitka. Although the essays in this section reach outward to other fields of artistic production, they are grounded in literary analysis, and approach McLuhan through the writing of Sheila Watson. In "Sheila Watson, Wyndham Lewis, and Men without Art," Dean Irvine reads Sheila Watson's oeuvre through the lens provided by two Watson texts: her frequently quoted essay, "What I'm Going to Do," the transcription of comments she made prior to an impromptu reading from *The Double Hook*; and her less-known doctoral study, *Wyndham Lewis and Expressionism*. "What I undertake here," Irvine writes,

is to recontextualize her oeuvre through her signature statement on aesthetics in "What I'm Going to Do," but with a view to her critique of expressionist aesthetics and her practice of satire and metasatire. Taking her oeuvre as a gestalt, in a manner somewhat analogous to Watson's approach to Lewis, I reconstruct the sequence of her published fiction....Each text in this reading is a part of a whole, a collection of increasingly critical portraits of expressionism... Watson's critique of expressionism in her thesis, essays, and fiction is, in this reading, an extension of Lewis's verbal assaults on dogmatic theories of expressionism in his own polemics and satires. (173–74)

In Irvine's view, Watson's *Deep Hollow Creek*, *The Double Hook*, and *Five Stories* are "analogous to Lewis's satire of modernity in his trilogy *The Human Age* (1928–1955)" (205). "Structured as a gestalt without redemption," he argues, "Watson's satiric oeuvre simply reinscribes the metanarrative of expressionism and its aesthetic mediations of the reified technological, social, and spiritual conditions of modernity as a fall without end" (206).

In "'His Name is Felix': Artist as Catalytic Agent and the Counter-Environment in Sheila Watson's *The Double Hook*," Linda M. Morra narrows the focus from Watson's oeuvre to a single text and, within that, to a single character. As the starting point for analysis, Morra offers McLuhan's comments (in an interview with Gerald E. Stearn) about the "exceedingly difficult" nature of communication:

In the sense of a mere point-to-point correspondence between what is said, done and thought and felt between people—this is the rarest thing in the world. If there is the slightest tangential area of touch, agreement, and so on among people, *that* is communication in a big way... Most people have the idea of communication as something matching between what is said and what is understood. In actual fact, communication is *making*. The person who sees or heeds or hears is engaged in making a response to a situation, which is mostly of his own fictional invention. (211)

Although, in her discussion of the role of art and counter-environment in communication, Morra is careful to distinguish Watson's "emphasis and terminology" from McLuhan's, she argues that the two writers shared "a conception about the integral function of the artist as an agent for change" and that both "would subscribe to Ezra Pound's sense that the artist operates as the 'antennae' of a people" (215). Consequently, Morra argues, "There is no better place...to observe the ideological affinities between McLuhan and Watson than in the characterization of the artist figure, Felix" in *The Double Hook*:

> An assessment of his character reveals that he is the artist figure, the key person who sees, heeds, and hears and forms a response to situations. He works beyond the community's dissonances because his heightened perception allows him to recognize their needs. His artistic endeavours (specifically, the playing of his fiddle), his ability to use and push beyond fragments of clichéd speech and Catholic liturgy, and his own benevolent actions eventually produce mutual engagement by members of the community—rather than violence. By the end of the novel, the characters move towards greater coherence, as initiated by Felix, and are compelled by him into organized forms of responding to others. (215–16)

In Morra's reading, Lenchen's decision to name her baby Felix is a sign of that "greater coherence," of communication as "making."

Kristine Smitka, in her essay "Magic, Monstrosity, and 'the Mechanization of Death': Sheila Watson and Marshall McLuhan's Dialogue on Photography," brings into significant relation three different bodies of work: Watson and McLuhan's decade-long discussion of photography and new media contained in letters they exchanged while she was writing her doctoral study on Lewis; her essay, "Michael Ondaatje: The Mechanization of Death," which focuses on photography as both content and form in *The Collected Work of Billy the Kid*; her last published short story,

"The Rumble Seat," which Smitka reads as the "culmination" of the writer's "decades of reflection on the ways in which photographs extend power and limit the body" (244–45). Following F.T. Flahiff's lead, Smitka is careful not "to misread McLuhan's and Watson's supervisor-supervisee relationship as one of influence." The relationship, she argues, is "far more complex."

> Watson was older than McLuhan when he accepted her as his student (Flahiff, *Always* 177), and their letters demonstrate a collegiality of mutual respect. They also prove Watson's ability to discuss, debate, and, at times, resist McLuhan's point of view. She brought to their conversation her own preoccupations, specifically the relationship between technology and power. (232)

Undoubtedly, Watson's most important preoccupation—at least, with regard to the arguments Smitka advances in the chapter— is an enduring concern with photography itself: "Watson's investigation of photography," Smitka argues, "preoccupied her for decades and eventually moved beyond her engagement with Lewis and McLuhan" (242). Smitka traces that enduring concern from Watson's dialogue with McLuhan to her essay on Ondaatje's long poem to the publication of "The Rumble Seat."

We use the connected "Analepsis" and "Prolepsis" to frame these nine chapters in a larger debate about English as a discipline: "Analepsis" begins with McLuhan's work as a teacher in Toronto, while "Prolepsis" opens towards the future of English studies. The contributions by Leon Surette and Darren Wershler consider McLuhan's deviations from habitual English department pedagogy, alongside contemporary applications of McLuhan's theories and methods in English studies. Articulating the ground from which McLuhan probed technology's effect on cognition, Surette reflects on his experience as a graduate student ill-prepared for McLuhan's departure from English's traditional lines of inquiry. This turn to disciplinarity highlights the sometimes ambiguous boundaries among English, communication studies, and media studies, and asks what Canadian vorticism might teach us about interdisciplinary studies (Wershler). These framing essays happen to be disproportionately focused on McLuhan as a reflection of the disproportionate attention paid to McLuhan's pedagogy and institutional critique. As mentioned above, Wershler's essay concludes by opening up the possibility of reinterpreting the work of Canadian vorticists through other academic perspectives. Indeed, the digitization work on Wilfred and Sheila Watson at the University of Alberta rather openly invites such considerations in the future.

ANALEPSIS

1

Remembering McLuhan

Leon Surette

THIS CHAPTER ATTEMPTS to recreate the cultural and academic atmosphere in which *The Gutenberg Galaxy* appeared on its publication in 1962. The University of Toronto where McLuhan taught was very different in 1961, when I was a fresh Honours BA (English and History) from Queen's University, than it is today. In 1961, the rivalry between the parochial colleges (Anglican, Catholic, and United Church) was still very much alive. New Criticism was the new mode of literary criticism, displacing the previous mode of historical scholarship. The leading exponent of historical scholarship at Toronto in 1961 was the Milton scholar, and head of University College (a secular college), A.S.P. Woodhouse, who was then nearing retirement. But the most famous literary scholar by far was Northrop Frye of Victoria College (United Church), whose seminal work, *Anatomy of Criticism*, had been published four years earlier. At the time, McLuhan had not published enough to attract much attention from anyone. The publication of *The Gutenberg Galaxy* in 1962 and *Understanding Media* two years later, made him the most famous man or woman on campus—though his fame was largely outside the magic circle of academe. It also made him the target of disparaging remarks from the university community.

As the first member of my extended family to finish high school—never mind university—I was a naïve young man whose professional ambition reached no further than to be a high school teacher. Despite my naïveté, or perhaps because of it, I imagined myself as a budding intellectual who would one day address the outstanding intellectual problems of the day—once I discovered what they were—in the ample spare time afforded a high school teacher. In short, I was a budding intellectual—easy prey for broad-brush cultural theories.

I elected to write a master's thesis on the "Conversation Poems" of Coleridge under the supervision of Milton Wilson of Trinity College. I did not take a course from Wilson, but chose F.E.L. Priestly's course on nineteenth-century British thinkers (I've forgotten the actual title) at University College, and Kathleen Coburn's class on Coleridge's prose at Victoria College. These choices served my nineteenth-century thesis focus. For my third course, I looked for something that would offer a little variety.

Someone—I think it was Michael Estok—suggested that I register in a course on New Criticism being offered by a professor at St. Michael's College of whom I had never heard. The professor in question was Marshall McLuhan. At the time, apart from a respectable number of articles on Victorian literature, McLuhan had published only two books—*The Mechanical Bride* (1951) and *Explorations in Communication* (1960), an anthology he edited with the anthropologist, E.S. Carpenter. I had heard of neither. The appeal of the course for me was the subject—New Criticism—not the professor. New Criticism was the darling of young and budding scholars like myself, no doubt because it was still regarded with suspicion by established scholars who had been raised in the tradition of historical scholarship or hermeneutics. I remember Malcolm Ross, then chair of English at Queen's, gingerly attempting to dismiss New Criticism as a passing fad in a course I had taken the year before.

In choosing McLuhan's course, I hoped to learn more of the principles and practices of New Criticism. As Ross's cautious dismissal of New Criticism indicates, it was still a novelty in the Canadian academy twenty years after the publication of John Crowe Ransom's 1941 book *The New Criticism*, which had labelled it, and forty years after the work of Eliot and Richards that inspired it. However, that hope was to be dashed. Unbeknownst to me and to the other registrants in his course, in the autumn of 1961 McLuhan was seeing *The Gutenberg Galaxy* through the press, and had already begun revising an earlier commissioned work, which subsequently appeared as *Understanding Media* (1964). Accordingly, we got the principal arguments of both those books straight from the horse's mouth as a kind of coda to the critical writings of Ezra Pound, T.S. Eliot, I.A. Richards, F.R. Leavis, René Wellek, Austin Warren, and Cleanth Brooks—whose critical theories were the ostensible subject of the course, and which received scant attention.

I should confess that my association with McLuhan did not end with that 1961–62 seminar. After two years as a lecturer at the University of British Columbia, I returned to Toronto to pursue a PhD under McLuhan's supervision, and took another course from him. The dissertation was on *The Cantos* of Ezra Pound, and had little directly to do with McLuhan's communication theories.

McLuhan's principal insight was the notion that modes of communication had cognitive consequences in addition to social ones. And "modes of communication" means everything from grunts and gestures, through speech, alphabetic writing, and print to the telephone, radio, television, and (after McLuhan's death) the Internet and the Web. It was a standard opinion at that time that the Greek creation of the full alphabet was a factor in their cultural efflorescence, as was the notion that the Northern Renaissance was jump started by Gutenberg's invention. But the idea that Greek *thought* was somehow *generated* by the alphabet, or that the peculiarities of the medieval world reflected its status as a scribal culture, were novel ideas that offended the standard supposition of Western culture—at least since the Enlightenment—that thought was autonomous of its mode of expression or communication. McLuhan went further, arguing that print had destroyed the enchanted world of the medieval scribal culture, and that electronic modes of expression and communication were destroying the secular and materialistic world of industrial societies that print had created.

These acts of creative destruction, which modes of communication brought about, were, McLuhan asserted, caused by those modes altering our sensory balance. Before the alphabet, language use was almost exclusively oral and auditory, thereby, he believed, enhancing the mind's auditory component. With the alphabet, the ear was at least partly supplanted by the eye insofar as language encoding and decoding was concerned. However, script was still rather difficult to read, and very few individuals were literate in the age of script, which scholars call the "chirographic" age. In McLuhan's story, it was not until Gutenberg's invention of moveable type that the dominance of the eye over the ear was fully established in European culture. That, in a nutshell, is the thesis of *The Gutenberg Galaxy*, with the addendum that electronic modes of communication—the telephone and radio—were about to restore the balance between eye and ear back to something like that obtaining in the medieval period.

Unfortunately, there was no neurological basis in the 1960s for McLuhan's assertions. It was assumed at that time that our neurological endowment was hardwired and essentially inalterable. In addition, the dominance of logical positivism within philosophy—an heir of philosophical idealism—held that cognitive behaviour—barring pathology—was independent of the flesh-and-blood vessel in which it was embodied. As I will note below, that radical separation of mind and body is no longer quite canonical. Nonetheless, McLuhan's notion of sensory balance had no support from either psychology or neuroscience at the time he articulated it. And even today, when the notion that brain architecture is malleable has been largely accepted, there is still no evidence that the enhancement of the rôle of one sense entails the suppression of another. There is no doubt that exercise of a sense can enhance it. Most of us cannot distinguish and identify scents with any accuracy, but those men and women who make a profession of it apparently can. However, it seems very unlikely that an expert oenophile suffers from diminished capacity in hearing or sight.

We were ill-equipped to deal with these sweeping assertions. Most of my fellow students were irritated by McLuhan's high-jacking of the course material so as to preach his own gospel. I was initially puzzled but became increasingly intrigued by the novel perspective McLuhan brought to literature and culture generally—though hard-pressed to make much sense of it. His ideas took the form of "probes," as he called them. McLuhan's probes were mostly about the relation between human cognition and the modalities of symbolization and communication, for which he is now famous. "The medium is the message" is his most famous probe. None of us in his graduate class had ever given any thought to the role of technology in determining cultural and cognitive modalities. We were astonished, offended, or just puzzled by the "probes" McLuhan dropped into classes, ostensibly to explore the critical views articulated in T.S. Eliot's "Tradition and Individual Talent" or I.A. Richards's *Practical Criticism*.

Unfortunately, I no longer have any of the notes I took in that course—which I attended in the academic year 1961–62. Accordingly, I will have to represent the sorts of things McLuhan said by having recourse to *The Gutenberg Galaxy* and *Understanding Media*, and attempt to reconstruct our response to them. The most general observation made in *Galaxy* is the following: "If a technology is introduced either from within or from without a culture, and if it gives new stress or ascendancy to one or another of our senses, the ratio among all of our senses is altered" (24). As literature students, most of us were familiar with the bifurcation of cognitive life between the emotional and the rational, or the aesthetic and the scientific that I.A. Richards and others had articulated in the 1920s. But we were not aware of anyone who had attributed such distinctions to the "ratio among all of our senses." Quite apart from the unfamiliarity of the notion that such a ratio existed and had cognitive consequences, it was even more astonishing to suppose that technology could alter that supposed ratio. It was all a complete novelty to us.

McLuhan was not alone in his claim that modes of communication impacted modes of thought. Lewis Mumford in his 1934 study *Technics and Civilization* noted that the clock, by dissociating "time from human events...helped create the belief in an independent world of mathematically measurable sequences: the special world of science" (15). McLuhan was a reader of Mumford and was undoubtedly influenced by him, but he chose to take a narrower view, complaining in *Understanding Media* that "Mumford, in fact, is unaware of the alphabet as the source of Western mechanism, just as he is unaware of mechanization as the translation of society from audile-tactile modes into visual values" (147).

Another theorist of technology who anticipated, and influenced, McLuhan is Sigfried Giedion. They met in St. Louis in the mid-1940s and again on numerous occasions thereafter. Giedion registered a McLuhan-like assessment of the cognitive effects of mechanization in his 1948 book *Mechanization Takes Command*:

> Mechanization is an agent, like water, fire, light. It is blind and without direction of its own. It must be canalized. Like the powers of nature, mechanization depends on man's capacity to make use of it and to protect himself against its inherent perils. Because mechanization sprang entirely from the mind of man, it is the more dangerous to him. Being less easily controlled than natural forces, mechanization reacts on the senses and on the mind of its creator. (714)

I recall neither of these men being invoked in our 1961–62 seminar, but they are included in a book list that McLuhan distributed and that I still have. Two names that were certainly not mentioned are Jack Goody and Ian Watt. They were to make claims very similar to McLuhan's about the impact of alphabetic writing and print in an article called "The Consequences of Literacy," which appeared in 1963, the year after *The Gutenberg Galaxy*. Eric A Havelock's *Preface to Plato*, also published in 1963, came to conclusions similar to McLuhan's about the cultural impact of the alphabet on Greek culture. Although Goody and Watt acknowledged neither Havelock nor McLuhan in their essay, Goody later acknowledged that they did know Havelock's book; however, he has not admitted any knowledge of McLuhan.[1] Neither Watt nor Goody pursued the McLuhanesque line of thought, leaving the field to McLuhan and Havelock.[2]

It was easy enough to get our heads around the assertion that the alphabet altered the sensory balance of literate individuals, by emphasizing the visual over the auditory. The alphabet gave us "an eye for an ear," as McLuhan put it. And the notion that Gutenberg's invention of print enlarged the alphabet's cultural footprint seemed plausible. As literature students we were accustomed to spending hours in dingy, acoustically deprived, library stacks poring over dusty tomes. In those days, Walkmans, MP3 players, and iPods were not even dreamt of. And, of course, we read by scanning pages of print without mouthing the words or otherwise registering their acoustic equivalents.

So far, we could follow McLuhan; our training had relied on print, to the near exclusion of iconic information such as that which movies and television provide, plus meagre doses of acoustic stimulation in lectures and seminars. The notion that literate people were somehow different from illiterate folks was not foreign to us. But we took the distinction to be essentially socioeconomic—in those cases where it was not caused by a cognitive deficit. Cognitively challenged and socially disadvantaged people were often illiterate, but none of us had supposed that such a deficit could be construed as the mark of a fundamental difference in the way they conceived the world. Even more difficult to swallow was McLuhan's claim that there were cognitive losses as well as gains from the rejigging of our sensory balance as a consequence of literacy.

We had no one to help us understand McLuhan's theory, since—except for a few of his colleagues such as Edward Carpenter and Harley Parker—no one else had yet been exposed to it. And we were getting it in bits and pieces that we had to knit together ourselves. Of course, it quickly became a game of one-upmanship between us as to who understood what McLuhan was getting at. That seminar was a microcosm of the squabbling that followed the totally unexpected celebrity of *Galaxy* and *Understanding Media*. We had detractors and enthusiasts, skeptics and cool explainers amongst us—and a few who stopped coming to class. I confess that I tended toward the cool explainer category, even though deep down, I knew that I was far from understanding McLuhan's views.

McLuhan gave us to understand that we young graduate students were on the cusp of an epochal cognitive shift analogous to that initiated by the alphabet in Greek culture. Here is how he expressed it in *The Gutenberg Galaxy*:

> All values apart, we must learn today that our electric technology has consequences for our most ordinary perceptions and habits of action *which are quickly recreating in us the mental processes of the most primitive men...* Certainly the electro-magnetic discoveries have recreated the simultaneous "field" in all human affairs so that the human family now exists under conditions of a "global village." We live in a single constricted space resonant with tribal drums. (30–31, emphasis added)

Today, the term "global village" is a cliché, but it was novel and puzzling in 1961, when there were no personal computers and no Internet. So far as we could make out, McLuhan was the only one in the room whose intellect was "resonant with tribal drums"—whatever that might mean. Nonetheless, it was exhilarating to think that—unbeknownst to us—we were recreating "the mental processes of the most primitive men"—even though we had no clear idea what those processes might be. We were not entirely comforted by the allegation that primitives didn't have clear ideas either.

We had grown up with the telephone, phonograph, radio, and movies, but not television, which had begun in North America only in 1948; and the CBC did not begin broadcasting until 1956, when we were all well along into our teens. The fact that movies—clearly a visual medium—had played a rather larger role in our childhood than had the acoustic medium of radio troubled us a little, but we set that aside. And it was pleasant to suppose that our synapses fired in a manner different than did those of our parents and grandparents—apparently rather more like those of primitive men and women, who, like blondes, had more fun.

While it was difficult to perceive a cognitive alteration from our elders in ourselves, we could see that radio broadcasts reached a widely dispersed audience simultaneously—something print could not do. And McLuhan's point that such simultaneity of reception was analogous to the performance of the rhapsodes in ancient Greece and of the nineteenth-century Balkan bards—whom Albert Lord studied in *The Singer of Tales*, published the year before I attended the seminar in 1961–62—seemed plausible. In those days, we listened to radio dramas as a family in a fully lit room, in contrast to solitary and silent reading, or even to watching movies in a darkened hall. Such group enjoyment was somewhat analogous to the ancient Greeks listening to a rhapsode recite Homer. But it was difficult to see how such a social difference between group and solitary enjoyment of narratives affected sensory balance. After all, we watched movies, listened to concerts, and attended plays collectively and acoustically. So what was the big deal about radio? It is true that radio lacked visual stimulation, but so also did silent, solitary reading.

Even if we granted that radio had altered our sensory balance toward the acoustic, looking ahead, it seemed that television would rejig the next generation's sensory balance back toward the visual. We had no difficulty seeing that television shared with radio the property of simultaneous reception over great spaces, thereby recreating a simultaneous "field"—as McLuhan liked to call a community of interlocutors. But we balked at McLuhan's assertion that television was not visual. It seemed visual to us—even though only black and white and low definition in those days.

He deployed an ingenious set of dodges to save the appearances. He told us that insofar as it affected sensory balance, television was not truly visual, but something else. One strategy was to point out that the television image consisted of a matrix of dots—something like a Byzantine mosaic, though monochrome. And the Byzantine world was undeniably pre-print. That seemed a pretty desperate dodge. A much better one involved the appeal to the nature of the cathode ray tube's generation of an image. It generates an image by scanning the screen from behind and side to side, proceeding from top to bottom of the screen, illuminating or not, the matrix of dots—thereby creating what appears to be a moving image. McLuhan likened the scanning ray to a finger tracing an image on paper. On these grounds, television could be characterized as *tactile*—or haptic as he sometimes said—rather than visual. Television, then, does not give us an ear for an eye as radio did, but rather a finger for an eye. If he had survived to the digital age, McLuhan would not doubt have pointed out that "digit" means "finger," thereby rendering HDTV haptic. And, of course, the digital image consists of a *mosaic* of pixels—although the image is no longer generated by a scanning electronic ray.

McLuhan claimed that primitives had difficulty with film because they inspected the image in detail, instead of taking it all in at a glance as literate folks do. This observation permitted him to contrast purportedly visual film to purportedly tactile television ingeniously: "With film you are the camera and non-literate man cannot use his eyes like a camera. But with TV you are the screen." This contrast is based on the fact that the cathode ray tube is projecting *toward* the viewer from behind the screen, while the movie projector is *behind* the viewer. It is difficult, even today, to see the relevance of this fact to the visual status of film and the tactile status of television. But McLuhan pressed on with the contrast: "And TV is two-dimensional and sculptural in its tactile contours. TV is not a narrative medium, is not so much visual as tactile. That is why the optimal mode of TV image is the cartoon...because it is a world in which the visual component is so small that the viewer has as much [work] to do as in a crossword puzzle." These remarks rely on the grainy nature of cathode ray tube television, which ostensibly requires the viewer to fill in fine details. McLuhan followed these remarks with what still seems to me to be a non sequitur: "More important still, with the bounding line of a cartoon, as with a cave painting, we tend to be in an area of the interplay of the senses, and hence of a strongly haptic or tactile character" (*Galaxy* 39).

While the foregoing remarks are taken from *The Gutenberg Galaxy*, they correspond very closely to what we heard in McLuhan's seminar. They intrigued and puzzled us then, and they still puzzle me. It is not easy to see how cartoons and cave paintings have a "strongly haptic or tactile character." And even if we can make that connection, what have either to do with the television image? *I Love Lucy*, *The Honeymooners*, and *The Ed Sullivan Show*—among the most popular shows in those days—although silly, were not cartoons.

We were unable to answer those questions, and left the seminar puzzled, but stimulated nonetheless. Much to my surprise, when *Galaxy* appeared, it was precisely such assertions about the nature and impact of television that were picked up by the media. McLuhan reiterated them even more loudly in *Understanding Media*, without adding any further evidence. The puzzlement, irritation, skepticism, or credulity felt by members of that 1961–62 graduate seminar anticipated the response of the wider community to McLuhan's predictions of the consequences of television. Despite the fact that those predictions were based on nothing but a general, and unproven, hypothesis that modes of communication had cognitive as well as social consequences, they have "had legs," as media folk say.

In retrospect, I can see McLuhan's tangled response to television reveals that he was not the dispassionate observer of cultural trends that he pretended to be. Television upset the symmetry of his sensory balance argument—the opposition of eye and ear. But instead of abandoning it, he revised it to an eye and touch opposition that permitted him to argue (with some strain) that television would bring about the demise of the secular, eye-dominated culture inaugurated by print. As print had destroyed the enchanted medieval world of faith, so electronic media would destroy the disenchanted secular world created by print. As an adult convert to Catholicism, despite his disclaimers, McLuhan was nostalgic for the enchanted medieval world of the ear.

Despite the problems with McLuhan's analysis, some fifty years later, we are told daily that a sea change in the fabric of culture analogous to those initiated by the alphabet and print, has taken place, or soon will, as a consequence of the new technologies to which children are exposed at an early age: computers and tablets, e-books, text messaging, and the Internet in general. Such prognostications are the legacy of McLuhan's style of cultural analysis. And it is difficult to imagine that some social and intellectual changes will not be occasioned by those technologies. It is less clear that such changes—if they take place—have anything to do with an alteration of our sensory balance.

However, McLuhan's notion—which he shared with Mumford, Giedion, and Havelock—that modes of communication can and do have cognitive consequences now has significant support from cognitive psychology. It is now the standard view within neuroscience that the brain possesses significant "plasticity," that is, the capacity of one part of the brain to adapt to new functions in response to injury to the part of the brain normally devoted to that function. Given such plasticity, it is plausible to assume that a lifelong practice of oral communication and memorization, or of reading alphabetic text, will reinforce the function of one or another part of the brain. And why would it not? We take it for granted that practice of athletic functions improves athletic performance, and such improvement would require improvements in co-ordination, which is a neurological function—albeit subcognitive—and not merely a muscular function.

The Canadian cognitive psychologist Merlin Donald acknowledges that McLuhan's ideas have served an heuristic function in the development of his own studies of the influence of technology on human thought. In *Origins of the Modern Mind: Three Stages in the Evolution of Culture and Cognition* (1993), Donald argues that cognitive practices such as speaking and hearing or reading and writing have consequences for brain structure: "There is a great deal of evidence in single-case neurological histories that these 'literacy support networks' [in the brain] are anatomically and functionally distinct from those that support oral-linguistic skills, as well as from those brain regions that support basic perceptual and motor functions" ("Précis" 746).

It is fair to say, then, that McLuhan's "probes," however dubious they are as contributions to cognitive psychology, did identify a truth about the variability of human cognition across cultures and technologies that were rejected out of hand by the positivistic cast of thought that dominated the academy in his day. McLuhan, after all, was a literary scholar, with no training in philosophy or neurology. His mind was a jackdaw that collected bits of insight from all over and threw them together without much regard for verifiability. Philip Marchand quotes Omar Solandt, a former chancellor of the University of Toronto, as observing of McLuhan, "It never disturbed him in the least when he got his facts wrong. He was never intimidated by facts" (*Marshall McLuhan*, 1989, 118).

McLuhan's importance, then, is as a sort of irritant, a grain of cognitive sand that gets under the skin of sociologists, psychologists, and maybe philosophers, causing them to deposit pearls of discovery in an attempt to accommodate or refute his often outrageous assertions. For my own part, I can say that he prompted me to look at our modes of thought in ways I never would have done without his influence.

Notes

1   In Goody's Introduction to *Literacy in Traditional Societies*, he wrote, "See in particular the somewhat extravagant work by Marshall McLuhan, formerly [*sic*] of Toronto, which elaborates on themes developed also at Toronto by Innis and later by E.A. Havelock (whose *Preface to Plato* appeared in 1963) and others... The work of Innis and Havelock influenced the paper that Watt and I wrote ["The Consequences of Literacy"] but our more concrete interest in the subject arose from the wartime deprivation of written matter we experienced in different parts of the world and our sojourn amongst non-literate, illiterate or semi-literate peoples" (1n1). However, there is no mention of Havelock, Innis, or McLuhan in the 1963 article.

2   Eric Havelock (1903–1988), a British classicist, taught at the University of Toronto from 1929 to 1947, in which year he left for Harvard. McLuhan came to the University of Toronto in 1946, but they did not meet. However, McLuhan greeted *Preface to Plato* with enthusiasm. Goody mistakenly places Havelock in Toronto at the time he published *Preface to Plato*, along with McLuhan and Harold Innis, whose work certainly influenced McLuhan, but Innis died in 1952, a decade before the appearance of *The Gutenberg Galaxy*.

I

The art

OF BEING

READ

2

Marshall McLuhan
and the Avant-Garde Function
of Counter-Environments

The New
Canadian
Vortex

Gregory Betts

One day I shall have some influence.

—Marshall McLuhan to Wyndham Lewis, 1944

If I thought it were merely private perception or
point of view, I would not bother to say it.

—Marshall McLuhan to Michael Wolff, 1964

MARSHALL MCLUHAN developed a unique sense
of the avant-garde that was notably different from more
common definitions and insinuations of other modernist and
postmodernist theorists. For McLuhan, the avant-garde was less
a revolutionary band of artists or political agents acting against
contemporary society in advance of a future civilization than it
was a perspective on contemporary cultural environments that
revealed its unconscious, unacknowledged forces. He used the
recurring metaphor of such artists being the "antennae of the
race"[1] to highlight their advanced perception of their cultural
context, not their ability to change that context as many revolutionary avant-garde artists have sought before him. The function
of avant-garde art and especially literature for McLuhan was
the momentary disruption of the flow of culture by revealing its
transformations as they occurred. In this way, McLuhan's notion
of the avant-garde becomes intertwined with pedagogy, cultural
analysis, and rhetoric in that the goal of such work is to teach an
awakened perspective and consciousness that returns the possibility of agency to the inhabitants of a virtual environment.

Teaching, in this sense, returns to its Old English etymological roots of pointing, showing, and, most appropriately, warning. Artist and teacher become intertwined in exposing the world-as-it-is-becoming to audiences and students alike, rather than seeking to help condition and, one might add, indoctrinate all to the world they inhabit. Such a perspective teaches resistance through elevated cultural consciousness and media awareness: or, as McLuhan writes (with Wyndham Lewis's theories in mind), "the role of the artist is to prevent our becoming adjusted, since to individualized Western society the Protean 'well-adjusted man' is an impercipient robot" (M. McLuhan and E. McLuhan 78). This avant-garde *perspective* was freely available to anybody (recalling Lautréamont's famous line that "poetry must be made by all and not by one"), though McLuhan tended to privilege the artists of a culture as the most likely to achieve this perspective independently. The rest of the population required what he called counter-environments—such as the classroom, such as art at its best—and instruction in order to see how the forms of culture determined or influenced its content.

Approaching McLuhan's scholarship as the expression of an avant-garde initiative helps to unravel a central paradox of his scholarly production: how a rather conservative mid-twentieth-century English professor of somewhat obscure literary texts at a famously conservative institution became the spokesperson for the emerging contemporary technological age. As with all paradoxes, however, the surface contradiction underscores a greater truth: as biographer Philip Marchand attests, while the young McLuhan resented the "low pay and lack of prestige" of the professoriate (*Marshall McLuhan* 68), the mature McLuhan sought to transform that vocation (and his host institution) into a culturally necessary function. Evidence of this transformative intent begins especially with his founding of the Centre for Culture and Technology in 1963 at the University of Toronto as an experimental pedagogical space committed to the emerging role of the University in the electric age as the "principal organs of perception for the entire community" (*Letters* 293). Following

his definition of the avant-garde, I herein address that function
that he sought to evoke and develop as an avant-garde pedagogy.

We encounter McLuhan's unique characterization of the avant-
garde early in his first and as of yet unpublished book *The New
American Vortex* (c. 1946). The book announces the possibility of a
new North American avant-garde movement that would build from
the pioneering efforts of England's rather truncated and tempes-
tuous vorticists. The proclamation by McLuhan was occasioned
by a series of lectures on the intersections of religion, philosophy,
and literature by the founder of vorticism Wyndham Lewis at
Assumption College in Windsor, Ontario in 1943. During those
lectures, which were collected and published as *America and Cosmic
Man* (1948), Lewis advanced the idea of a new kind of "Cosmic Man"
that was being forged in the cultural turmoil of the American nation;
that is to say, a new kind of consciousness was emerging that could
precipitate "the first entire cosmopolis...the first of a new species
of man" defined by the amalgamation of the world's cultures (16).

McLuhan had visited Lewis during the exiled author's resi-
dency at Assumption College, and was familiar with the lectures
and their content (Murphy 13); indeed, after this meeting, McLuhan
(working with his colleague Felix Giovanelli) lured Lewis down to
St. Louis for a rather unsuccessful six-month stint. Lewis returned
the "favour" by luring McLuhan to Windsor with the promise of
working on a magazine together, and then himself departed shortly
after McLuhan's arrival (see Marchand, *Marshall McLuhan* 79–85).
Despite their somewhat perhaps predictably strained relations, it
was, as William Toye has documented, from the global consciousness metaphor that Lewis developed in Windsor that McLuhan
developed his famous aphorism of the global village (Toye 253n3).
McLuhan accepted the notion of the cosmopolis and positioned
himself as a member of a nascent avant-garde that would or could
help to forge the great possibilities of the new transnational culture
that was arising.[2] "After Joyce, Eliot, Pound and Lewis it is for us
in America to form the new vortex in which a totally new assimilation of human traditions must occur. The initial steps have been

taken by them. Their work provides the tools and analogies for the new effort and perception" (*New American Vortex* 13). The key element of the new effort that would empower future generations was precisely the possibility of a new way of seeing and rendering contemporary individual experience in relation to the transnational, impersonal impact of technologies and media. The linear modality of pre- and early modernism no longer sufficiently accounted for the networked virtuality of culture in the electric environment. Disrupting linearity, individuality, and cultural participation begins with encountering counter-environments, a concept he associated with the disruptive power of art and the classroom.

McLuhan's idiosyncratic *perspectival* avant-garde model develops naturally from Lewis's description of the potential cosmopolis as an effect of transnational experience: already "the earth has become one big village" (*America and Cosmic Man* 21). Lewis argued that one needed only to stand in America and regard the world from there in order to access the new consciousness, which he characterized as the "spirit of the spectator" of global affairs (22). The task of the artist changes in light of this new spectatorship from presenting the epiphanic triumph of a private vision or forging an individual style to providing audiences with an access point to participate in the new global environment.[3] The goal of this garde, as outlined by Lewis, was nothing less than the total cultural alignment of the entire planet: a giant post-racial, post-individual, post-national melting pot. Hence traditionally defined art, even avant-garde art, was not necessarily the most effective means of realizing the cosmopolis. Poignantly considering McLuhan's extended attention to the implication and interpretation of advertisements from the 1950s and on, Lewis noted that the "best" modern art in America could be found in the advertisements of its newspapers and magazines (214). Though he had important reservations about capitalist cultures, this kind of work met with Lewis's approval for its vitality, its innovation, and, perhaps most importantly, for its unconscious promotion of modern transnational cultures— behaviour he found to be in sharp contrast to America's "cultural nationalists" bent on erecting borders between ideas ("did they mean that Durer and Bach should be 'foreigners' to anyone except a German, Dante and Giotto 'foreigners' to all but Italians—was that what they meant? and if so, it was nonsense—*yes*, that *was* just what they meant!" [214]). The line to McLuhan's writing and thought is easy to trace: this new avant-garde was being led by those plugged into the globalized electric environment rather than by those outside who remained treading the well-established paths of sequestered aesthetic activity or whose politics amounted to nothing more than thinly veiled nationalism. Such divisions were irrelevant to a future shaped by the total involvement of all people on the planet.

In contrast to this universalist position, the majority of theorists define the avant-garde through the trope of political and polem-ical antagonism. Renato Poggioli begins his influential treatise by defining the concept as a whole as "an argument of self-assertion or self-defense used by a society in the strict sense against society in the larger sense" (4). In Matei Calinescu's theory, this antagonism is focalized against "the practical modernity of bourgeois civilization" (4) and is characterized by "varieties of polemicism and...the wide-spread use of subversive or openly disruptive artistic techniques" (96), whereas in John Weightman's theory it is conceptualized in opposition to "the static or cyclical view of human existence" (20). Charles Russell locates the "high point" of avant-gardism in the "culturally antagonistic and visionary impulses [that] generated a vital tradition of social radicalism and aesthetic innovation" (4). Meanwhile, Martin Puchner has documented attempts by various aesthetic avant-gardes to literalize the militaristic metaphor by actively embracing and advocating war and truculence (see his chapter "From Revolution to War" 79–84). In considering the historical antagonism of the avant-garde, Calinescu notes that one consistent failing has been too much attention paid to battling the existing conditions to the distraction of their futurist mandate (98). The futurist orientation of the historical avant-garde, and here is where McLuhan's avant-gardism reconnects with his histor-ical precedents, includes an assimilating cultural program in the redeemed, post-revolutionary culture; likewise, McLuhan's new vorticism was shaped by a "rigorously intellectual...simultaneity of vision, vertical and horizontal, which devours and digests every kind of experience" (*New American* 15). The animus of his new kind of avant-garde subject position, however, and its performance in the present differs by his insistence that it proceed non-antagonistically: it must be "an affair of intellectual daylight in which the action of the storm can be studied and conducted with complete objectivity" (1–2). In this guise, avant-gardism becomes less a radical or revolutionary force contesting a degraded Western civilization than a displaced subject position through which might emerge a countervailing environment and ideology: ultimately, a similar avant-garde result achieved through a very different approach. McLuhan would later characterize this meteorological perspective through the spatial metaphor of a place apart and outside the dominant culture as a classroom of sorts in which the workings and potentials of that culture could be taught, analyzed "objectively," and, perhaps, potentially, harnessed. McLuhan proposed the classroom as a literal and metaphorical embodiment of an avant-garde counter-environment: "the classroom educator can recover his role only by enlarging it beyond anything it ever was in any previous culture" (*Counterblast* 134).[4] In this expansion, the role of the teacher and the artist therein begin to merge. Both have the potential to become the antennae of the race, the principal organs of perception, and both have the opportunity to wrest control of society away from the unconscious machinations that govern social behaviour.

The intellectual thug avant-garde model almost entirely disappeared as McLuhan's career advanced and new opportunities in the classroom developed. His conception of cultural perspective and the function of the counter-environments entirely shape his evaluation of art. In his 1967 Marfleet lecture at the University of Toronto, McLuhan extended the cultural vantage provoked by avant-garde eruptions to the cultural vantage created by Canada:

> What all of us do, only the artist makes visible. The ordinary procedures and environmental patterns of a society don't become visible until the artist creates this counter-environment of art objects. This is a frontier problem that

relates to Canada's position as a frontier country, giving
Canada a kind of world art role in making visible the vast,
man-made American environment that is becoming a world
environment.

I don't know whether that makes much sense at first, but
as the United States becomes a world environment, some
means is needed to make it visible and capable of appraisal,
appreciation, and criticism—that, only the artist can do—and
Canada is essentially in this artistic role. ("Canada" 119)

While McLuhan's comments are best characterized as probes more
suited for further consideration, the fact that he used part of his
lecture to even consider the possibility of extending the avant-garde
function to an entire nation signals his distance from the artist-
as-hero model of the historical avant-garde. In its place, art (and
Canada) is valued for what it reveals and makes open to criticism:
for shifting perceptions and provoking debate and evaluation. The
optimal function of art is indistinguishable from the optimal function of the classroom in the creation of counter-environments.

Complimenting this avant-garde pedagogical function, McLuhan
developed another recurring metaphor to explain the need for a
general awakening; to describe the greater portion of the people
who make up the spectrum of contemporary life he used the trope
of a sleepwalking, somnambulant public. His image builds from
T.S. Eliot's characterization of the modern clime as an ether-
ized patient laid out upon a table, but in McLuhan's rendering it
becomes the task of the avant-garde to rouse the sleeping patient
and make him or her aware of the table upon which he or she sleeps.
Revivifying the tribe thus goes beyond the poetic task of "cleansing
and renewal of speech and language" championed by Mallarmé,
Eliot, Pound, Joyce, and Lewis (*From Cliché* 115). The new task of
the avant-garde must be understood in environmental terms: "the
arts have reversed their traditional function from integrating, which
leads to a kind of mechanistic death, to rectifying sensibility by
providing counter-environments" (*The Book* n. pag.). This is an idea
that McLuhan would revisit and refine in his most characteristically

vorticist works such as *The Mechanical Bride* (1951), *Counterblast* (1954/1969 with Harley Parker), *Through the Vanishing Point* (1968 with Harley Parker), and *From Cliché to Archetype* (1970 with Wilfred Watson). Each iteration of the trope privileges the avant-garde artist not for his or her militancy or bombast but for robust wakefulness—a consciousness revealed in the ability to see the culture he or she inhabits as a simultaneous, dynamic whole.

It was his unique contribution to the evolution of vorticism that McLuhan merged the antagonistic vision of the British Vortex with the "cool" philosophy implied by Edgar Allan Poe's short story "A Descent into the Maelström"—his was, poignantly, a move-ment predicated upon a pun.[5] McLuhan used Poe's story as a parable of the present, arguing through it that survival in the electronic environment depended on abandoning large total-izing, over-detailed theories in favour of more selective, smaller theories that were particularly responsive to features of the culture rather than to the culture as a whole. Of course, his own writing embodied this relativistic nimbleness (leading to the "pseudo-Einsteinian" charge by Paul Riesman in 1966 [175]) in his attempt to shift from moralism to neutrality. He was not always successful in achieving neutrality, especially in letting the odd openly ideological slur into his writing (most visible in racist, homophobic, or sexist utterances; see Coupland [104] for a small collection of McLuhan's reactionary statements), but detachment was consistently his stated ambition—a fact that distinguishes him from the historically engaged role of the avant-garde.

Many scholars have responded to McLuhan's recurring invoca-tion of avant-gardism by making the obvious connection to his own practice as an experimental literary scholar. As Donald F. Theall notes in *The Virtual McLuhan*, this recurring theme keenly inter-sects with McLuhan's self-conscious endeavour to merge the subject of his scholarly work with "the power of the poetic" as a formalist experiment in research—and thereby to become an example of the phenomena he tracks: "The multiple motifs of modern commu-nication, modernist poetry, avant-garde anarchism, and the man of letters as media star permeate not only McLuhan's analysis of the 'media world' but his ultimate desire to become one of its stars" (32). But to what extent, and through what theory besides his own, can McLuhan's style be said to be avant-garde? It has been noted by many that his prose style strategically served to include the multitude of oftentimes contradictory complexities that circulate in his writing, which become in the process trace evidence of the dynamic avant-garde consciousness that he championed. In his early correspondence, McLuhan was rarely circumspect about his ambitions to participate in the twentieth century's avant-garde current. He admitted as much in a letter to Ezra Pound in 1951 when he wrote, "I am an intellectual thug who has been slowly accumulating a private arsenal with every intention of using it. In a mindless age every insight takes on the character of a lethal weapon" (227). His desire for influence and position within the ranks of the avant-garde can be measured in this and many other similar proclamations from the first half of his career.

Despite this militaristic private discourse, however, but in keeping with what we can begin to recognize as his unique characterization of the new function of the avant-garde, in *The Mechanical Bride* from the same year McLuhan used the image of the vortex, from Poe's maelstrom and Lewis/Pound's vortex, to argue *against* revolutionary provocation. The book instead presents an attempt to "assist the public to observe consciously the drama which is intended to operate upon it unconsciously...to set the reader at the center of the revolving picture created by these affairs where he may observe the action that is in progress and in which everybody is involved" (v). This spirit of the spectator contrasts the habitual rhetoric of the avant-garde, especially as found in such vituperations as André Breton's open call to social "revolt" (132) or Marinetti's desire to "violently / purge Italy of parasitic peace" (53) or even Wyndham Lewis's call to "Blast" and "Curse" "England" ("Manifesto" 11), while simultaneously blessing various known terrorists in London (28).

Forty years later, McLuhan echoed Lewis's bless/blast model in *Counterblast* by presenting such witticisms as "Blast the Canadian Beaver, apt symbol of our damned up creativity" (66). But in McLuhan's satire of Canadian symbols, the openly militant dynamic of the early avant-garde is overrun, indeed neutered, by his coy punning. Similarly, McLuhan's *Mechanical Bride* does not offer any strategies to contest the disapproved somnambulance and even explicitly rejects "moral indignation" (v). Instead, he proposes the careful, dispassionate construction of a counter-environment defined by a heightened consciousness of the surrounding culture. Many years later, he would use this subject position to distinguish himself from Pound: "My metaphysical approach is not moral" (*Letters* 413). This was not a significant deviation from McLuhan's original conception of the new avant-garde, but it can be sharply distinguished from the iconic avant-garde embrace of irrationalism and violence—even from Pound's criticism of modernists like James Joyce for political disengagement. McLuhan's dominant trope of wakefulness contra public somnambulance can be recognized, in this context, as a poignant inversion of the Surrealist and Joycean interest in dreams and the creativity of the sleeping brain.

Even in *The New American Vortex*, despite his professed intellectual thuggishness, McLuhan's new avant-garde consciousness was already from the outset imagined as a metaphysical, non-confrontational, and cosmic enterprise, defined explicitly through the spirit of the spectator: "Instead of moving radially or unilaterally the cubist spectator circulates around the object so that what may begin as a view from above or from the side may suddenly become a view from everywhere at once. For the 'line of development' or 'line of investigation' there is substituted the 'frame of reference' with lo spettator nel centro del quadro" (17–18). With this new avant-garde spectator occupying the centre of an immersive picture, the militaristic and/or spatial metaphor of the avant-garde breaks down—for in an immersive environment there is no linear movement in which to be avant of anything anymore; there are no frontlines of an everywhere-at-once battle. This nonlinear conceptualization of culture has come to characterize postmodern theories of the avant-garde (increasingly truncated as "post-avant" or "post-avant-garde" theories[6]) in distinction from modernist antagonistic, masculinist, and linear models.

McLuhan's dispassionate intellectualism, however, remains recognizably avant-garde in its connection to the habitual avant-garde ambition, whether postmodernist, modernist, or otherwise, to dissolve the boundary between life and art by participating wholly in the world through their work. As he explains in his anti-sequestration experiment *Culture Is Our Business*, "There is no past or future, just an inclusive present" (112). By the publication of *The Mechanical Bride* in 1951, McLuhan had already begun conceptualizing what role his writing could play in this inclusive present. This book, much more effectively than the *New American Vortex*, concocts a "circulating point of view" (vi) to match the experience of the avant-garde involved spectator. The book departs from academic practice by organizing its chapters haphazardly in a nonlinear fashion—a technique that would become something of a trademark of McLuhan's prose. He explicitly invites his readers to start anywhere and work concentrically, for "there is no need for it to be read in any special order. Any part of the book provides one or more views of the same social landscape" (*Mechanical Bride* vi). The overall impact of the text is one of complex simultaneity: a cultural collage of the myths and folklore that structure contemporary experience.

McLuhan produced a number of books that expanded on this atemporal collage-like perspective—what could also be described as the vorticist effect of *The Mechanical Bride*. Some of these books were written in collaboration with other Canadians who were sympathetic or enthusiastic about vorticism: *Counterblast* and *Through the Vanishing Point* were produced in collaboration with Harley Parker, a Toronto-based designer, painter, and critic, while *From Cliché to Archetype* was written in collaboration with Edmonton's iconic avant-garde poet and playwright Wilfred Watson. I've argued elsewhere that these three, alongside a core group of other writers and artists, including the novelists Sheila Watson and John Reid, constitute a Canadian vorticist school.[7] One of the characteristics of this group's writing is precisely the simultaneous experience of multiple phenomena coalescing into the centre of a great power. The writing uses a nonlinear form to represent and embody the perspective of the immersed spectator. McLuhan's sense of Canada as a whole as a (potential) counter-environment surely stemmed from his ambitions for this group, and the broader circle of like-minded individuals in the McLuhan orbit, from Harold Innis before him to the legion of students who packed his classrooms.

Of course, as with any avant-garde writing, the novel effects of the style tend to disorient and befuddle readers (and students) or else, ideally, make them feel as if they had encountered a new kind of consciousness. Urban theorist Jane Jacobs, who worked on a short film with McLuhan in 1970, was one of the ones left behind; she confessed, "I'm still bewildered about Marshall" (123). In contrast, his provocative disorientation led avant-garde composer John Cage to praise McLuhan's literary style: "I don't always understand McLuhan, nor do I understand anything else that I actually need and can use...In his writings I like the way he leaps from one paragraph to the next without transition... [leaving] space in his work in which a reader, stimulated, can do his or her own thinking" (n. pag.). Cage's positive experience with disorientation can perhaps be understood as a creative and itself avant-garde engagement with McLuhan's work and style. American avant-garde poet and theorist Richard Kostelanetz iden- tifies both Jacob's and Cage's type of experience of disorientation as predictable outcomes of an encounter with any genuinely avant- garde work: "One explanation for why avant-garde works should be initially hard to comprehend is not that they are intrinsically inscrutable but that they challenge the perceptual procedures of artistically educated people" (6). By definition, the interpretive tools and established vocabularies of audiences, scholars, and artists provide no comfort or insight into the new categories and orientations of avant-garde art. Such work appears meaningless, or even opposed to meaning (or parodic of meaningful exchange, as was sometimes charged of McLuhan's texts) because the means of accessing meaning must change with the new mode of production.

The initial resistance to McLuhan from the academy as from established literary figures (such as Norman Mailer, who described McLuhan's writing as "repellant" and "Faustian" and "ultimately Totalitarian" [Davis]) highlights the fact that his writing worked from a new consciousness as much as it tried to articulate the utility of that new consciousness. In the televised debate in which Mailer made the charges above, McLuhan's rebuttal outlined the role of the avant-garde artist in a manner commensurate with his own ambitions as an experimental scholar:

> The present is only ever faced in any generation by the artist. The artist is prepared to study [the present] as his material because it is the area of challenge to the whole sensory life and, therefore, it is anti-utopian. It is a world of anti-values. And the artist who comes into contact with the present produces an avant-garde image that is terrifying to his contemporaries...The artist alone in the encounter with the present has the sensory awareness necessary to tell us what our world is made of. He is more important than the scientist.

Though in the same interview he dismissed the notion that he himself was an artist, it was precisely McLuhan's ambition as a scholar to create virtual and physical classrooms through which students could face the present, and by which confrontation could shift their sensory awareness to discover/uncover what the world is made of. His creation of the Centre for Culture and Technology at the University of Toronto in 1963 was, as he explained to the university's president, Claude Bissell, precisely designed "to establish the sensory typology or preferences of entire populations, starting with our own population" (*Letters* 319). The centre was an amoral anti-environment in which students could attune themselves to the semiotics of the cosmopolis.[8] In pursuit of this mandate, McLuhan experimented with various methods of disrupting the old consciousness in favour of the new such as his famous "probes" that were used to investigate possibilities and provoke insight rather than provide concrete answers.[9] The disorienting stylistics of his academic work can be traced back to this ambition, which we can recognize through McLuhan's adaptation of the concept as developing from the historical avant-garde.

McLuhan's unique vortex of literary, historical, and cultural allusions, puns, probes, and aphorisms further intersects with conventional definitions of avant-gardism in how it manages to create an immersive environment through which seemingly disconnected, even contradictory, aspects of Western culture coalesce. Newspapers, comic strips, professional sports, and politics became aspects of a unified culture that could be read in relation to one another. The desire for a multiple vision led McLuhan to experiment with "mosaic" style essays and books, as well as typographical experiments that shattered what he called "the flat earth approach" of visually oriented media (*Counterblast* 22). While he commented on the sensory-impact of technology, it was the sensory-impact of his collagist literary techniques—a technique that can itself be thought of as providing or provoking a counter-environment—that pushed him beyond the detached role of academic observer or commentator. Indeed, his writing has a characteristically avant-garde effect in the perspectival shift it precipitated on and within his readers and students.

McLuhan himself openly acknowledged his formal experiments with academic discourse as an extension of the vorticist movement. It was for this reason that he sought to "update" the founding vorticist manifesto through his radically experimental text *Counterblast*, first self-published in 1954 as a short chapbook and then developed into a book-length experiment and published by McClelland & Stewart in 1969. The prefatory note explicitly situates the book as the continuation of the vorticist line from *Blast* in 1914 to Lewis's later Canadian works, including the novel *Self Condemned* and most importantly *America and Cosmic Man*. *Counterblast* begins by blasting "the printed page" and proceeds in a visually striking manner to concoct a counter-environment through the disorienting effects of typographic experiments, complex literary allusions, and McLuhan's idiosyncratic nonlinear aphoristic manner. Fredric Jameson once described James Joyce's writing as following "a derivative personal style" comprised of pastiche and parody all while working "toward something which transcends both style and pastiche altogether" (*Marxism and Form* 34). Jameson, in the same study, pauses to acknowledge a similar "streamlined modernistic form, in the works of Marshall McLuhan" (74). *Counterblast* explores a comparable derivative style in its stated attempt to use cultural reference to transcend "all goals and objectives and points of view" (12). The book describes the current cultural moment in a manner that evokes Lewis's cosmopolis. We are entering, McLuhan writes, the "directionless, horizonless" world of acoustic space: "it is a cosmic, invisible architecture of the human dark" (13). As "the content fades and the medium itself looms large" (22), the work of the avant-garde, like *Counterblast* itself, comes to resemble the "all-inclusive nowness...[of the] mosaic image" (27).

McLuhan's second book with Parker, *Through the Vanishing Point: Space in Poetry and Painting*, also experiments with vorticist form by pairing iconic visual art images with short ekphrastic essays on the similar use of physical space in painting and poetry. The book, which McLuhan described as "quite a new kind of approach to language and literature and painting" (*Letters* 304), repeatedly connects art to the paradigm shift associated with the electric age and the cosmopolis. Intriguingly, this book begins with a rather conventional free-verse poem co-written by the collaborators. The poem uses mostly images rather than explication or aphorism to highlight the importance of immersive consciousness, but pauses to explicate itself: "No question here of privacy or private identity, but a free flow of corporate identity" (33). In the poem, as in the book as a whole, language itself becomes the key technology by which the speaker is able to access and accept an emerging immersive, mosaical consciousness.

McLuhan consistently theorized that language and even literature had the potential and thus the mandate to adapt to the new consciousness he envisioned. Indeed, it became an important dimension of his Canadian vorticism to note that language already had a heteroglossic power and flexibility: he was keenly aware that "language alone includes all the senses and interplay at all times" (*Letters* 304). This rich excess and multiplicity of language led him to consider the pun as "a metaphysical technique for 'swarming over' the diversity of perception that is in any part of language" (413). In contrast to the cosmopolitan future potential of the pun, this consideration of language led him to consider the cliché as the ideological bedrock of the existing or "literate" culture. As we store clichés in our imagination, they orient our sensorium and become the archetypes of a civilization. Even while this implies a kind of rigidity of thought, McLuhan and Watson argue in their book *From Cliché to Archetype* that we deploy these archetypes mosaically: "When we consciously set out to retrieve one archetype, we unconsciously retrieve others; and this retrieval recurs in infinite regress" (21). In other words, the cliché reveals that the mosaic model already structures our experience of knowledge. Both authors were ultimately disappointed with the book, but even still they clearly articulate the new Canadian vorticist consciousness that recognizes language as "a technology which extends all of the human senses simultaneously" (20). It falls to the artist, especially the avant-garde artist, "to contrive situations that will dislocate the mind into awareness" (63) of the link between the mosaical structure of the imagination and the mosaical nature of our technologies, especially language.

McLuhan's avant-gardism was thus deeply integrated into the critical vantage from which he oriented his communications theories and other scholarly activities. Though he muttered protests against the charge, he was, of course, also recognized by other avant-gardists as one of their ilk. For instance, in 1966, McLuhan published a short essay called "Culture and Technology" in a San Francisco publication delightfully titled *Astronauts of Inner Space*. The ambition of the book as declared by its subtitle was to present an "international collection of avant-garde activity"; as such, it collected manifestos, essays, and original creative work by acclaimed avant-garde artists like Allen Ginsberg, Raoul Hausmann, Bruno Munari, William Burroughs, Dom Sylvester Houedard, Jackson Mac Low, Emmett Williams, Jean Arp, Ian Hamilton Finley, and many more. While

McLuhan's work is far more formalistically accessible than many of the other entries, his clarity must be read in the context of his explanation of the function of the contemporary avant-garde: "The new art and architecture and poetry of the 20th century had their roots in the new kind of perceptual discipline...[as] a means of perceiving the entire structure and values of a civilization" (18). He outlines his commonly stated belief that the entire sensory environment must be approached as a "luminous work of art" by an "inclusive perception." He concludes the article by describing the Centre for Culture and Technology as the culmination of that perception—an avant-garde sensibility made manifest in bricks and mortar. Through the work of the centre, and the dissemination of the perspective it teaches its students, there arises "the possibility of a human environment sensorially programmed for the maximal use of the human powers of learning" (18). In other words, he writes "straight" compared to the other avant-garde artists in the magazines not because he is less formalistically ambitious than they, but because the form of his ambition extends beyond his prose mosaics to the avant-garde classroom he was building in Toronto. The article's faith in the possibilities of the future, in breaking down the division of art and life, and in his own role in fostering that change all imply the avant-garde function animating McLuhan's scholarly work.

Starting in the mid-1940s, McLuhan developed from Wyndham Lewis, James Joyce, and the historical vorticist movement a sense of a new mode of consciousness. The orientation of this consciousness was decidedly nonlinear, atemporal, and simultaneous. McLuhan variously used the figure of the vortex, the maelstrom, and the mosaic to characterize its orientation. While this new consciousness deviates from the historical avant-garde in the tenor and rhetorical presentation, it still resonates with the avant-garde ambition of breaking down the division between art and life by creating an immersive total environment. Furthermore, his pedagogical goal was to facilitate survival and empowerment within the environment in which we, his students, are already immersed. To be clear: to think of McLuhan as an artist in the traditional sense is to decidedly mischaracterize his work. He produced the odd deliberate poem, a few decidedly literary experiments such as his aphoristic playing cards *Distant Early Warning* (1969), and might even have dabbled in the seven arts proper, but such productions are ephemeral when compared to the distinctly avant-garde character of his scholarship and pedagogy. Recognizing his production as participating in the avant-garde he studied makes the alienation of his academic peers and students, who protested his disorienting didacticism, rather predictable. Recognizing his work within that frame also helps to underscore the broadly socio-political ambition of his project: as he writes in "14"—an *Explorations* essay that includes extensive citations from manifestos by Marinetti, Lewis, and others—"The handwriting is on the celluloid walls of Hollywood; the Age of Writing has passed. We must invent a NEW METAPHOR, restructure our thoughts and feelings. The new media are not bridges between man and nature: they are nature" (210).

McLuhan's response to Lewis, to Joyce, and to the idea of the cosmopolis can be finally registered in the development of his iconic nonlinear, collage-like form. Considering his formalistic differences from his vorticist influences and paratactic predecessors, and considering that he recognized the avant-garde as the receptors (the antennae) of common mediated environments, by way of conclusion it is worth considering McLuhan's parallels to other late modernist avant-gardisms. Ironically, and lending credence to his belief that Canada engendered counter-environments, McLuhan's interest in perceptual revolution and mosaical forms connects him to another Edmonton-raised avant-gardist who helped to pioneer the postmodern assault on nonlinear consciousness: Brion Gysin, the Canadian inventor of the literary cut-up method that William Burroughs made famous. McLuhan never wrote about Gysin, but he did recognize a link between Gysin's cut-up method as used by Burroughs and the new consciousness of the cosmopolis: this form attempts "to reproduce in prose what we accommodate every day as a commonplace aspect of life in the electric age. If the corporate life is to be rendered on paper, the method of discontinuous nonstory must be employed" ("Notes on Burroughs" 69). The shift from Lewis to Gysin as a point of comparison highlights McLuhan's difference from the historical avant-garde and his compatibility with the new models of avant-gardism that emerged early in the postmodern era. The cut-up is a useful correlative to McLuhan's theories and experiments with academic style and highlights the compatibility between the conceptualization and realization of his project and the literary avant-garde of the mid-twentieth century and beyond.

Notes

1   Philip Marchand attributes McLuhan's metphor to Ezra Pound (*Marshall McLuhan* 178).

2   In fact, McLuhan was aware of the failure of the previous generation to steer or shape the rising social milieu. In a letter to Ezra Pound, he compared the lamentable impact of *America and Cosmic Man* to "an H-bomb let off in the desert. Impact nil" (*Letters* 227).

3   The task of the philosopher and of the religious also changes as a result of global *mediated* consciousness, which fact was the overarching subject of Lewis's various lectures at Assumption College in 1942 and 1943.

4   All citations from *Counterblast* refer to McClelland & Stewart's 1969 edition.

5   The concept has oddly befuddled critics of McLuhan's work, but his meaning was rather straightforward, colloquial even, and often repeated: "'Cool' in the slang form has come to mean involved, deeply participative, deeply engaged" ("The Future" 70). He often explained the theory with reference to comics and cartoons where, because the detail is low, the audience must get more involved to complete the image.

6   See Ben Highmore (243–62) for an account of the debate and development in post-avant-garde theory since Peter Bürger first articulated the term in reference to what he perceived as the inevitable failure of the avant-garde.

7   See "Canadian Vorticism" in *Avant-Garde Canadian Literature*.

8   Norman Mailer recognized the amorality that McLuhan had embraced as method: "In all of McLuhanland, you never find the words 'good' or 'bad'" (Davis).

9   W. Terrance Gordon draws an important link between McLuhan's vorticism and the metaphor of his probes: "McLuhan's probes were drills. He used them to pierce the crust of mankind's dulled perceptions, but his principal interest was rarely, if ever, in getting a hole finished, for that would be a goal-oriented and linear activity. The drill, after all, is a spiral, and what it churns up is the important matter to McLuhan" (*McLuhan: A Guide* 23).

3

Watson,

McLuhan

[& Lewis]

Elena Lamberti

Challenging Canadians

WYNDHAM LEWIS, Sheila Watson, and Marshall McLuhan are master figures in the (modernist) Canadian cultural and artistic scenario; their works are now part of the literary Canadian national "syllabus," often praised for their investigations of universal themes and for their successful attempts to bring Canadian voices into the international literary arena. The paradox is revealing: they are part of the Canadian legacy also (if not mostly) because their works transcend Canada and challenge what, in the middle of the previous century, many critics still felt as a typical Canadian cultural isolationism. Critics have called them "solitary outlaws" and their works have often been labelled as "obscure," "difficult," "eccentric," or even "nonsensical." I like to think of them as conscious, solitary intellectuals challenging Canadians or as challenging solitary Canadians consciously breaking through established cultural patterns.

The definition that McLuhan gave of Lewis as early as 1944 captures the essence of these three writers' long-term poetics, which today's readers may grasp more readily than past generations: "Lewis pleases nobody because he is like an intruder at a feast who quietly explains that dinner must be temporarily abandoned since the food has been poisoned and the guests must be detached from their dinners by a stomach pump" ("Wyndham Lewis: Lemuel" 179). Obviously, if you are a guest at that dinner, you would immediately resent the person who intrudes and ruins the party; however, later on you cannot but be grateful to the intruder who saved your life, even though through a very unpleasant remedy. Similarly, we often have an ambiguous attitude towards those writers who make us "see, hear and above all feel," that is, for those writers who, as

39

Joseph Conrad would put it, force us to face our "Africa within"; we resent their frankness, even when ironically disguised through a witty use of language, because nothing is more trouble than to look things in the face. However, over time we cannot but be grateful to them because they treated us not as spoiled children, but as grownup readers who no longer inhabit the (too soon lost) wonder-land. Lewis, Watson, and McLuhan were intruders who told their (world) readers—and their fellow Canadians—things that clashed with the commonly accepted ideas of their time and denied rest to those minds longing more for a creed than for original thoughts.

To label these three writers *tout court* as "modernist" in fact risks limiting their reception. Rightly, Sheila Watson defined Wyndham Lewis as a post-expressionist writer and artist—as someone in between cultural moments. Similarly, Marshall McLuhan found an interest in both Lewis's theory of art and his theory of communication, discussing his works against both the modernist and the "postmodernist" cultural and technological scenario.[1] By so doing, Watson and McLuhan were among the first to fully grasp both the complexity and the potentialities of Lewis's productions; a possible reason for that might lay in the fact that they, too, were thinkers inhabiting a broader setting than the one offered by clearly cut territories such as modernism, postmodernism, or, even, Canada. Watson and McLuhan were (Canadian) intellectuals crossing the twentieth century: to stabilize them into too rigid canons and definitions would be incorrect, as they trespassed too many onto-logical borders, always posing new challenges to their readers and critics. Just like Lewis before,[2] they, too, consciously embraced the challenge of being intellectuals in a shifting hyper-technological world. Even though they lived and experienced different Canadian and world realities, and even though their works belong to different genres, they nevertheless seemed to share a common tenet: when society is itself an evolving vortex, the intellectual's, and the artist's, task is not to provide comfort through a complacent repetition of reassuring patterns. Mannerism, in fact, would equal collective suicide. The intellectual's task is to show you what is going on under the opalescent surface of things, no matter how irritating or uncanny that might seem. Prose, poetry, criticism must then show you not only the vortex and its evolving spirals but also their entangled progression, and their side effects. Prose, poetry, criticism must warn you that you are now entering a *terra incognita* and that you have to reset most of what you knew before in order to develop new ways to look at/through the new situation, and face it. In other words, at a time of change, the conscious intellectual, just like the conscious artist or critic, must warn you that you are entering the Africa *within* yourself, and that you must start to map it *by* yourself. As a journey, it might not be that pleasant; perhaps it is not as unpleasant as a stomach pump, but it inevitably unsettles you, your sensibility and your habits as it turns you into a cultural transient shifting from a collective narcosis to a solitary awakening. Yes: Lewis, Watson, and McLuhan were...challenging Canadians.

Inhabiting or Embedding "Canadian Modernism"? Or Transcending It?

To define Lewis, Watson, and McLuhan as Canadian modernists is therefore both true and a limitation. It is certainly true that both Watson and McLuhan appreciated Lewis's lesson on formal experiments, a tenet of modernism, and that they, too, walked along the uncanny road of experimental writing. Certainly, if compared to more traditional productions of their time, their work *is* obscure, difficult, eccentric, or even nonsensical. I will return to that later on in this chapter. Inevitably, both their works and the reactions that they provoked in a variety of readers helped reveal the Canadian society of their time and the solitude of the intellectuals moving countercurrent. McLuhan's letters to Watson often lamented this condition, something he overcame as he developed a network across Canada and abroad. To Watson, he writes on January 26, 1976,

> One of many thoughts I had as I read your Lewis essay
> was how stupid of people with our interests to scatter to
> the four winds. There is no way in which serious work

can be promoted without team effort. In isolation, it is
ground to powder. My own position here at the University
of Toronto is no better than yours at the University of
Alberta. Total isolation and futility! However, thanks
to my publications, I can have serious and satisfactory
relations with people off campus and abroad, leaving
the local yokels to gnash their molars! (*Letters* 516)

The key words in this passage are in fact "team effort"; they
become quite relevant to a discussion on Watson and McLuhan as
Canadian modernist writers, as they question not only the idea of
Canadian modernism as a conscious movement, but also its periodization. (Well, McLuhan's passage also offers some ground for
speculating on academic egos and rivalries, but I leave that for
another time). As a matter of fact, it is a statement that makes me
think that more than *inhabiting* Canadian modernism, Watson
and McLuhan might have *embedded* it, especially if we consider
modernism as an *attitude* for interfacing one's own world, and
not simply as a (variable) period of time containing a series of
cultural and artistic processes. Watson and McLuhan did not share
an aesthetic impulse to simply give form to a precise philosophy,
an opinion, or just their temperament; they did not dwell in the
comfort of a movement that, even though disruptive, still creates
a bond and makes you feel you belong to a community. Instead,
they incarnated change as their way of being: their intellectual
curiosity made them explore unknown territories that were, in fact,
extensions of their dynamic interior landscapes; at the same time,
their unique sensibilities made them often act ahead of their time
and often as solitary intellectuals. If modernism is to be defined
as the attitude to "make it new," through an awareness of evolving
cultural, technological, political, and social factors, then Watson
and McLuhan embed it fully. If modernism is to be defined as a
series of movements evolving within a time frame and expressing
a conscious and shared artistic rebellion, then they do not. It is
even more complicated than that: modernism is now introduced

as a transnational and cosmopolitan moment in the cultural and artistic history of the twentieth century, bringing artists together across national borders and across the arts, in turn inhabiting different cities and always turning them into the heart of a lively republic of/for creativity. No matter the place (be it Wien, London, Paris, Milan, or New York), the constant feature of modernism was the "international community" of artists gathering together and defying established canons. How does the very idea of *Canadian* modernism stand against such a commonly accepted definition?

Let me better explain what I mean. Outside Canada, the idea of a specific Canadian modernism remains relatively new; believe it or not, it still surprises scholars. For one thing: Canadian voices— writers and poets—are still not so well represented in non-Canadian anthologies and syllabi. And for another thing: even when Canadian writers and poets are mentioned, it is the idea of a *shared* and *conscious* Canadian modernist movement that is usually missing. The pioneering role of the the *McGill Fortnightly Review* and of the *Canadian Mercury*, as well as of writers such as F.R. Scott, A.J.M. Smith, and Leo Kennedy, is still almost unknown outside of Canada.[3] A few names stand out, of course (Morley Callaghan, Martha Ostenso, Frederick Philip Grove, or even Malcolm Lowry), but with the exception of the Group of Seven (painters), modernist Canada is often perceived as a land inhabited by isolated figures, by solitary "outlaws," challenging both natural and creative wilderness in isolation. From the 1960s, the Canadian renaissance started to reveal a new scenario of cultural, artistic, and literary achievements to international audiences. But, at that time, modernism was no longer so central; postmodernism was already on its way (Leonard Cohen's *Beautiful Losers* published in the mid-1960s is considered as a "forerunner of Canadian post-modern fiction" [Hutcheon 14] and rightly so). In our international scholarly imagination, the Canadian renaissance overlaps with postmodernism, as well as with a series of other new critical and artistic approaches that consolidated in the last decades of the twentieth century (postcolonial studies, cultural studies, women's studies, etc.). Hence, the issue of the periodization of modernism, which is, of course, an age-old issue,[4] is further complicated if set against the Canadian scene: it is true that Watson published her short story "Rough Answer" in 1938, but all her other productions were released from the 1950s onward. McLuhan published his first book *The Mechanical Bride* in 1951, and all his others in the 1960s and 1970s. Can we still consider those works as Canadian modernist productions? As I have said above, the answer could be at once yes and no.

Certainly, studied together, the cases of Lewis, Watson, and McLuhan can perhaps help to work out an innovative approach to modernism, or at least they can offer some ground for a more specific connotation of "Canadian" modernism—that is, not through a traditional periodization, but by juxtaposing periodization with both the making of an artistic and intellectual shared consciousness and the establishment of a national intellectual landscape capable of becoming part of the international scenario. If we do that, Canadian modernism cannot but extend after the Second World War, which is one of the conventionally accepted dates that marks the end of modernism.[5] After all, it is only since 1947 that Canadians are named "citizens" and not "subjects" of the British Crown. Before that date, Canadian modernist productions, while promoting the literary, artistic, and intellectual awakening inside Canada, also pursued a broader agenda: to create a collective, though still in progress, Canadian identity different from the still too British one. At the time, to rebel against the so-called Victorian (another definition that has been constantly challenged)[6] canons had both aesthetic and political implications. It is only after that date that art was, finally, freed from a contingent political agenda and could in fact return to a more universal search. Hence, soon after 1947, to experiment with words, images, ideas, and form was not just a way to consolidate the new Canadian cultural identity (which, of course, it was), but also a way to try to better understand the new spirit of the time— that is, the *universal* transcending the *local* contingency. It was a brand and a brave new world that artists and writers were called to explore and assess, and not just within Canada. While Canada was finally being celebrated as a new and (almost) independent nation, a certain idea of nationalism was being superseded by a series of facts worldwide, including new technological factors. The postwar world, in fact, was evolving into the global village, the new electric world that McLuhan soon defined as "the fourth world":

> It is the electric world that goes around the first, the second and the third worlds. The first is the industrial world of the nineteenth century; the second is Russian socialism; the third is the rest of the world where industrial institutions have not established themselves yet. And the fourth world is a world that goes around *all of them*. The fourth world is us, it is the electric world, it is the computer world. (*Video McLuhan* 6)

However, it was not easy to perceive and accept Canada's post-nationalism without celebrating it as a fully accomplished one. Watson and McLuhan did. For this reason it is a limitation just to consider them as modernist writers *tout court*. As said, they certainly embedded modernism by breaking previously established canons. Still, what makes them more than just Canadian modernist writers is their standing as intellectuals linking the modernist will to "make it new" with the postmodernist "deliberate refusal to resolve contradictions" (Hutcheon x). Like Lewis, they straddled the late modernist and the proto postmodernist motions; they were self-displaced individuals who tried to negotiate "the contradictions between [their] self-reflexivity and its historical grounding" (Hutcheon xiii) through parody and irony (Watson), and through humour (McLuhan), while Lewis had recourse to bitter sarcasm and satire. It is for this reason that I think that Watson and McLuhan (as well as Lewis) transcend modernism; they are better read as representatives of a universal search that transcends the local and temporal dimension, and reaches a more international scenario and broader spectrum of interpretive possibilities. They are torchbearers of an epistemological progression bringing the Canadian landscape into the international setting and the international setting into the Canadian landscape.

Conscious (Modernist) Solitudes

Watson, McLuhan (and of course Lewis) were conscious solitary intellectuals for several reasons. In their professions they broke previously established canons and searched for new ways to be teachers, writers, artists, and critics. By so doing they became public figures who established their own charisma and did not perform to please authority but to challenge their audiences. Also, their solid and vast knowledge made them somewhat suspicious or "difficult" to follow and understand, in turn hermetic or nonsensical. Finally, in their works they did not praise Canada *tout court*, they did not celebrate the Canadian wilderness, but turned that very landscape into a perturbing setting for exploring the universal condition of human beings. In Lewis's fiction, Toronto becomes a prison for the individual who does not comply, and in his criticism Canada is presented as a "monstrous empty habitat" that dominates people "psychologically and so culturally" (Lewis, "Canadian Nature" 268). In Watson's short stories and her most famous novel, *The Double Hook*, Canada is presented as "cattle country" as if confirming Lewis's statement that "Canada is first and foremost an agricultural nation, and, still more importantly, is everywhere on the frontiers of the wilderness" (267). In her fiction, violence is often part of the Canadian landscape: some times physically so (as in *The Double Hook*, a novel that opens with the killing of "the Old Lady," in fact the mother of the killer himself); at other times verbally (as in the cynical dialogues the reader finds in most of her short stories, such as "The Black Farm" or "Brother Oedipus"). In Watson's literary territory, Canada is therefore the setting where human relationships implode and design a sad metaphysical version of people's inner landscapes. Finally, McLuhan gave a definition of Canada that, even though it leads to a more dynamic interpretation of the metaphor associated with the nation, somehow remains rooted in a paradox also introducing a negative connotation: he spoke of the "Canadian *Nobody*," not to diminish Canada, but to emphasize the unique perspective granted to the nation by its geopolitical location. Canada can combine the best of two worlds, he wrote, taking advantage of both the more human dimension of a small nation, and the immediate benefits of its proximity to a superpower ("Canada, The Borderline Case"). However, the dialogue between the local and the global dimensions takes place through an idea of a mobile "nobody," which in fact displeased more than one Canadian because *nobody* is a term that at once denies both physical (no-body) and metaphysical identity.

The above shows that these three writers fought both mannerism and intellectual conformity; their works can therefore be read as attempts to preserve individual and original thinking at a time when society was moving fast towards a massive commodification of culture. This major goal was developed by approaching Canada metonymically—that is, as a location exemplifying the new world dynamics. In this sense, they (especially Watson and McLuhan) brought the Canadian scenario into the global village and vice versa. Their go-between was their shared universal knowledge as found in classic literary and philosophical sources, in myths and in the performative functions of the liberal arts. In particular, the ancient *paideia* (an ancient Greek term that means "to educate" and is associated with the idea of a rounded cultural education inclusive of a view of public life, invested in the greater good or public interest) was the operative tool they retrieved to work out the patterns of change. Also, for them literature was the mode through which the ancient *paideia* could be re-energized. When mass culture was entering its prime, these writers used ancient educative tools to warn their readers: to standardized forms of communication they opposed complex verbal experiments; to the folklore of the industrial man, they juxtaposed more mythical narratives. While readers were getting used to *Reader's Digest* storytelling, Watson, McLuhan (and before them Lewis) resurrected Oedipus, Europa, Daedalus, or pre-Socratic philosophers to create their uncanny plots.

Working from Canada, they employed their humanistic knowledge to probe the evolving human condition of people now inhabiting the fourth world, knowing that the new culture of the time was more and more a transnational affair. No matter how far or vast Canada was, it was not spared new cultural cross-pollinations as they were now coming impromptu and through invisible waves. "In the folds of the hills / under Coyote's eyes" (Watson, *Double Hook* 3) lived the old lady, her children, and many others with them; no matter how secluded their world was, the storm arrived nonetheless and changed things once and forever. What makes things even more uncanny is the fact that such a storm can take different shapes and come in disguise, as in Watson's short story "Rough Answer": Margaret and Joe can send the young school teacher away to protect their silent suppers. Still, all they can do is cling to an illusion as their silence is no longer unbroken. The same could be said for the young girl. It does not matter that she is not "ready to meet herself yet" (10) and wants to go home: change has already overtaken her; her world, just like Margaret and Joe's, will never be the same again. They pretend not to notice the coyote howling and the dog barking, but nature is on the move and so are they. To keep their ears shut or their doors closed will not change their destiny.

While Canada was being consolidated as a nation, by a team of politicians, thinkers, artists, and media agencies alike, Watson and McLuhan chose to act from a different perspective and learnt from Lewis (and from others) to imagine their old/new nation as part of a more global scenario. Their concern was not to judge but to warn or, better, to understand the impact of a more and more globalized actuality on human consciousness and on societies. Fearing cultural homologation, they set off to awaken their audience through literary counterblasts, which resonated too obscurely or weirdly for many readers. Theirs was not a snobbish but a conscious choice because to achieve their goal form was as important as content; this is perhaps the tenet that mostly relates to modernism in the works of Watson and McLuhan (and, of course, Lewis). If, as T.S. Eliot explained, the real meaning of a poem is what that poem does to you while you are distracted by its content,[7] then how you consciously develop your narrative as a writer requires both a heuristic and a social (if not political) function. It sounds so familiar: the medium is the message, is it not?

Blowing the Dust Aside: Counterblasting *Kulchur* (in Canada and Elsewhere)

When exploring the literary achievements of McLuhan, Watson, and Lewis in relation to both the Canadian and the world scene, the year 1954 can be considered an *annus mirabilis*; that year stands, in fact, as a crossroad of creative experiments produced by three intellectuals representing three different personalities that nonetheless shared, as said, a similar understanding of the role and function of literature at a time of deep cultural change. As F.T. Flahiff recalls in his famous Afterword to Watson's novel *The Double Hook*, it is in the autumn of 1954 that Watson moved to Edmonton from Calgary and sent a copy of the manuscript she had completed a year before to Frederick M. Salter, "a distinguished professor and authority on medieval and Shakespearean drama" (Flahiff, Afterword 128). According to Flahiff, "Salter's reaction was as precise and detailed as it was generous and enthusiastic"; he soon became her *miglior fabbro*, her best craftsman, playing "a crucial part in the final shaping of *The Double Hook*" (128). It is, therefore, in 1954 that Watson began a series of revisions leading to a text that stands now as a milestone in Canadian literature; her renewed attention to form led her to deal "with things eternal and not transitory" (Frederick M. Salter to Sheila Watson, December 12, 1954, qtd. in Flahiff, Afterword 120). That same year, Lewis published his novel, *Self Condemned*, set in a fictional Toronto (Momaco) and investigating the universal theme of the solitude of the individual who does not conform to the new consumerist world. As for McLuhan, in 1954 he published the pamphlet version of what would later become another of his most famous pocket books, *Counterblast*. In the introduction to his 1954 work, McLuhan explicitly acknowledges Lewis's North American productions as a key to his own intent as a writer and a would be media explorer:

> In 1954 Wyndham Lewis blasted Toronto in the novel SELF CONDEMNED. His René (reborn) seeking his true spiritual

self selects Toronto, Momaco: (Mom & Co.) as a colonial
cyclotron in which to annihilate his human ego. He succeeds.

In AMERICA AND COSMIC MAN Lewis saw North
America as a benign rock crusher in which all remnants
of European nationalism and individualism were happily
reduced to cosmic baby powder. The new media are
blowing a lot of this baby powder around the pendant
cradle of the New Man Today. The dust gets in our eyes.

COUNTERBLAST 1954 blows aside this
dust for a few moments and offers a view of the
cradle, the bough, and the direction of the winds
of the new media in these latitudes. (n. pag.)

Hence, the year 1954 catalyses these three writers' renewed
consciousness of where they stood, even though in different ways:
Lewis, then an old and accomplished "enemy writer," had returned
to the novel form and was pursuing a new political vision now
rooted in an enthusiastic approach to internationalism, which also
affected his stylistic developments;[8] McLuhan and Watson started
to elaborate their original forms of writing, embarking on a lifelong
search, which often took the works of Lewis as a point of reference.

As late as 1971, McLuhan and Watson were still questioning Lewis's
"spatial philosophy" in terms of audile-tactile sensorial perception, as
their correspondence reveals. On February 17, 1971 McLuhan writes,

Apropos the French request for a note on Wyndham Lewis, I
was wondering about doing a short piece on his mis-naming
of "the eye" and its world. When Lewis opts for eye values
and rationality and civilization, he was at the same time
creating and sponsoring, graphically and verbally, art
forms that are audile-tactile. Do you think that he really
understood that icons and bounding lines are not visual but
audile-tactile? Did he understand that "touch" is the acoustic
interval? The other point I had in mind is the characters of
The Human Age as *angels*. Electrically, it is the sender who

is sent, whether on the telephone, or on radio, or TV. We are transported electrically and bodily. Thus the people of the Magnetic City are angels, literally. Good or bad, disembodied intelligences. Lewis seems to have grasped this, perhaps as early as *The Enemy of the Stars*. (*Letters* 424)

In 1954, McLuhan had known Lewis for about a decade; coincidentally, Watson entered the University of Toronto two years later, in 1956, the year before Lewis's death, and completed her PhD with a thesis called "Wyndham Lewis and Expressionism" under McLuhan's supervision in 1965. Therefore, she officially started her own lifelong engagement with Lewis's poetic as a crossroad of artistic and literary expressions, while she was still revising her first novel, which she finally published in 1959. Since 1954, and throughout the rest of their lives, but especially through their collaboration at the time of Watson's PhD work, McLuhan and Watson acted as intellectuals who blew aside the dust and started to walk in the opposite direction than the wind; by so doing, they committed to unveiling something that their audience might not necessary wish to see. Just like Lewis had done before, but with more animosity.

Certainly, Canadians did not like what Lewis showed them about Toronto and its inhabitants in his semi-autobiographical novel *Self Condemned*: in fact, that book displeased a broader audience than just Canadians, because Lewis's fictionalized Toronto transcended Canada to display what Lewis portrayed as the unfortunate and mortal condition of a hyper-industrialized mass society. When the Western world was finally overcoming the disaster of the Second World War, entering the economic boom, Lewis denounced the vacuum of the new consumerist society, despising its cultural conformism as civic death. In the novel, his protagonist René Harding starts as a Nietzschean superman and ends as a defeated everyman inhabiting the new North American cities. After attempting to resist the overwhelming effects of the new *Kulchur*,[9] he in fact adjusts to the new consumerist world, from then onwards living his life as a cultural zombie. In a similar way, not all Canadians appreciated what Watson showed them in her novel *The Double Hook*, as rural Canada is introduced as a ghostly reality inhabited by moral corruption and social disintegration. The possible redemption suggested at the very end of the novel through the birth of an innocent child is nonetheless blurred by the coyote's last words in the novel, which, in fact, impose the fear of an inescapable destiny on all characters' hope:

> I have set his feet on soft ground;
> I have set his feet on the sloping shoulders
> of the world. (134)

Watson's rural village is but an allegory of McLuhan's global one, or vice versa. In both perspectives, the idea of a village community epitomizes an environment in which individuals are forced to confront a new moment in their social evolution: old values and new forces juxtapose and clash, and violently (that is, suddenly) change a status quo. Fear and excitement accompany those who find themselves within the vortex (the terrible storm in Watson's novel, a classic image that also borrows from the *Sturm und Drang*, romantic tradition, the electric vortex in McLuhan's media analysis): they have to decide how to inhabit it. This is the point: the goal is not to survive change—the vortex, the storm, the clash of old and new— but to consciously inhabit it. And this is the merit of Watson and McLuhan (and Lewis, too): they did not simply intrude at the feast and tell the guests about the poisoned food; instead, they offered an antidote through their (disturbing, obscure, nonsensical) works. By so doing, they also offered a strategy to develop antibodies. Their writing embeds change by triggering a renewed interplay of sensorial patterns that make reader experience their shifting environment and not just read about it. To fully grasp their writings, readers must reconsider more traditional approaches to reading so to perceive all the nuances of meaning hidden in their multilayered storytelling; it means to refuse the standardized and reassuring approach to communication typical of more intelligible or traditional works. This is why reading Watson, McLuhan, and Lewis implies not looking *at* their pages but looking *through* them and entering the acoustic dimension of a form that works also in depth and becomes three-dimensional, not just metaphorically, but truly so.

Today, we know very well that to actually interface with 3D environments we need special glasses: if we do not wear them, then what we see appears out of focus and makes us dizzy. Something similar happens when reading Watson, McLuhan, and of course Lewis. If we read them without wearing the right glasses, the uncanny, nonsensical, or obscure elements of their prose convey a foggy patina to their cosmogonies. It is true that they developed different forms to achieve a similar goal: to make people aware of the deep cultural change then in progress, yet their styles and poetics have, in fact, been defined in different ways. We refer to Lewis's spatial philosophy, to McLuhan's mosaic-like writing style, and to Watson's allusive or mythical prose; and yet these different terms indicate writing strategies that nonetheless have something in common: they all rely on the grotesque as a key to awakening. The grotesque is, in fact, the tool that opens up the three-dimensional dynamics of these writers' pages.

From its original use in Roman architecture, to its retrieval in Renaissance Europe, to its later interpretation as a Gothic variable, the grotesque has evolved into an expression for all that is incongruous, disharmonic, or even ugly—that is, into all that disturbs us and makes us see things under a different shadow. In modernist literary experiments, it became a strategy to oppose the overwhelming mannerism of a more traditional prose: if the latter was meant to preserve accepted ideas—the approved moral of the time—the former was adopted to make people see their own reality as *it really was* (that is, as a moving, evolving, 3D image, not as a fixed setting). The grotesque became a preferred strategy to stop the mainstream societal flow and offer mobile snapshots of what it, in fact, concealed; within different modernist poetics, expressions such as moments of beings (Woolf), epiphanies (Joyce), or impressions (Ford, Conrad) point out the suspended instant that becomes the mirror distorting an otherwise reassuring image. Lewis's space-time philosophy, as expressed in his *Time and Western Man*, relies on "the experience of arrest" (McLuhan, *Interior Landscape* 85) to induce consciousness, an expressive strategy that Lewis developed both as a painter and as a writer; the distorted grimaces that result from the arrested flow challenge and disturb the passive reader, but fuel the active one who might even find amusement in the revealing grotesque.[10] Similarly, learning from both Lewis and Joyce, McLuhan relied on the grotesque technique to vivisect society and to arrest the flow; his mosaic-like approach to his material was consciously developed as a new form of critical writing that, through an intentional disharmony, forces the reader to reconsider what was previously perceived as a uniform and harmonic ground. Already in his *The Mechanical Bride*, he uses the technique of vivisection to combine different forms of serious art with popular art, as well as with new forms of mass communication: the aesthetic clash is what leads to the ethical and engaging discovery.

Being less funambulist or overtly juxtapositive, Watson's form of writing might not immediately be associated with a clear-cut grotesque strategy; irony is certainly a most evident key to interpret her allusive and symbolic prose. However, her use of myth is clearly grotesque; it is her strategy to arrest the flow and offer illuminations. As Glenn Willmott writes, in Watson's prose, "Not only are myths 'alive' to rewrite themselves in new worlds, they are permeable by other such myths. What this means practically is that the reader needs not struggle to bend character or story to mythic allusions. The myths themselves are bending, blending, and growing" (Afterword 91). In other words, they are distorted (bending), confused or clashing with other images (blending), and evolve (growing) into something else, therefore guiding us to new epiphanies. Exemplarily, in one of her short stories, "Brother Oedipus," Oedipus, who cannot "ignore" his mother, takes refuge "in the arched earth cave" and finds peace only by the willow tree that his mother wants to cut (15). His name puzzles his siblings who content themselves with "learning to pronounce" it, but who prefer to playfully call him Old Puss, or Puss-Puss, or Boots: through continuous shifts from myth to fairy tales to the reality of brother Oedipus's life, Watson's storytelling opens up a myriad of paths and triggers uncanny epiphanies; or, better, it constantly bends, blends, and grows our Western, *civilized* common sense. In fact, it turns that upside down: "A surgeon...*interferes* with the natural cycle of growth and decay"; the "age of *reason*" is a "*barbarous* age"; school masters have taught us "to look through a microscope, to accept the evidence of our eyes, and to reconcile ourselves to our inferiority" ("Brother Oedipus" 22–23, emphasis added). Brother Oedipus would make the perfect champion of ecocriticism; but that would be a limit, too, because on Watson's pages his ability to bend, blend, and grow myth transcends closed interpretive clichés. The grotesque clashing of juxtaposing images in Watson's prose remains mobile and relates to a multitude of differing readers. As Willmott continues, when reading Sheila Watson, "We approach her garden of symbols...as co-creators, with Pan and Oedipus. We put elements together; we place growing things side by side, in sun or shade...But the task of gluing such fragments—as we might in Ezra Pound's *Cantos* for instance—here defeats us. Hence we learn that what we have are not fragments at all; they are not puzzle pieces whose meaning refers back to a given, allegorical all, but seeds or genes which mix together in a new, fertile context" (Afterword 91). We are asked to provide new meaning and to create a new composition starting from her fragments, which in fact takes us back to more universal stories—not only Greek myths or fairy tales, but also native ones (the coyote character is as frequent as Oedipus in her stories). In any case, they are fragments relating to pristine moments in human history, as if detecting a universal and transcending unconscious.

Watson's writing strategy, as well as McLuhan's (and before them Lewis's) reminds us that history is always in the making and that we are "all primitives of an unknown culture" (Umberto Boccioni qtd. in McLuhan, *Understanding Media* 141). Watson's cattle country, her rural Canada, was no more familiar to her readers than the new evolving global village was to McLuhan's readers, because at a time of change, individuals are on their making, too. The grotesque rendering in Watson's, McLuhan's, and Lewis's narratives at once vivisects and recreates reality; distortion is what blows aside the dust "for a few moments and offers a view of the cradle, the bough, and the direction of the winds" thereby revealing new societal challenges. As non-complacent explorations with form, Watson's and McLuhan's writings were certainly modulated inside modernist experiments and achievements; certainly, they both learnt from Lewis. But they also moved farther in time and space, challenging Canadians still inhabiting cattle country, as well as all other individuals experiencing the fourth world. They left their guests free to choose to abandon dinner or not; they left them free to choose which role to play: "The world is a vast amphitheatre...We are all actors in a rite. My sensible brother here is a mere spectator." (Watson, "Brother Oedipus" 26). So goes Watson's Oedipus, Old Puss, Puss-Puss, or Boots, who, no doubt, was one of the first to disobey the father's rule: "Father said we never should / Play with madmen in the wood" (Watson, "Antigone" 60). No doubt that most spectators— and perhaps even his brother—judged Oedipus mad and left him alone in the woods; perhaps he still sits by the rose bush and scorns those who pass by with his grotesque grimace. But if we look at the world through his eyes, we cannot but acknowledge that his solitude inhabits all spaces, transcends all times and embeds our own.

The intruders were right: the feast was over and you had to learnt how to digest that poisoned food. Blowing the dust aside and engaging with a dynamic situation through the grotesque clash of different moving images were the steps these intruders consciously took to awaken their readers, in Canada and elsewhere. "What a scene about nothing"—[Oedipus] said—"The individual unconscious scorns such complications" (Watson, "Brother Oedipus" 27).

So it goes.

Notes

1 See the chapter on Wyndham Lewis in *The Interior*.

2 For a discussion on Lewis as a literary figure shifting in between modernism and postmodernism, see E. Lamberti, "Wyndham Lewis: Blasting Time, Blessing Space."

3 See Dudek and Gnarowski's "The Beginnings of the Modern School" The Precursors: 1910–1925" and "The Initiator (1926–1936)" in *The Making of Modern Poetry in Canada*; Stevens's *The McGill Movement*, and Norris's "The Beginning of Canadian Modernism."

4 See Orr, "Modernism and the Issue of Periodization."

5 See Bradbury and McFarlane, eds., *Modernism. A Guide to European Literature 1890–1930*.

6 See Armstrong, "When Is a Victorian Poet Not a Victorian Poet?"

7 See T.S. Eliot, *The Use of Poetry and the Use of Criticism*.

8 See Gregory Betts's and Adam Hammond's contributions in this collection.

9 The term *Kulchur* was used by Ezra Pound in his 1938 volume *Guide to Kulchur* to comment on and revise the idea of "culture" in his time. In his Preface, Pound writes, "This book is not written for the over-fed. It is written for men who have not been able to afford a university education or for young men, whether or not threatened with universities, who want to know more at the age of fifty than I know today, and whom I might conceivably aid to that object" (6). Pound's volume is therefore introduced as a refined but antagonistic cultural Baedeker fighting all cultural and intellectual common places of his time (forming not culture but *kulchur*). Even though he is "fully aware of the dangers inherent in attempt such utility" to his readers (6), Pound's writes his volume to restore *culture* (see Lamberti, "Ezra Pound's *Guide to Kulchur*"). Consistently, the term *Kulchur* is often understood as indicating a decadent or *commodified* culture when discussing modernist works that criticize the materialist take of their time, as in the case of Lewis's novel *Self Condemned*.

10 See Lamberti, "Wyndham Lewis."

4

How Sheila Watson and
Marshall McLuhan Made
Wyndham Lewis Influential

Excellent
Inter-
nationalists

Adam Hammond

THE CANADIAN CONNECTIONS of Wyndham Lewis
are by now well known. Lewis—born in Nova Scotia in 1882, bred
in Britain—was associated with his homeland primarily through
the two Great Wars. During the first, he worked as an artist for
the Canadian army. He spent the duration of the second in a
six-year self-imposed North American exile, living primarily in
Toronto—where he painted and produced a political pamphlet called
Anglosaxony: A League That Works (1941)—and Windsor—where
he gave lectures at Assumption College that formed the basis of
America and Cosmic Man (1948). Though the latter work demonstrates a passionate enthusiasm for North American society and
politics, Lewis's Canadian correspondence is most remarkable
for the stylish contempt he showers upon the country of his birth,
which he calls, among other equally colourful epithets, a "blasted
ice-box," a "sanctimonious bush-babylon," and "the most parochial
nationette on earth" (*Letters of Wyndham Lewis*, 311, 339, 311).

Lewis's influence on the arts and letters of the nation he so
disdained is now equally well established, thanks to the diligent work
of several generations of Canadian scholars. A first wave of interest
in Lewis occurred in the late 1960s, when Sheila Watson edited
a 1967 *artscanada* special issue on Lewis, and George Woodcock
produced a "Wyndham Lewis in Canada" special issue of *Canadian
Literature* (1968), later expanded into a book (1971). A second wave
occurred in the 1990s, with Donna Pennee's analysis of the Lewisian
influence in Watson's *The Double Hook* ("Canadian Letters, Dead
Referents," 1993/94) and the monumental "*The Talented Intruder*":
Wyndham Lewis in Canada (1992) edited by Catharine M. Mastin,
Robert Stacey, and Thomas Dilworth. In the latter, Dilworth went
so far as to claim, "By crossing the Atlantic in 1939, Lewis brought
Canada into the history of literary modernism" (157)—a bold

59

assertion that more recent scholarship on Canadian modernism has done much to justify. Paul Tiessen, Elena Lamberti, and Gregory Betts have focused in particular on the important role Lewis played in the intellectual development of three influential Canadian modernists: Marshall McLuhan, Sheila Watson, and Wilfred Watson. Owing to the decisive influence of the founder of vorticism on their work, Betts names them "Canadian Vorticists" (*Avant-Garde*).

While this body of scholarship has contributed valuable understanding to a central figure in the development of Canadian social and literary thought, it has tended to concentrate on one side of the story. Whether the Lewisian influence is regarded as an infection (as in Mastin and Pennee), a stimulating injection (as in Tiessen and Betts), or some irresolvable combination of the two (as in Lamberti), the primary focus of these accounts is unidirectional: on the way that Lewis impacted Canada and Canadian artists, rather than on how Canada and Canadian artists impacted Lewis. Here, I look at the flipside of the Lewis/Canada relationship. Let us begin from Lewis's own most positive statement of the way North America changed him: in *America and Cosmic Man*, he tells his English readership about the "*something* that is to be found there, and not here in Britain, that is very impressive: so much so that once you have grasped what it means, it must affect profoundly your outlook." For his part, he claims, "it will influence everything I think and write henceforth," adding, "It has tended to transform me from a good European into an excellent internationalist" (11–12). The first part of my argument explores Lewis's political conversion to internationalism during his North American years, and relates it to another important transformation that occurred in his work at the level of style. In her essay "Global Modernisms," Melba Cuddy-Keane argues the "close relation between critical *paradigms* of globality and modernist *aesthetics*": "The crucial stylistic modernist features of perspectivism, reflexivity, parataxis, and ambiguity parallel the complex interactive systems of globalist thought, leading us to consider both how modernism models globalism and, conversely, how increasing global connections exerted a formative influence on modernist literary styles" (561). With typical defiance, Lewis's twofold conversion follows precisely the opposite trajectory: prior to his arrival in Canada, he tended to express nationalist sentiments in complex modernist style, while after arriving, he celebrated internationalism in a straightforward, decidedly non-modernist manner. The second part of this chapter shows how two major Canadian modernists, Marshall McLuhan and Sheila Watson, substantially resolved this incoherence in Lewis's artistic and critical practice. The relationships, I argue, cannot simply be described as ones of "influence." Rather, McLuhan and Watson—in highly individual ways—reshaped and transformed Lewis, taking what was best in his North American internationalist thought and synthesizing it with his earlier modernist style. By adapting his ideas to meet the needs and realities of an increasingly multicultural post–Second World War Canada, they made Lewis *useful* to the cultural life of the nation, giving him a powerful, if indirect, role in shaping Canada's multicultural identity. Watson and McLuhan were not simply influenced by Lewis; they turned him into an influence.

A Promiscuous Grave: Lewis's Conversion to Internationalism

At both the major sites of his Canadian exile, Lewis's reputation as a nationalist—more specifically, as a supporter of fascism and of Hitler—preceded him. A.Y. Jackson, an acquaintance in Toronto, recalled that Lewis "left England after he had written an article in which he said that some of the Nazi ideas weren't bad at all," noting, "It was very bad form of course, when England was at war with the Germans, and feeling ran pretty high" (qtd. in Mastin 31). In Windsor, Lewis initiated legal action against one Mr. Kibble, janitor at the Lewis's Sandwich Street apartment complex, for spreading rumours among tenants that Lewis was a Nazi spy (O'Keefe 470–72). In the life of a figure so consistently eager to antagonize, and so quick to suspect persecution, these stand among the relatively few instances in which Lewis was justified in sensing himself ill-treated. The "article" mentioned by Jackson—in fact a full-length book, *Hitler*—had been published in 1931, some ten years before Lewis arrived in Toronto and three years before Hitler declared himself Führer. Before he had left England, Lewis had in fact firmly recanted any vestiges of support for Hitler in *The Hitler Cult* (1939); and while in Toronto and Windsor, he was going further still, writing a pair of works in passionate defence of internationalism.

The extent of Lewis's North American political conversion is fully registered only when considered in relation to his notorious nationalism of the decade preceding his arrival. Though written from the claimed perspective of "an exponent—not as critic nor yet as advocate—of German Nationalism, Hitlerism" (4), Lewis's *Hitler* is at least a mild ode. It founds its support on a fatally wrongheaded belief that nationalism—particularly the Nazi emphasis on "race"—could prevent another European war, and in fact made "Adolf Hitler a Man of Peace," as one of Lewis's chapter headings declared. Lewis describes the Nazi policy of *Blutsgefühl*, or "blood-feeling," as a means of producing cultural homogeneity by emphasizing biological uniformity:

> What the doctrine of *Blutsgefühl* aims at...is this. It desires a closer and closer drawing together of the people of one race and culture, by means of bodily attraction. It must be a truly bodily solidarity. Identical rhythms in the arteries and muscles, and in the effective neural instrument— that should provide us with a passionate *exclusiveness*, with a homogeneous social framework. (106–7)

This homogeneity, he continues, promises peace:

> What I think it is safe to affirm is that "Race," used as a propagandist engine, must tend to simplify and concentrate. It promises political unity, at all events. It would, if followed out, draw people together, rather than thrust them apart—at least the people of the same race. Thus it would secure greater social efficiency. (85)

The argument of *Hitler* is littered with admissions of argumentative weakness and inconsistency, as the disturbing qualification "at least people of the same race" demonstrates. But Lewis—who experienced firsthand the First World War—repeatedly brushes them off in deference to what he regards as the historical urgency of promoting unity among the European nations and so preventing another European war. At one point Lewis says that the development of "love and understanding of blood-brothers, of one culture, children of the same tradition" represents "the only sane and realistic policy in the midst of a disintegrating world" (109).

By the late 1930s, Lewis was prepared to admit that he was wrong. In *The Hitler Cult*, he says of his earlier book, "I confess, I was badly taken in" (37), and belatedly declares "Herr Hitler...a 'villain'" (132). *The Hitler Cult* marks a turn not only in Lewis's personal feelings towards Hitler but also the tentative beginnings of his embrace of internationalism. "Wherever I go to-day," Lewis writes,

> I hear people talking about a Federal scheme, the
> object of which is to induce the great democratic states,
> especially Great Britain and America, to abandon
> their national sovereignty, pool their resources, have a
> common Parliament and armies under one direction...
> Let me say at once that I am in favour of such a scheme:
> and if France, Spain, Portugal, and the Scandinavian
> countries would join it so much the better. (239)

If this "post-sovereign" grouping of nations seems suspiciously Eurocentric, the elegiac tone in which Lewis discusses it suggests that he considered it a genuine mixture. "Some years ago," he writes, "I hoped to be only with the English—for us to be distinct. Now, after a great deal of close observation, I see that it is impossible. I have to have my England diluted, or mixed. Dear old Great Britain has to take in partners" (241). *The Hitler Cult* announces Lewis's recognition that nationalism was not, after all, what he wanted, and his attendant acceptance that internationalism was a policy worth investigating. It was not until he arrived in North America, however, that Lewis began to regard the post-nationalist future as something worthy of outright celebration.

The major document of Lewis's time in Toronto, the political pamphlet *Anglosaxony: A League That Works* (published in 1941 by Lorne Pierce of the Ryerson Press) devotes most of its energy to defending democracy against totalitarianism. In doing so, it initiates a major Lewisian cultural metaphor: the idea of "rootlessness" as a strategy for peace. One of the many reasons Lewis gives for calling democracy "a very good thing indeed" (10) is its flexible conception of citizenship. In a marked departure from the argument of *Hitler*, Lewis contrasts fascism and democracy through the contrasting symbols of "soil" and "the Wave": "If the 'soil' plays a leading part in national-socialist propaganda—if 'Blut und Boden' is *their* watchword—then 'the Wave' should, perhaps, be *ours*: with all that the ocean-wave takes with it of elasticity and freedom, of intangibility and in a sense rootlessness" (50). This praise of flexible democratic inclusiveness seems to have resulted in part—and negatively rather than positively—from Lewis's personal experiences in Toronto. In an article published in 1940 in *Saturday Night*, he complained of the "pride in being repellent, rather than attractive, to the stranger within-the-gate" that persisted in "Upper Canada"; he recommended that "'Toronto the Beautiful' should forget about being English" ("On Canada," 24–25). It also owed something to his analysis of French–English relations in Canada, reflecting the sentiments of the 1940 "Address to French-Canada" Lewis broadcast on the Société radio-Canada, in which he described Canada as "une collaboration émouvante," emphasizing the "intérêts primordiaux" that tie French and English Canada, and concluding, "C'est nationalisme...c'est *racisme*, que nous voudrons bannir du monde" (qtd. in Mastin 31).[1]

It is in the works ensuing from Lewis's time as lecturer at Assumption College in Windsor, however, that his enthusiasm for "rootless" internationalism reached its crescendo. In a 1943 third-person account of plans for upcoming lectures, Lewis provides the outlines of his new political position:

> The hope for the world lies, he thinks, in abolition of differences, rather than in their cultivation. He believes in one

world...But he thinks it very important that this political
Monism in-the-making should be of a higher dimension than
the barbarous plurality out of which it must emerge; not just
a mechanical act of standardization. ("Mr. Lewis's Plans" 2)

As in his nationalist works of the 1930s, Lewis looks to unification
and the elimination of difference as a strategy for peace. There are,
however, two fundamental differences. The first—one that also
distinguishes Lewisian internationalism from multiculturalism—is
that unity is now imagined as being achieved by dissolving, rather
than emphasizing, national and ethnic differences. The second is
that this political "Monism" occupies a middle ground between
complete "standardization," on the one hand, and the "barbarous
plurality" of the nationalist model of mutually distinct groups
in violent competition, on the other. In "The Cosmic Uniform of
Peace"—an elaboration of his Windsor lectures published in 1945 in
The Sewanee Review—Lewis rapturously describes America (a term
which in Lewis's genuinely "post-national" employment generally
includes Canada as well as the United States)[2] as "the great big
promiscuous grave into which tumble and there disintegrate all
that was formerly race, class, or nationhood" (509). In "American
Melting Pot" (1946), another offshoot of his Windsor lectures, Lewis
employed the image of the melting pot to describe American society
as made up of disparate parts, each of which surrenders its differences in becoming part of the mixture: "The Irish, the German,
the Jewish, the Italian, the Negro, the Polish, the Scandinavian,
the Indian, the French, the Chinese, have merged their minds and
sensibilities" (57). In one of his 1943 lectures, "'The Frontiers of Art'
or 'the Cultural Melting Pot,'" he described this society as "a preview
of an international culture" (2); in *America and Cosmic Man*
(1948), the book that finally resulted from his time in Windsor, he
described America as "a human laboratory for the manufacture
of Cosmic Man" (201–2), the latter being the "perfectly eclectic,
non-national, internationally minded creature" he now took as his
ideal citizen, with "blood...drawn...from all corners of the earth, with
no more geographical or cultural roots than a chameleon" (203).

If Lewis's conception of internationalism appears, from the perspective of the present-day multicultural Canada, to lay too strong an emphasis on the dissolution of difference in the establishment of a post-national society, it nonetheless represents a genuine and dramatic shift from his political thought of the 1930s. *America and Cosmic Man*, the major product of his Canadian period, stands as the most exuberant political work Lewis ever produced, and the most relevant to the international world of today.

Settle Down and Snooze: Lewis's Abandonment of Modernism

Lewis's North American political conversion was accompanied by a stylistic transformation. Taken together, they represent a chiasmic reversal of the trajectory described by Cuddy-Keane: when his politics became internationalist, espousing a complex social tension between unity and diversity, his style abandoned its dialogic modernist complexity, becoming increasingly straightforward. Lewis's stylistic reversal is most compactly visible in the strikingly dissimilar volumes of his trilogy, *The Human Age*. The first volume, *The Childermass* (1928), is typical of the polyvalent experimental style Lewis developed through the first four decades of the twentieth century. While W.B. Yeats approved of its complexities, calling it "as powerful as 'Gulliver' and much more exciting to a modern mind" (*Letters of Wyndham Lewis* 182), I.A. Richards called it incomprehensible, complaining, "We don't know—to an agonizing degree we are not allowed to know—what it is all about" (60). When Lewis finally completed the trilogy following his return to England after the Second World War, stylistic experimentation had vanished. Reviewing *Monstre Gai* and *Malign Fiesta* (1955) in *The Kenyon Review*, Thomas H. Carter called Lewis's prose "an economical, transparent instrument devoted self-effacingly to rendering the somber action from which it takes its tone" (331). The turning point in this remarkable transformation was, once again, Lewis's experience in North America, and was tied directly to his newfound enthusiasm for "Cosmic Man." From the beginning of his career, Lewis had conceived style in social and political terms, often employing dialogic, polyvalent style as a means of training his reader to resist dominant social discourses. Lewis's magazine *Blast*, employing a strategically self-contradictory modernist style, provides a case in point. *Blast* 1 (1914) contains two manifestos, the first of which repeatedly both "blasts" and "blesses" the same target, and the second of which acknowledges such inconsistencies as deliberate: "We start from opposite statements of a chosen world. Set up violent structure of adolescent clearness between two extremes. / We discharge ourselves on both sides" (30). Lewis's ironically titled contribution to *Blast* 2, "Be Thyself" (1915), begins by espousing and demonstrating stylistic complexity, stating, "You must talk with two tongues if you do not wish to cause confusion." It then proceeds to a theoretical justification of such double-voicedness, which Lewis employs to incite a state of active, alert engagement with the text: "You must catch the clearness and logic in the midst of contradictions," he tells his readers, "<u>not</u> settle down and snooze on an acquired, easily possessed and mastered, satisfying shape" (91). A similar stylistic logic undergirds Lewis's major political work of the 1920s, *The Art of Being Ruled* (1926). A sentence from the notorious chapter "Fascism as an Alternative" provides a demonstration of the work's pointedly contradictory style. Repeatedly and deliberately confusing Mussolini's fascism with its putative opposites, socialism and communism, Lewis writes, "[Italian fascism] is *the sort of socialism* that this essay would indicate as the most suitable for anglo-saxon countries or colonies, with as much of *sovietic proletarian sentiment* as could be got into it without impairing its discipline, and as little coercion as is compatible with good sense" (321, emphasis added). In his autobiography *Rude Assignment* (1954), Lewis explained that the stylistic aim of *The Art of Being Ruled* was to "state, here and there, both sides of the question to be debated, and allow these opposites to struggle in the reader's mind for the ascendancy and there to find their synthesis" (183). Reed Way Dasenbrock argues that Lewis's "shifting, mobile perspective" (436) trains its reader to engage critically with the discourses of modern life—"to separate the wheat from the chaff in Lewis's discourse, to follow the 'manifold byways' of his argument, and sort things out for himself" (437–38).

Whatever the merits of Lewis's dialogic political style, he began to
abandon it immediately after the publication of *The Art of Being
Ruled*. Whereas Lewis wrote in the latter's preface, "It must of necessity make its own audience; for it aims at no audience already there
with which I am acquainted" (13), he began the next year's more
straightforward *Time and Western Man* (1927) by declaring, "It has
been my object, from the start, to secure an audience of people not
usually attentive to abstract discussion, the general educated man
or woman" (xi). As readers of this nonetheless occasionally baffling
work will attest, however, the transition was gradual; throughout
the 1930s, Lewis's creative and nonfiction output vacillated
between the experimental and the straightforward. It was not until
his North American period that the movement was completed.

Paul Edwards argues that *The Vulgar Streak*, written in New
York in 1940, represents the true turning point: the novel, he
says, "can be seen as marking a great change in Wyndham Lewis's
fictional writing," effecting a definite break with experimental style
and standing as the first of Lewis's straightforwardly realist novels.
Fittingly, the theme of the novel is the politics of voice. This is
manifest in the novel's principal plot, which recounts the efforts of
its hero, Vincent Penhale, to escape from his class-bound Cockney
accent. Vincent, in a line later quoted by George Orwell, describes
himself as one whose "very tongue is branded" (38);[3] calling Cockney
English a "slave jargon" (133) and the English lower classes "a dark
and tonguetied multitude" (31), Vincent argues that such impov-
erished dialects serve politically to keep the working classes in
their place. Cockney English is, for Vincent, "the way our rulers
wanted us to speak" (137). A second development of the theme
occurs in the novel's exploration of the politics of the fascist voice.
In a lengthy scene, the protagonists gather to listen to Hitler's 1938
speech from the Berlin Sportspalast. Lewis's narrator recounts,

> The famous voice droned on. April sat in a bored and
> melancholy dream, wishing that that horrible voice
> would stop. Four other English guests listened sternly

and blankly to the voice of Fate. But since Fate unfortunately spoke a language which they were unable
to understand, they inclined their ears towards
the instrument in the hope that they might at least
discover if fate was in a bad temper to-night. (54)

In both aspects of its analysis of the politics of voice, *The Vulgar Streak* emphasizes clarity of expression. Bafflement is not a positive attribute in the listeners' response to Hitler's incomprehensible speech, which effectively presents a demonic parody of Lewis's earlier political style; both the reception Hitler's voice and the problem of the "tonguetied multitude" suggest the importance of transparent communication, stressing that, both within and across nations, citizens must speak the same language and understand one another if they are to coexist peacefully.

This realization marked the definitive end of Lewis's politically motivated experiments in dialogic modernist style. He took the lesson very much to heart in his North American writings; both *Anglosaxony* and *America and Cosmic Man* are written in a clear, direct style that leaves minimal room for readerly "synthesis." In one of the articles derived from his Windsor lectures, however, Lewis suggested an alternate vision of what an "international style" might look like—a vision more in line with Cuddy-Keane's analysis of modernist style and internationalist politics. In "Towards an Earth Culture" (1946), primarily concerned with painting, Lewis praises the lack of stylistic coherence in the art of the incipient post–Second World War period: "Although there is no unity of style or purpose in contemporary art," he argues, "that does not matter. It could not be otherwise." Warning against conceptions that equate unity with uniformity, he argues for "a more comprehensive dynamism" (7). "We have to live in chaos," he concludes: "Let us wear our motley to the best advantage, and let us pride ourselves on the number of different patches we display, the more the better" (11). This motley, diverse, dynamic style was not the one Lewis himself employed in his North American works. It bears a strong resemblance, however, to the styles adopted by two of his most important Canadian interpreters, Marshall McLuhan and Sheila Watson.

Marshall McLuhan's Lewisian Bricolage

We need not rely on the accounts of critics and historians to establish the enormity of Lewis's influence of Marshall McLuhan; McLuhan repeatedly went out of his way to assert it himself.[4] In an essay written at the beginning of his career, "Wyndham Lewis: Lemuel in Liliput" (1944), McLuhan made his admiration hyperbolically plain, calling Lewis "the greatest political thinker and observer since Machiavelli" (197) and "the only serious painter England has had in the past fifty years" (180). In an interview given at the height of his fame, distributed on a flexidisc supplement to the 1967 Wyndham Lewis special issue of *artscanada*, McLuhan was equally effusive, responding to a question about Lewis's influence by stating, "Good heavens—that's where I got it!":

> It was Lewis who put me on to all this study of the environment as an educational—as a teaching machine. To use our more recent terminology, Lewis was the person who showed me that the manmade environment was a teaching machine—a programmed teaching machine. Earlier, you see, the Symbolists had discovered that the work of art is a programmed teaching machine. It's a mechanism for shaping sensibility. Well, Lewis simply extended this private art activity to the corporate activity of the whole society in making environments that basically were artifacts or works of art and that acted as teaching machines upon the whole population.

In an essay published shortly before his death, "Lewis's Prose Style" (1980), McLuhan praised Lewis in terms remarkably similar to those of the essay published thirty-six years before: "Lewis was an *avant garde* all by himself, the greatest pictorial draughtsman of his time, the most controversial prose stylist of our day" (64). The Lewis–McLuhan relationship, however, was far from one of passive influence. McLuhan's response to Lewis is best characterized as an act of intellectual bricolage: McLuhan did not hesitate to take the best elements of Lewis's thought and style, to recombine them in novel ways, and unceremoniously to abandon the remainder.

Among the most important and best known of McLuhan's borrowings from Lewis is the famous concept of "the global village," which Lewis elaborated throughout his Canadian period. As early as 1929, Lewis had written, "the Earth has become ONE place instead of a romantic tribal patch work of places" (qtd. in Fox 45). Given his interest in internationalism, however, the notion of the global village became a particular focus during Lewis's time in North America. In a plan for a 1943 lecture entitled "'The Frontiers of Art' or 'the Cultural Melting Pot,'" Lewis (again adopting the third person) wrote,

> With television tomorrow causing us to be physically present (in our living-room, with one of its walls a screen for long-distance projections) at contemporaneous happenings all over the earth: with the vast development in the immediate future of air-travel, which will abolish distance, and strangeness: with the cultural standardization which has already resulted, and must in the future increasingly result, from this—with all these and many other technological devices expanding our horizons and making a nonsense of the oldfashioned partitions and locked doors of our earthly habitat, it is Mr. Lewis's belief that national or nationalist (for it always comes to that) cultures must disappear. (1)

Lewis reiterated this vision of an internationalist culture connected—and produced—by new technologies in "Towards an Earth Culture," describing the "comprehensive revolution brought about by those great Twentieth Century techniques, of flying, radio, cinematography, rotary photogravure, and so forth, unifying the nations in spite of themselves," and adding, "We should all give thanks for, and in any way we can promote, this union" (3). The final expression came in *America and Cosmic Man*, where Lewis wrote, "the earth has become one big village, with telephones laid from one end to the other, and air transport, both speedy and safe" (21). McLuhan—who in *The Gutenberg Galaxy* (1962) stated, "The new electronic interdependence recreates the world in the image of a global village" (36)—was clearly listening to Lewis's North American pronouncements on technology and internationalism. More than this, however, he actively assisted Lewis in formulating them. McLuhan and Lewis were close acquaintances throughout Lewis's Windsor period, and McLuhan indeed provided Lewis with reading suggestions for *America and Cosmic Man* (Mastin 80). In a 1951 letter to Ezra Pound, McLuhan complained that *America and Cosmic Man* was "an H-bomb let off in the desert". (*Letters* 227)—a work of fundamental importance that had failed to find its audience. McLuhan himself subsequently remedied this situation. Though not, like Lewis, a committed internationalist, McLuhan provided the major conduit through which Lewis's ideas on inter-nationalism were disseminated; and through him they exerted a tremendous—one might almost say thermonuclear—impact.

While McLuhan adopted and adapted important elements of Lewis's internationalism—the major intellectual fruit of his engagement with North American society—he was conspicuously *not* influenced by Lewis's major North American stylistic devel-opment: his turn from experimental, dialogic modernist forms to clear, straightforward prose. As Elena Lamberti has argued, McLuhan's style was a crucial aspect of his work; she asks us to take seriously his famous assertion, "the medium is the message," and to move from a focus on "what McLuhan said" to "*how* he said what he said." Lamberti describes McLuhan's works as

> open to several interpretations, since they are built on poly-semic "images" or fragments, and the act of juxtaposition, which leads to a discontinuous form, is that which triggers new semantic combinations and, therefore, new epiphanies: it is the "gap," the leap from one passage to the other that, paradoxically, contributes to the making of sense, since it is conceived as a "resonant internal" enhancing knowl-edge. ("McLuhan and the Modernist Writers' Legacy" 72)

This could just as well serve as a description of Lewis's early, modernist style—particularly in works like *The Art of Being Ruled*, where Lewis employed strategic argumentative contradictions and "gaps" to "trigger" active engagement, active reconfiguration, and "new epiphanies" in the minds of his readers. McLuhan himself indeed described Lewis's early style in strikingly similar terms:

> For readers who are accustomed to action in prose narra-
> tive Lewis is baffling. Especially his early novels provide
> passage after passage which are like nothing so much as a
> package of materials with directions for making a painting.
> As Dr Johnson said of Richardson's novels: "If you were
> to read them for the story, Sir, you would hang yourself."
> A good deal of work is left for the reader. But the result
> enables the reader to see. And the effect is finally more vivid
> than a ready-made painting. ("Lewis's Prose Style" 64)

Lamberti calls McLuhan's "non-linear form of writing" a "mosaic" (*McLuhan's Mosaic* 43)—much as Lewis in "Towards an Earth Culture" had called mixed, chaotic, non-unified inter-nationalist style a "motley" composed of "different patches." While Lewis influenced the development of McLuhan's mosaic style, as Lamberti explores in her chapter on Lewis in *Marshall McLuhan's Mosaic*, it was decidedly not Lewis's straightforward North American style that provided the impetus. In the act I have described as one of bricolage, McLuhan combined Lewis's later internationalism with his earlier stylistic dialogism, and in so doing resolved an important incoherence in Lewis's thought.

McLuhan's reconfiguration of Lewis is nowhere clearer than the 1954 *Counterblast*, the first of his two responses to Lewis's *Blast*.[5] *Counterblast* incorporates and develops many of Lewis's insights about internationalism. In the preface, McLuhan writes,

> In AMERICA AND COSMIC MAN Lewis saw North
> America as a benign rock crusher in which all remnants
> of European nationalism and individualism were happily

reduced to cosmic baby powder. The new media are
blowing a lot of this baby powder around the pendant
cradle of New Man today. The dust gets in our eyes.

COUNTERBLAST 1954 blows aside this
dust for a few moments and offers a view of the
cradle, the bough, and the direction of the winds
of the new media in these latitudes. (n. pag.)

As McLuhan's prefatory "plan de guerre" makes clear, the "content"
of *Counterblast* is inspired by the North American Lewis, sharing
his interests in technology's role in creating a post-nationalist
global culture. But its "form," with its bombastic and energetic prose ("benign rock crusher") and showily vorticist pose
(blowing aside the dust to look objectively at the swirling media
landscape from a point of stillness) bears a strong similarly to
early Lewis. The passage in which McLuhan praises "The crafty
cubist JIVE of the / daily press awakening the political appetite
of / COSMIC MAN" finds him espousing late-Lewis politics by
means of a vigorous early-Lewisian style. Perhaps the most telling
example of the juxtaposition occurs when McLuhan employs
Lewis's *Blast*-era strategy of deliberate self-contradiction to challenge his readers to reflect actively on the Massey Report, that
monument of Canadian cultural nationalism. On facing pages,
McLuhan writes, "Oh BLAST / The MASSEY REPORT damp
cultural igloo / for canadian devotees of / TIME / & / LIFE" and,
"BLESS / The MASSEY REPORT, / HUGE RED HERRING for /
derailing Canadian kulcha while it is / absorbed by American ART
& Technology." Bringing together internationalist politics and
modernist style much in the manner described by Cuddy-Keane,
McLuhan's *Counterblast* achieves a combination never encountered in Lewis's work itself. Some of McLuhan's associates noted a
waning of Lewisian influence in his work beginning in the 1960s;
Paul Tiessen, for example, records Wilfred Watson's disappointment
that James Joyce replaced Lewis as McLuhan's major modernist
touchstone ("Shall I Say" 116). McLuhan's continued employment
of the mosaic method and persistent interest in the global village,

however, attest to the enduring importance of those two poles of Lewisian thought—dialogic modernist style and internationalist politics—that McLuhan ingeniously and actively integrated, and in so doing put to use in post–Second World War Canada.

Nationalism of the Predominant Culture: Sheila Watson's Reworking of Lewis

As with McLuhan, the importance of Lewis to Sheila Watson is easily demonstrated.[6] Watson's doctoral dissertation, supervised by McLuhan, was titled "Wyndham Lewis and Expressionism." Watson organized and edited the 1967 Lewis special issue of *artscanada* and supplied it with a long essay, "The Great War: Wyndham Lewis and the Underground Press." In the late 1960s, Watson briefly planned a biography of Lewis. To describe the specific influence of Lewis on Watson—particularly of his North American writings—is, however, a more difficult task than with McLuhan. Although her work enacts cultural diversity through polyphonic modernist style,[7] Watson assuredly did not derive her artistic practice from any McLuhan-like process of Lewis-derived bricolage. While Watson's thoughts on internationalism and on style were profoundly affected by her engagement with Lewis, she arrived at her own positions primarily by resisting and reworking—rather than by straightforwardly embracing or adopting—those of Lewis.

Watson's view of internationalism, indeed, is far less enthusiastic than Lewis's, and effects a powerful critique of the skewed balance of unity and diversity that Lewis advances in his vision of an international culture. Watson cites *America and Cosmic Man* only once in her dissertation; although she quotes the famous "global village" passage, her interpretation of Lewis is so pessimistic, and her quotation so selective, as to amount almost to a misreading:

> After the second war Lewis observed "that the earth has in fact become one big village with telephones laid from one end to the other, and air transport both safe and speedy." The village, however, was hardly the result of creative compulsion. What had been nations he said "were bankrupt

dumps" infested by black-marketeers squabbling for control of the site. America had addressed itself to the "austere if eccentric task of taking over the world...and running it as a sort of poorhouse, disciplined by atomic fission." (252)[8]

In an equally pessimistic formulation, she wrote in her essay "A Question of Portraiture,"

In *The Art of Being Ruled* [Lewis] observes that a revolutionary state of mind has become instinctive and automatic because of the pattern of commodity production, superannuation, and sabotage, imposed on the human mind by the techniques of industry. Elsewhere he suggests that this state of mind will spread as the language of technology becomes a universal idiom and the earth "a big village with telephones laid from one end to the other." (44–45)

The global village—decidedly positive for both Lewis and McLuhan, who employed it as a symbol of collapsing national boundaries and increased international intercourse—becomes almost demonic in Watson's reading, where it is transformed into an image of standardization and uniformity. If Watson's is a misreading, it is one that highlights an important blindness in Lewis's frenzied support for internationalism: his over-eagerness, in describing the "political Monism in-the-making," to celebrate the melting away of difference and corresponding lack of concern for what he passingly identified as the threat of "a mechanical act of standardization." For Watson, who recognized that so-called internationalism could easily become a disguised form of imperialism, the dangers of standardization precluded any such reckless celebration. Fred Flahiff records Watson's statement, in the early 1970s,

Internationalism means the nationalism of the predominant culture, and if you've lived in Western Canada you've suffered through several imperialisms. You've suffered through British imperialism, when nothing was valid unless it had come from Oxford or Cambridge or London. Then you suffered through domestic imperialism, which said nothing was important unless it had roots in eastern Canada. And so for me American imperialism, the new internationalism, is simply a third wave. (*Always* 258)

Watson does not, in this passage, specifically reject the idea of internationalism that Lewis celebrates—the abandonment of national attachment and embrace of a unifying, post-national consciousness. However, focusing on how this idea functions in political practice, she shows how the label "internationalism" often functions as little more than a attractive label to disguise cultural imperialism. At a 1973 reading of *The Double Hook*, Watson argued that her novel stood as an attempt to resist such forces of "internationalist" standardization:

It was at a time, I suppose, when people were thinking that if you wrote a novel it had to be, in some mysterious way, international. It had to be about what I would call something *else*. And so I thought, I don't see why: how do you...how are you international if you're not international? if you're very provincial, very local, and very much part of your own milieu. ("What I'm Going" 182)

Watson's answer to this rhetorical question was not, however, that one should be purely and proudly provincial—as *The Double Hook* itself clearly demonstrates. Stephen Scobie argues that the novel defies any conception of the regional and international as alternatives in an either/or choice: Watson "clearly... resisted" McLuhan's (and Lewis's) insistence "that regional differences and particularities were being rendered irrelevant as the world became the 'global village'"—but "At the same time, paradoxically as always, she recognize[d] the need to go beyond the limitations of the *merely* 'regional' novel" (21).[9] In *The Double Hook*, as Scobie suggests, Watson responded to Lewis by producing not an "anti-internationalist" or "pro-regional" novel, but one that presents the regional and the international together, on equal terms, neither subordinated to the other. She did so by using some of Lewis's own stylistic tools.

The question of whether *The Double Hook*'s modernist style is somehow at odds with its depiction of a rural community is, by now, a very old one. John Grube, reading international modernism as incompatible with sincere representation of the rural, describes *The Double Hook* in his 1965 Introduction as a "symbolic novel" that—like works by Morley Callaghan and Ernest Hemingway— "appears to be written in the clichés of the regional idyll" but whose "use of cliché is ironic" (5). Donna Pennee, blaming where Grube praised, sees *The Double Hook* as a regional novel colonized by the alien, universalizing aesthetic of literary modernism: both in its "style and themes," she argues, the novel yields to "modernist prescriptions of the mythic method and objective correlative," and in so doing "sacrifices historical, ethnic, and gendered specificity in the name of cosmopolitanism." Pennee attributes Watson's lamentable incorporation of the "repressive principles of high anglomodernism" to the influence of Lewis. Indeed, genetic criticism confirms some of Pennee's suspicions, suggesting that Lewis loomed large as Watson performed the dramatic final revisions to *The Double Hook*. Margaret Morriss has described these revisions—which included the excision of regional detail and the removal of much omniscient narration—as moving the text "from the potential stereotype of the regional novel, to a universal and archetypal pattern of action" ("'No Short Cuts'" 69). As Gregory Betts shows in *Avant-Garde Canadian Literature*, Watson's reading of Lewis's *Human Age* trilogy was a major instigator of this movement. In her diary entry of November 18, 1955, Watson described Lewis's novels as "the best thing I've read for some time." Though the final volumes of *The Human Age* belong very much to Lewis's post-transformation realist phase and bear little relation, stylistically, either to Lewis's early work or to *The Double Hook*, Watson responded to perhaps their only characteristically modernist feature: the employment of a detached narrator. In Lewis's novels, Watson noted, "There is no malice, no excitement, no castigation" (Flahiff *Always* 125). Betts ties this remark to one made shortly before Watson began her final revisions: "It is absolutely necessary to liquidate anger, chagrin or contempt before writing" (136). This Lewis-derived insight, Betts argues, inspired a process of revision that led to Watson's "taking out the narrator as a Joycean personality, taking out the history of the characters, taking out cultural references and backgrounds" (Betts, *Avant-Garde* 273).

Watson's decisions to eliminate regional detail and intrusive narration from the final version of *The Double Hook* were undoubtedly guided by her reading of modernist fiction in general and of Lewis in particular. This is not to say, however, that Watson succumbed to modernist universalism or Lewisian internationalism in making these revisions—or that in doing so she committed her own sin of denying the "validity" of the local. Instead, Watson's formal maneuvers should be seen as serving to maintain a *balance* in the novel between the international and the regional; unlike Lewis, who vacillated between poles of nationalism/internationalism and modernism/realism, Watson developed a hybrid style in order to keep the opposition of local and global in play, without resolving it. What attracted Watson in Lewis's style was not any of the characteristics listed by Pennee in her caricature summary of modernism—its supposed hardness, universalism, and indifference to context—but rather its dialogism. In "A Question of Portraiture," Watson says of Lewis,

> His art is essentially the art of dialogue and can be called "polemical" or "disputatious" only by those who have rejected open dialogue as a mode of awareness. Lewis's training as a visual artist, or perhaps the peculiar sensibility which allowed him to speak "two dialects of the same language" simultaneously, helped him to create a type of dramatic critical writing which was peculiarly his own. (47)

Watson's elimination of regional detail and intrusive narration are consistent with this conception of modernist dialogism. By removing

the normalizing presence of the narrator, Watson allows us to hear
more of her characters' actual words, transforming the novel into
"a spare, poetic, highly imagistic narrative delivered by a chorus of
disparate voices," as Philip Marchand describes it ("Reflections").
The removal of regional details follows from this same desire to
allow characters to speak for themselves. It is in part simply a matter
of accuracy: in their own speech and thoughts, the characters of
The Double Hook would not use the names that appear on maps
when referring to their local environment; for them, the valley
is simply "the valley," the river "the river." Only the narrator
would supply such map names; and the narrator would only do
so for the benefit of the reader, to help her locate the action of
The Double Hook within the spatial and temporal co-ordinates
of her world. Providing these details would, however, unbalance
the relationship between character and reader. The characters
in *The Double Hook* have only the vaguest notions of the outside
world; when Lenchen tells her brother, "I've had enough of this
place, but I don't know where to go," for instance, he replies,
"Place is the word," admitting that his own geographic imagination extends only as far as the nearby town: "I only know a place
where men drink beer" (11). By withholding local descriptions
and background, Watson ensures that the reader's experience of
looking in to the novel is just as disorienting and uncertain as
the characters' experience of *looking out* at the wider world. Far
from subordinating the regional to the international, Watson's
technique stands as a refusal to serve up the local for easy outside
consumption. Rather than translating the local into terms easily
comprehensible to the outside world, rather than making the
local easily assimilable into the international, Watson places the
local and the international as equal participants in dialogue.

One of the text's most memorable images of the interdependence of the local and the global is introduced when William
reminds Heinrich that Theophil, despite his strident indepen-
dence, "drinks coffee like the rest of us," adding, "A man who
drinks coffee is dependent on something outside himself" (129).
A similar image—one that can be seen as Watson's response to

Lewis's motley and McLuhan's mosaic—is the plaid shirt James wears at the end of the novel.[10] When Heinrich sees the shirt, immediately following his conversation with William about coffee, he reads it as a symbol of James's intercourse with the outside world. He asks, "Where have you been that you left the two of them alone at such a time, and come back two nights and a day later dressed up in a new shirt?" (131). Scobie perceptively reads plaid—"a weaving together of various elements into a unified pattern" (31)—as a symbol of the way *The Double Hook* embraces "both sides of the paradox—the sense of a *particular* locality, the sense of a *universal* setting" (29). That the particular plaid James chooses is a mixture of green and blue—the colours of the planet— only underscores the particular effect that Watson achieves (96). Whereas Lewis abandoned his own modernist style to advocate melting-pot unification, Watson in *The Double Hook* employs elements of Lewisian modernist style to envision and enact a genuine internationalism in which the local is interweaved with the global, but with all its strangeness and specificity intact.

Internationalism, Multiculturalism, and the Global Brain

The flipside of the Lewis/Canada story—the story of how Canada shaped Lewis and Canadian modernism reshaped him—is one intimately tied to Canadian national narratives past, present, and future. Sheila Watson, by resisting Lewis's unifying conception of internationalism and by arguing for a pluralistic model of distinct, interacting cultures, adapted Lewis to the enduring post–Second World War vision of Canadian society: multiculturalism. McLuhan—who, as Janine Marchessault has argued, himself placed multiculturalism at the "core" of his critical project (129)—recombined, reconfigured, and cross-pollinated Lewisian insights to produce a distinctly Canadian vision of cultural interconnection that reverberated well beyond our borders. McLuhan's and Watson's reshaping of Lewis turned him into a refracted influence on Canadian society: by leaving out what was worst in Lewis and adapting what was best, they introduced his thought into the heart of the Canadian national conversation.

The present moment is a propitious one in which to begin our own rereading of Lewis's work—to look again at his version of modernist internationalism, and to see how we might make use of it in shaping the new cultural narratives that are emerging in the twenty-first century. At a time when technology is challenging national borders and promoting new networked forms of association, and at a time when state policies of multiculturalism are undergoing widespread reconsideration both at home and abroad, the two questions posed by Lewis's North American writings— where must the balance fall between unity and diversity in a global society, and what forms of discourse are best suited to expressing and enacting this post-national society?—remain as relevant to us today as they were to Watson and McLuhan. Achille Mbembe has argued that whereas the primary task of twentieth-century postcolonial criticism was the protection of threatened national identities against universalizing imperialist discourses, the most pressing need today is to reconcile distinct national identities with a more universal "politics of the fellow-creature" (3)—to develop, as he says, "a *polis* that is universal because ethnically diverse" (11). This need for discourses able to emphasize what is shared in common between diverse groups has been spurred powerfully by the spread of the Internet and wireless technologies, which have promoted new forms of global consciousness in ways that neither McLuhan nor Lewis could fully have imagined. Nowhere is this need more apparent than in Canada, which Charles Foran has recently described as a country "poised somewhere between a nation-state and a post-nation configuration with no easy name for it." As we begin to construct the new cultural narratives that can hold together the complex strands of unity and diversity, Lewis's Cosmic Man and modernist dialogic style remain for us, as they were for McLuhan and Watson, excellent starting points.

Notes

1 He described Canada as a "dynamic collaboration," emphasizing the "fundamental interests" that tie English and French Canada, and concluding, "It's nationalism...it's *racism*, that we wish to banish from the world."

2 Catharine M. Mastin, quoting a passage from *America and Cosmic Man*, responds to Lewis's persistent unwillingness to treat Canada as a distinct entity: "No Canadian reading these words can fail to regret that Lewis did not acknowledge that his Canadian experience and acquaintances—in particular his mutually stimulating relationship with Marshall McLuhan—had a...revelatory and transformative effect" (102).

3 In his 1942 essay "The English People," Orwell wrote, "The English working class, as Mr Wyndham Lewis has put it, are 'branded on the tongue'" (5).

4 For excellent elaborations of Lewis's influence on McLuhan, see Betts, *Avant-Garde Canadian Literature*; Cavell, *McLuhan in Space*; Willmott, *McLuhan, or Modernism in Reverse*; Tiessen, "From Literary Modernism to the Tantramar Marshes."

5 McLuhan's second response to *Blast*—and the major document of his persistent interest in Lewis's ideas and critical style in the late 1960s—is the 1969 second version of *Counterblast*, designed by Harley Parker. It continues the Lewisian strategy of deliberate self-contradiction, paradoxically blasting "the printed page" (the paradoxical nature of the statement registered by a diagonal row of question marks), and inverting some of the valuations of the earlier *Counterblast*. Whereas the 1954 manifesto declared "BLESS the sports page, upholder of / HOMERIC CULTURE / the comic strips, pantheon of / PICKLED GODS and / ARCHETYPES," the 1969 text performs a double inversion, chiasmically reordering the words and revaluing the sentiments: "BLAST / The Sports Page / pantheon of pickled / gods and archetypes / & / The Comic Strip / upholder of / HOMERIC CULTURE."

6 For critical elaborations and discussions of this relationship, see, for example, Betts, *Avant-Garde Canadian Literature* and Pennee, "Canadian Letters, Dead Referents."

7 See, for example, Glenn Willmott's argument in "Sheila Watson, Aboriginal Discourse, and Cosmopolitan Modernism."

8 The same passage is incorporated into Watson's essay "Myth and Counter-Myth" (131).

9 Gregory Betts, in his article "Media, McLuhan, and the Dawn of the Electric Age," also notes the intertwining of the local and the global, the individual and the communal, in Watson's novels. Focusing specifically on the role that technologies plays in *The Double Hook* and *Deep Hollow Creek*, Betts argues that they "participate in the formation of a new culture by connecting the European settlers to the Aboriginal characters and ritual systems," producing "a hybrid of the First Nations and European diasporic cultures" (255).

10 The famous typo in early editions of *The Double Hook*, "plaid *skirt*," has served to divert critical attention from the adjective to the noun. Scobie is thus truly perceptive in noting this lovely image of cultural intermingling.

II

THE
ANTENNAE
of
the
race

5

McLuhan, Anti-Environments, and Visual Art across the Canada–US Border, 1966–1973

Dispatches from the DEW Line

Adam Welch

"**WHAT ALL OF US DO,**" Marshall McLuhan proposed
in his Marfleet lecture from 1967, "only the artist makes
visible." "The ordinary procedures and environmental patterns
of a society don't become visible until the artist creates this
counter-environment of art objects" ("The Marfleet Lectures" 119).
Initially, McLuhan's invocation of the artist seems out of place in
an account of Canadian–American relations. However, in this first
of the two-part lecture entitled "Canada, the Borderline Case,"
McLuhan proposes this striking correspondence, positing Canada
itself as an artist figure; the country, in other words, as a maker of
global anti- or counter-environments.[1] Reflecting on what it meant to
share a border with the United States, over the course of the lecture
McLuhan argues that as America becomes the "world environment"
through its global reach of "resources, technology and enterprises,"
Canada's principal role is to lay bare such newfound configurations.[2]

Speaking at a time of intense geopolitical transformation—fears
of American cultural imperialism and a concomitant Canadian
nationalism—McLuhan, tellingly and rather curiously, points
to the indispensability of artists. That he would marry transnational politics and the function of the artist in 1967 is significant:
it was a moment when centennial celebrations in Canada fostered
a heightened cultural nationalism and unprecedented levels of
state sponsorship in the arts. In the years following, programs and
agencies such as Opportunities for Youth, the Local Initiatives
Program, the Canada Council for the Arts, National Museums,
Explorations, and the Art Bank, among others, indelibly marked
the Canadian arts landscape. These initiatives owed much to Pierre
Elliott Trudeau's policies of "decentralization and democratization,"

inspired by the politics of André Malraux during his time as French minister of culture under Charles de Gaulle (Danzker 216).[3] This remarkable meeting of art and politics in Canada has attracted considerable interest as of late. Curator and writer Vincent Bonin, for one, in the catalogue accompanying his exhibition *Documentary Protocols* (2010), details this "cybernetic welfare state," where artists "banked on the exceptional convergence of their projects with the decentralized governance policies" (44).[4]

We would do well to read McLuhan's Marfleet lecture against this context and, moreover, to situate his political argument along-side period artists' practices. Taking up McLuhan's analogy of Canada as a global artist figure, in this chapter I argue that visual artists working in Canada through the late 1960s and 1970s served an important role as creators of anti-environments to the pervasive American ground. In this way, I follow McLuhan's collapsing of transnational politics and the function of the artist. Through projects that engaged explicitly with the Canadian–US border—as well as those taking up transnational relations in a more abstract sense—we might understand McLuhan's lecture as addressing not only polit-ical relations at the close of the 1960s but artistic relations as well.

McLuhan's understanding of Canada as an artist figure grew out of his earlier and extensive thinking about environments and counter-environments—this central argument in the Marfleet lecture arising out of a conjunction of two seemingly disparate ideas. These two ideas are Canada as a counter-environment, and artists as makers of counter-environments. The former first appears, as Richard Cavell details, with McLuhan's hasty response to the Massey Commission Report, in an essay enti-tled "Defrosting Canadian Culture" published in the *American Mercury* in March 1952. Quoting McLuhan, Cavell suggests,

> While Canada's economic relations with the United States have thus placed Canada in "a state of perpetual anxiety and expediency," those conditions have granted the Canadian "a power of acute observation and the ability to

comment shrewdly on the ebullient comings and goings of his rich friend to the south of him." ("Defrosting" 92–93 qtd. in Cavell, *McLuhan in Space* 200)

The second idea, that of artists as makers of counter-environments, would arrive over a decade later, with the text "Art as Anti-Environment," published in the 1966 issue of *Art News Annual*. That same year, he draws these two seemingly disparate lines of inquiry—Canada as a counter-environment and artists as makers of counter-environments—together as the notion of Canada as an artist figure.

The development of this crucial, hybrid notion is elaborated in a series of letters between McLuhan and Claude Bissell, then president of the University of Toronto. Writing to Bissell on March 4, 1965, McLuhan shares "a new idea of [his] on which [he has] just begun to work":

> It is this, that the U.S.A. is socially and informationally the environment of Canada. Canada is, by way of being anti-environment, a prepared situation that permits perception of the environment...Canada as anti-environment to the U.S.A. is able to perceive many of the ground rules and operational effects of the American environment that are quite imperceptible to the U.S.A. If the U.S.A. has built its distant-early-warning system in Canada for military use, let us observe that we can be of far greater use to the U.S.A. as an early-warning system in the social and political spheres generally. (*Letters* 319)

By relating Canada as an anti-environment, McLuhan stresses a critical distance necessary for the perception of the "American environment." For McLuhan, at least, American apperception is an impossibility. McLuhan offers this précis of his latest thinking, as he often did for Bissell, following a letter from the president congratulating him on a favourable review of *Understanding*

Media (1964) by the celebrated art critic Harold Rosenberg in *The New Yorker*. On his frequent speaking engagements, Bissell often remarked on his star faculty member's latest projects.

The following year, McLuhan noted Bissell's tendency to cite his work in a letter from January 28, 1966. Referring to a speech Bissell made to the Canadian Society of Los Angeles two days earlier, McLuhan begins, "I thought your remarks about the U.S. well timed and valuable" (*Letters* 333). (Bissell had alluded to Canada as a "distant-early-warning system.") McLuhan elaborates:

> Canada as a cultural DEW line, or distant early warning system, has a large untouched potential in relation to the U.S. The U.S.A. as our environment, tends to be an area of unconsciousness. We, as an anti-environment of the U.S. should, naturally, tend to push it up into archetypal form... As the U.S.A. becomes a world environment, our status as anti-environment to the U.S.A. becomes an invaluable asset. We are best situated to create and to provide aware- ness of the process of being and making Americans. (333)

Following this, McLuhan makes an explicit connection to art as anti-environment, saying, "I have found that to consider art as an anti-environment or as a means of perceiving the hidden dimension of the environment, is exceedingly useful...art has an indispensable function in cognition, and that men without art strongly tend to be automata, or somnambulists, imprisoned in a dream" (333).[5]

It is here that McLuhan draws together the two previously distinct threads in his thinking: on the one hand, Canada as counter-environment to the United States, and on the other, art as counter-environment. In this letter to Bissell, we see the link being forged between the two ideas. It is the result of this almost casual connection shared in correspondence that figures two years later as the crux of the Marfleet lecture.

Ever prolific, around the same time as the Marfleet lecture,

McLuhan penned an essay for the Toronto-based journal *artscanada*—the foremost arts periodical in Canada at the time. Titled "Technology and Environment," the essay begins by suggesting that the "really total and saturating environments are invisible. The ones we notice are quite fragmentary and insignificant compared to the ones we don't see" (5). McLuhan continues by further developing the role of the artist as maker of counter-environments: "One related consideration is that anti-environments, or counter-environments created by the artist, are indispensable means of becoming aware of the environment in which we live and of the environments we create for ourselves technically" (5). Citing the artist and musician John Cage's text *Silence* (1961), McLuhan reads the ambient noise in an environment as crucial to our functioning within it—never intended, but nonetheless pervasive and powerful. In sum, "the artist, as a creator of anti-environments... has a very peculiar role in our society" (5). Just as Cage's radical rethinking of how silence is understood—as in works such as a *4'33"* (1952; conceived 1947–1948)—McLuhan sees the artist as drawing our attention to the barely perceptible qualities in our surroundings. Silence, in other words, within which one finds a great deal of noise.

McLuhan's argument in "Technology and Environment" extends his earlier and frequently cited aphoristic reading from *Understanding Media* (1964) of "art, at its most significant, as a DEW line, a Distant Early Warning system that can always be relied on to tell the old culture what is beginning to happen to it" (69). Indeed, here we find a similarly crossed analogy of the military-industrial complex with the visual arts as encountered in the Marfleet lecture. If artists are prophetic and their work visionary, for McLuhan this was also Canada's role in the postwar global landscape.

Borderline Research Request

Published by the Toronto-based artist collective General Idea, the inaugural issue of *FILE Megazine* (1972–1989) presented readers with a curious, multi-part survey. On the verso of one page, readers were—somewhat predictably—asked to list their "ten favorite artists this month," recommend their friends for subscription, and make suggestions for future issues. On the recto, however, General Idea and their collaborator, Californian artist Robert Cumming, asked readers to take part in a far more unusual geopolitical exercise. Presented with a basic outline of the northern part of North America, the reader was asked to "locate and draw from memory the Canadian/American border." Left to sketch the borderline from memory, the map was headed with the caption, "behind a big story there may be another one" (General Idea, "Borderline Research" 31).

Formed in Toronto in 1969, and made up of the pseudonymous Felix Partz, Jorge Zontal, and AA Bronson, General Idea's practice of the late 1960s and early 1970s was founded on such collaborative, participatory models. Prior to founding *FILE* in 1972, General Idea had circulated other surveys through their mail network, including the *Orgasm Energy Chart* (1970). In this work, the artists distributed charts asking respondents to record the occasion and frequency of their sexual activity for a given period.[6] In many ways, *FILE Megazine* arose out of such early mail-based projects. However, it also developed as a response to General Idea's own "absence in the Canadian art press," and more broadly because of an "absence of a 'fanzine' for contemporary art in Canada" (Fischer, "Introduction" 22). As Barbara Fischer has argued, "*FILE* responded to the need for a mirror and the giddy discovery of the self-appointed power to reflect" (22). That this mirror was modelled on *LIFE* magazine speaks to the collective's larger concern for—as AA Bronson has put it more recently—injecting "ourselves into the mainstream of this infectious culture, and liv[ing], as parasites, off our monstrous host" ("Copyright" 27). Such *détournements* would remain a hallmark of their work throughout the 1970s and 1980s. Despite the fact that *FILE* is now regarded as a crucial early document of artist-initiated culture in Canada, at the time some held it as suspect, considering it little more than an elaborate inside joke.[7]

Critics at the time might be forgiven for thinking of the

Megazine as insiderish and flippant, but such levity masked a far more profound politics. With their *Borderline Research Project*, General Idea and Robert Cumming elicited telling responses from their readership. The submissions they received—now deposited in the General Idea fonds at the National Gallery of Canada— sketch a divide between Canada and the United States in turn absurd, playful, and deeply perceptive. Some were decidedly conceptual—Sharon Kulik determined the border by the fold line in her entry, while Ian Murray responded, "Art knows no national boundaries." Others were more markedly geopolitical: Robert Cumming's own submission provided what he called a "Chilean national geographic sensibility," with "a country squashed along a coastline of a major continent." He imagines an elaborate system of tariffs and tolls to use the ports or traverse the "vast inner power." Others still signal a looming American imperialism: Anna Banana, in Vancouver, draws a somewhat accurate borderline, captioned "the maps put it about so," then an arrow drawn to the furthest north, "but for all practical purposes it's around here."

From these submissions and some eighty others, General Idea superimposed selected responses and reprinted them as a single image—a collaborative topography—in the second issue of the *Megazine*. The large number of responses where the border is reimagined entirely points to a far deeper engagement with political borders in what at first appears rather frivolous—what some critics at the time would have undoubtedly dismissed as a cartographic gag. As boundaries drawn through consensus, and not governmental fiat, submissions from both sides of the border convey a fraught transnational situation. It is signifi- cant that the project comes at a time when the border was being contested and reimagined, if not actually, at least conceptually.

General Idea's *Borderline Research Project* drew from the very same ground as McLuhan did in developing in his lecture, "Canada, The Borderline Case." Central to McLuhan's argument in the Marfleet lecture is art's role in making "the corporate and communal accessible to the individual, whose task it is to assimilate the tradition, to modify it in relation to the new situations that are continuously forming" ("Marfleet" 119). Following this, we might imagine the Canadian–US political boundary as just such a "corporate and communal" reality—a reality made visible through General Idea's project. In his lecture, McLuhan provides historical examples of the communal being made accessible to the individual—Emily Carr conveying the experience of British Columbia through her work, or the Group of Seven making Canada perceptible to its inhabitants. Afforded historical distance, artists' practices contemporaneous to McLuhan's writing—though in all likelihood unknown to him—capture the sensibility much more accurately. Unlike paintings by Carr or members of the Group of Seven, painted by artists to be viewed by an audience, the *Borderline Research Project* is participatory. *FILE*'s readership at once makes and receives the work; with its two parts taken together, the project constitutes a correspondence-based feedback loop. "The artist," McLuhan suggests, provides insight to the individual "by creating counter-environments as mirrors of the present" (119). That the resulting "mirror" in *FILE*'s second issue, the single compiled map, is collaborative does not mean that it seeks consensus. As the outrageously drawn and conflicting lines attest, General Idea, Robert Cumming, and the nearly one hundred contributors reflect a border and a geopolitical situation in flux.

That the analogue of a mirror served as a crucial impetus for General Idea's founding of *FILE* and for McLuhan's understanding of the role of the artist seems, in hindsight, more than coincidental. Taking seriously McLuhan's suggestion that artworks lead us to a new awareness of current situations, General Idea addressed debates over Canadian nationalism and American cultural imperialism that were pervasive at the time.

DEW Lines and Contacts

While peripherally related to General Idea in Toronto, the Montreal-based conceptual artist Bill Vazan worked in Esso Imperial Oil's accounting department by day, and developed and carried out his work largely in his off-hours. By his own account, his day job put him at a distance from experimental art activities even in Montreal, let alone elsewhere in Canada (Vazan, Interview).[8] While he attended the Ontario College of Art, and spent a brief period at the École des beaux-arts in Paris, both in the early 1950s, Vazan ceased making work for nearly a decade, only beginning again in 1962. A more sustained practice followed later in the decade, and of particular interest for us in the context of McLuhan's writing is the especially fertile period toward the end of the 1960s and early 1970s. During this time, Vazan realized of a number of works, including a series of conceptual works that often took up geographical space and political boundaries in novel ways.

One such work is *Land Filling* (1966–1969): using a cast-off Esso map from work as his ready-made support, Vazan excised and repositioned American land over Canadian ground—reclaiming for Canada cartographically, if not actually, land marked as American. Here, Vazan anticipates the malleability of the border as in General Idea's *Borderline Research* request, reimagining the political division between the two countries. Cutting out a section of Buffalo and the nearby southwest shore of Lake Ontario, Vazan displaces it, ever so slightly, north. Immediately below Toronto now appears "See Esso Dealer for map of New York." Detroit, Michigan, too, is drawn into Canada, excised and placed north of Windsor, Ontario.

The process of reclaiming land also, however, has the additional effect of obscuring the Canadian ground now hidden beneath the collaged element. It becomes not so much an additive exercise, as an unwitting obliteration, a covering over of Canada by American landmasses. If Vazan's intent was to reclaim now-American land, it also has the effect of remapping a pervasive American imperialism on southern Ontario: Windsor is blotted out by Detroit, Hamilton by Buffalo's environs.

Land Filling is a relatively little-known work by Vazan from this period, though it does broach similar concerns to those of General Idea's project from a few years later. Far better known are those projects, beginning in 1969, where Vazan produced works taking up concerns shared by both conceptual and land art of the time. (According to contemporary accounts, Vazan was largely unaware of land art practices in the United States when he began his own peripatetic and somewhat happenstance interventions.) Among the earliest of these works is *Canada in Parentheses* (1969), realized with the help of the artist Ian Wallace. For this piece, on August 13, 1969, Vazan in Paul's Bluff, Prince Edward Island, and Wallace in Spanish Banks, Vancouver "bracketed" Canada by drawing in the sand large, open parenthetical marks, inclined toward the centre of the country. While ostensibly simultaneous (both were carried out on the same day), the temporal and spatial slippage owing to twice-daily tides and foot traffic on the beaches, means the works may have only been realized in an ideational sense. As Vazan recounted in a recent conversation with me, he considered it less a performance than making "visible a thought process."

This imagined connectivity—a link forged across thousands of kilometres—would lead to the far more ambitious and multitudinous works *Canada Line* (1969–1970) and *Worldline* (1969–1971).[9] Conceiving both over a number of years, the former drew together eight collaborators in Canada, and the latter extended the project to some twenty-five around the world. For the former, Vazan drew an imaginary line coast-to-coast, and solicited the help of galleries and museums across the country to realize his work. In each location, black tape marked out the angles leading from the previous and to the next point in the imagined itinerary. Building ambitiously off this first *Line*, the following year, on March 5, 1971, twenty-five institutions from Australia, Brazil, Chile, Denmark, Finland, Nigeria, Sierra Leone, the United States, and Yugoslavia participated in *Worldline*. In the publication that forms a part of the work, correspondence, installation photographs, and notes are reproduced, prefaced by Vazan's own handwritten introduction to the project.

In a lengthy article in the "Maps and Mapmaking" issue of *artscanada*, Joe Bodolai reads these and similar works as "attempts to translate the language of maps into the real world by rendering them visible in the same form as they appear on maps" (71). In his critique, he suggests the work as an "interesting form of graffiti but if it renders anything visible, or conceptual at all, it is surely less meaningful than, say, a road sign marking a provincial boundary, a customs post or a barbed wire fence at an international border, or even a tourist plaque marking the highest point in Saskatchewan" (71). What Bodolai fails to recognize in Vazan's work, however, is precisely how these geographical markers made real in the landscape are of a kind with *Canada Line* or *Worldline*. The very fact that Vazan intervenes in such institutional spaces suggests an awareness of the politics of place that makes the works so compelling. Anticipating Bodolai's reservations about the work three years later, Vazan wrote in *Worldline*,

> Imaginary lines a reality? Think of surveying triangulation marks and base lines; global parallels and meridians (space and time) (International Date Line); flight corridors and water channels (navigation); political demarcations (borders); high-way lane indicators; plotted satellite and space probe trajectories; proxemics, etc.

Bodolai's criticism of the work as "surely less meaningful than...a barbed wire fence at an international border" is forestalled and effectively countered by Vazan's litany of geopolitical markers. Meaning resides in these official marks in the landscape, and by focusing our attention on such signs, sites, and lines, Vazan's work troubles them.[10]

Such a reading has larger implications when considered alongside McLuhan's Marfleet lecture, and indeed, his broader thinking of Canada itself as a kind of DEW Line. The Distant

Early Warning Line was developed as an early detection system by the American military, and consisted of radar stations throughout the North, including Canada, Alaska, the Faroe Islands, Greenland, and Iceland. Intended to provide advance warning of incoming Soviet planes during the Cold War, it became obsolete when nuclear attacks no longer required planes to travel in close proximity to their targets (Coupland 165).

As addressed above, McLuhan had invoked the DEW Line as an enduring metaphor in *Understanding Media*, saying "art, at its most significant, [is] a DEW line, a Distant Early Warning system that can always be relied on to tell the old culture what is beginning to happen to it" (69). As with McLuhan's crossed analogy of artist as maker of counter-environments and Canada as an artist figure, the DEW Line, too, would apply both to art and Canada through McLuhan's writing in the 1960s.[11]

McLuhan and Bruce Powers revisited these associations in "The United States and Canada: The Border as a Resonating Interval," arguing that the DEW Line

> points up a major Canadian role in the twentieth century— the role of hidden ground for big powers. Since the United States has become a world environment, Canada has become the anti-environment that renders the United States more acceptable and intelligible to many small countries of the world; anti-environments are indispensable for making an environment understandable. (McLuhan and Powers 149)

This reading conflates the physical presence of radar stations across Canada's North with a far more intangible presence—that of the transnational relationship shared by the two countries. Like a string of radar stations, Vazan's *Lines* take the form of specific—and cultural significant—positions. Like government detector stations, the galleries and museums that participated in Vazan's project were recognized sites of culture, institutions where works of art were sanctioned through research, display, and dissemination.

It was precisely this institutional dependency of *Canada Line* and *Worldline* that led Vazan to his subsequent project. Institutional critique in the visual arts was beginning to question, and indeed undermine, the power of such spaces and their particular conventions. In *Contacts* (1971–1973) (or *X Contacts*, as it is variously titled), individuals serve as the connections in a global mapping exercise instead of institutions. As Johanne Sloan suggests, *Contacts* provided an "easy exchange of images, information and personal stories across borders and across art movements, while sidestepping already established museums, galleries and other institutional structures" (89). This sidestepping was in direct response to criticism from Vazan's peers as to the institutional basis of the *Line* projects (Vazan, "Interview").

Contacts was premised on the formation and documentation of "a vast network of total communication among many people on a global scale" (Vazan qtd. in Jean 59). Starting in 1971, Vazan asked artists around the world to contribute documents incorporating the sign *X* by mail or telex. A sign ancient and pre-linguistic, "a configuration indicating core, the heart, the meeting of directions," an *X* was "an identified place, object or event, and the balance between polarities" (Vazan qtd. in Jean 59). Vazan compiled these varied submissions together and published them as a book, to disseminate once again geographically specific markers. In doing so, Vazan's project "held out the promise of a de-centred art world, one that no longer awaited the okay from institutions in New York or Paris to make art public or to determine the relative value of art objects" (Sloan 89). This artist-centred exchange network served as an early warning system of another kind: heralding a radically altered means of communicating only fully realized with the advent of the Internet decades later.

Image Bank between the "Native and the Cosmopolitan"

If Bill Vazan and General Idea both relied on the postal system in their practices to circulate and collect ideas, in doing so they also broached contemporary debates of cultural centres and peripheries. In both cases, there is a degree of permeability between centres of art world production, such as New York, and rather more peripheral outposts (particularly in the 1960s) such as Montreal and Toronto. This permeability is at the basis of their practices, and the relative ease with which the mail system facilitated exchanges among artists—particularly across the Canada–US border—is at the core of this last case, as well.

While Vazan and General Idea used mail often in their work, nowhere in Canada was this type of activity more concentrated than in Vancouver toward the end of the 1960s and early 1970s. Arising out of a countercultural milieu, where mudflats communities provided respite and an outside to the affluent culture of 1960s capitalism, Image Bank was founded in 1969 as a hybrid form of artist collective and proto-artist-run centre. It had its roots in the earlier Intermedia Society, founded in 1966 around the painter Jack Shadbolt. Unlike Intermedia's mandate to build an artist community in Vancouver, however, Image Bank's principals Michael Morris and Vincent Trasov looked considerably further afield.[12] Image Bank, which operated from 1969 through 1973, served primarily as a postal directory for artists to exchange clippings, images, and mail art. Following General Idea's founding of *FILE Megazine*'s founding in 1972 by General Idea, Image Bank began publishing parts of their "Image Request Directory" quarterly in the periodical, and annually in its entirety. Submitting one's name, address, and interests to the Bank would serve as a solicitation to collaborators throughout the network. In this way, artists could request submissions of various types of material from other artists. Though ostensibly global, much of the mail passed over the Canada–US border.

In general, artist-led activities of this kind in Canada were founded on the twinned and deeply imbricated models of

Ray Johnson's New York Correspondence School on the one hand, and the "Eternal Network" as imagined by Robert Filliou and Georges Brecht in the wake of May 1968, on the other. Producing and exchanging works of art internationally, by mail, this gift economy served to connect Canadian artists to activities from which they otherwise would have been geographically isolated. Although Image Bank was quite consciously modelled on Johnson's work, and inspired by the example of William Burroughs, it was ultimately from Claude Lévi-Strauss's *The Savage Mind* (1962, trans. 1966) that they derived their name.

Image Bank's facilitation of transnational artistic exchange and collaboration is clearly different from that of General Idea's *Borderline Research Project*. There is no mapping exercise, no explicit acknowledgement of the border in the work. However, it, along with other correspondence art activities across Canada at the time, does speak to a crucial aspect of McLuhan's theory of Canada as a borderline case. Richard Cavell, writing in *McLuhan in Space*, understands McLuhan's theory as effectively dispensing with "notions of the native *and* the cosmopolitan" (212). Just as the country might be understood as liminal, so too might the practices of its artists: even if Image Bank was based in Vancouver, the directory facilitated exchanges between any two points listed within it. General Idea's solicitations to their mail network produced similar results: the correspondence collected, edited, and redistributed through the periodical. These activities— limited neither to Toronto or Vancouver, nor diffused in an entirely "dematerialized," global practice—are best situated in the interstitial space that is a mail network. This liminality has its advantages. As McLuhan argues in "Defrosting Canadian Culture," those "in the centers of change have less opportunity for appraisal and invention than those on the periphery" (95).

This relationship between centres and peripheries to which McLuhan was attuned was of similar interest to many artists working in Canada at the time. As Vancouver-based critic and curator Keith Wallace has argued, the mail network that served as a ground for much of Image Bank's work clearly challenged the assumption that "certain cities constituted geographical art centres"; instead, "correspondence art was able to mark out new means of communicating and exchanging ideas outside of the centre" (Wallace 3). As Wallace suggests, this was not simply a question of ready access to the centre and its ideas, but an ability to engage in a fully collaborative process of exchange, often without recourse to New York. As Morris himself reflected toward the end of the 1970s, "each artist's concerns are personal but open to cross-referencing with those of others who are willing to share their research for the purpose of creating art." He continues by saying that the purpose of Image Bank's activity "was not to hoard or collect, rather it was and is *research*, carried out by prac- ticing artists, using individual methods of communication and expression" (Morris 41). Anticipating technologies we now take for granted—crowd-sourcing and Google Image search, to name but two—artists could conduct research by soliciting other artists for images of whatever subject interested them. A collabora- tive research model that fulfilled, not coincidentally, McLuhan's expectation of art "in the new age...not as self-expression, but as a feedback loop" ("Art as Anti-Environment" 56).

That this research and feedback took place across national boundaries, with little regard for centres and peripheries as such— the request went out to the network and was fulfilled by any other member, regardless of their location—prefigured our present globalized art world. While markets still tend to reside in major centres (art fairs in this respect are the exception that proves the rule), the rise of peripatetic artists, curators, dealers, and collectors attests to the general disregard for political borders. "The artist is by nature a boundary-hopper and a claim-jumper," McLuhan said in the Marfleet lecture, a "frontier boundary-hopper has often been regarded as a kind of enemy of society because he makes things, he points out things that many people would rather not notice" (120). This actual and metaphorical boundary hopping was, for McLuhan as much as Morris and Trasov, the purview of artists.

On newsstands, in mailbags, and on gallery walls across Canada, artists took up the border as method and subject, engaging with contemporary debates around transnationalism. They were not only thinking of centres and peripheries, but especially following centennial celebrations, addressing questions of cultural nationalism and American imperialism in their work. That these practices found parity in McLuhan's own theory of Canada as a borderline case is telling. "Any environment," McLuhan suggests in the Marfleet lecture, "tends to be imperceptible to its users and occupants except to the degree that counter-environments are created by the artist" (106). McLuhan's reading of the country as an artist figure in his lecture and elsewhere in his writing resonates strongly with the interaction and occasional interrogation of the United States carried out by artists in Canada during the period.

Considering these varied projects in tandem with McLuhan's writing on Canadian–US relations we should be reminded of the continued role of artists in elaborating political realities. Counter-environments made by artists still serve to make perceptible the powerful American ground: tactical media artists such as The Yes Men explicitly take to task right-wing politicians and multinational corporations such as Halliburton. As pranksters who adopt corporate and political identities, they make declarations that their adopted hosts would never imagine, what they call "identity correction."[13] Just as the strategies have changed, so too have the subjects: many artists aware of the ends to which nationalism has been used in recent decades seem less intent on interrogating the nation than on working outside its reach. That the moment described above is now past makes it no less compelling: artists and their counter-environments are still much needed, and sometimes show surprising power in keeping governments and corporations to account.

Notes

1   McLuhan used the two terms—*anti-* and *counter-environment*—interchangeably, in spite of the subtle definitional differences of the prefixes. For instance, "the artist, as a creator of anti-environments, or counter-environments...has a very peculiar role in our society" ("Technology and Environment" 6).

2   This lecture would later reappear in various guises, including in David Staines's *The Canadian Imagination: Dimensions of a Literary Culture* (1977), and reworked with Bruce Powers as "The United States and Canada: The Border as a Resonating Interval" (1989).

3   On Opportunities for Youth and Local Initiatives Program, artist Paul Wong would later reflect, "The programs created a false market and a boom for social programs and cultural services; at the same time they provided important bases for development of non-static production and exhibition of art and art processes" (307).

4   Such convergence was short lived, as Bonin goes on to argue; by 1975, many grants were suspended to new organizations in order to fund those already established (48).

5   McLuhan's reference to Wyndham Lewis's collection of essays, *Men Without Art* (1934), however fleeting, alludes to the close friendship of the two men during the 1940s and 1950s.

6   For a discussion of this project and similar early mailers by the group, see Barbara Fischer, ed., *General Idea: Editions 1967–1995*.

7   Writing in 1977, Russell Keziere described *FILE* as "either a large in-joke for those in the know, or an ironic yet compassionate and slightly jealous celebration of contemporary sensibility, i.e. non-art-world sensibility" (11).

8   Vazan did, however, receive early issues of *FILE Megazine* from AA Bronson. In spite of Vazan's declaration of his peripheral status in the Montreal arts scene, he was nevertheless part of major exhibitions and organizations, including co-organizing the seminal *45° 30' N – 73° 36' W* exhibition at Sir George Williams Art Galleries and the Saidye Bronfman Centre for the Arts, and a pro forma founding member of the artist-run centre Véhicule Art.

9   *Canada Line* was first titled *Trans Canada Tape Line*, then subsequently *Canada Tape Line*. A similar work, *North American Line*, was planned but never realized (Vazan, Interview).

10 Indeed, as Marie-Josée Jean has suggested, "The virtual line comprising *Worldline* was no less real than national borders, airline corridors, satellite communications, or geodesic coordinates. It manifested a new, simultaneous form of space-time in a burgeoning society of global communications" (59).

11 McLuhan also published the *DEW-Line*, beginning in summer 1968, with his son Eric McLuhan, and the New York-based Eugene Schwartz. Lasting only briefly (it ceased publication in 1970), it was targeted at corporate officers, and was paired with a retreat to the Bahamas, organized by Schwartz, with talks by McLuhan and others (Coupland 165).

12 It is hardly incidental that McLuhan's work was of major influence to many of the artists affiliated with Intermedia Society (Cavell 180).

13 For a discussion of The Yes Men, see Blake Stimson, "For the Love of Abstraction" and Tom Vanderbilt, "Affirmative Action."

5

Writing (to) **McLuhan**

Wilfred Watson, Playwright

Paul Tiessen

The most fascinating playwright in the modern Canadian theatre and one of its most controversial, Wilfred Watson continues to attract our attention and our respect...A poet turned playwright, he found a congenial environment for his work at Edmonton's University of Alberta Studio Theatre, which in the 1960s, along with the experimental home provided by the Yardbird Suite, first produced the majority of his major works. It was on the University of Alberta campus that he first became aware of the potential use for a playwright of the acting company ensemble. He recognized the effect that a training approach and a clearly articulated artistic philosophy could have on the presentation of his work...In some instances Watson anticipated the electronic age of Marshall McLuhan for he was already probing the use of media as a valid supporter and extension of dialogue. He saw the total performance as the text...Watson jolted the complacencies of middle-class theatre in Alberta and the blithe optimism of entrepreneurs... His plunge into the irrational and magical is surreal, for although his work defies categorization surely his vision in part at least is the vision of the new surrealism.

—Gordon Peacock, "Wilfred Watson and the Modern Canadian Theatre"

M.M. (Marshall McLuhan) electrified me at a time when I was
serving an apprenticeship to U of A's Studio Theatre, under
Gordon Peacock, based on a modernism of adversary
eclecticism, very receptive to M.M.'s theoria and eager to
test it in praxis. My question—our question from 1960 on at
Studio Theatre was, what rôle does theatre play in an age of
motion picture, radio, acoustic tape, and TV?...In 1961 the
Learned Societies met in Montreal. Marshall gave a paper
on "The Humanities in the Electronic Age"...From 1957
on, I had read M.M. via Sheila [Watson] and Wyndham
Lewis.—I then in 1961 encountered M.M.'s theoria from his
own lips. I recall sitting next to Hilda Neatby to hear him
read his paper; she turned to me and said, "I don't understand a word of it." I found it dazzling—instant theatre,
in Hamlet's sense, that it gave to the age its "form and
pressure."

—Wilfred Watson, draft of a letter to William Toye, 05/02/87[1]

I

IN 1959 Wilfred Watson began a letter-writing
relationship with Marshall McLuhan; it developed into a
happy friendship over the next nine years, to the summer of
1968. Both men were English professors at Canadian universities, Watson at Alberta, McLuhan at Toronto. When they
began their epistolary conversation, both were poised to enjoy
not only academic accomplishment but also public renown.
But while their conversations held them together for those
nine years, their individual reputations diverged dramatically.
Today Watson is barely known; McLuhan remains (or has again
become) world famous, a giant figure of the twentieth century.
In biographies of McLuhan, Watson is hardly mentioned.

The letters they wrote one another from 1959 to 1968 suggest a
mutually energizing friendship, stimulated by their work on what
early on became their joint book-writing project, From *Cliché to*

Archetype (often referred to as *C/A* or *C-A*). Their hopes for the book's success expanded throughout the 1960s, reaching a crescendo of anticipation in 1967–1968. During 1968–1969, however, in the course of a months-long, face-to-face dialogue to finalize the manuscript, their partnership became mutually disillusioning and exhausting. Their discussion—about media and technologies, language and art, theatre and culture, space and time, sense ratios and multi-consciousness, cliché and archetype—barely survived.

This chapter is part of my larger project to establish a portrait of Watson within the context of his relationship with and his thinking about McLuhan. It largely restricts itself to the letters they exchanged with one another and, indeed, to a single thread running here and there through those letters: references to Watson's plays, to the writing, the production, and the reception of his scripts.

It was Watson, of course, who made his theatre work a recurring topic. Thereby he held McLuhan as audience of some of his day-to-day experimental concerns. The theatre trope provided him with a demonstrable means of asserting his separate identity. It marked off a terrain where he felt himself flourishing within a community of artists. It let him reveal to McLuhan that as artist— indeed, avant-garde artist—he thrived within a collaborative working environment such as he hoped he and McLuhan were forging.[2]

To be sure, McLuhan claimed to value Watson specifically as artist/poet, one whose first book, *Friday's Child,* a collection of poems, had been praised and published by T.S. Eliot. As McLuhan biographer Philip Marchand notes, Marshall saw Wilfred as "a Canadian poet of great wit, erudition, and virtuosity" (Marchand, *Marshall McLuhan* [1989] 219) and wanted to benefit from his ways of seeing. For his part, Wilfred, already throughout the 1950s—first at the Calgary (1951–1954), then the Edmonton campus of the University of Alberta—in exploring varied approaches to theatrical production, was keen to learn all he could from Marshall about media, art, and technology. In 1955–1956—with Sheila Watson, his intellectual soulmate who was to become known as the author of the 1959 novel *The Double Hook*—he went to Paris to study the reception

in France of Beckett, Genet, Artaud, Cocteau, and Ionesco, play-
wrights whose works were being produced in Edmonton (Tiessen,
"'Shall I Say'" 108–9). In 1956–1957—with Sheila entering graduate
studies at Toronto, where McLuhan became her supervisor and, also,
her close friend and admirer—Wilfred returned to Edmonton eager
to attach himself to "a small theatre group" (WW to SW, 03/11/56),
in fact, finding such a group at the University's Studio Theatre.

In the 1960s—when he was exceedingly prolific as playwright—
he increasingly embedded elements of Marshall's thinking into
his scripts and other writing, and liked to tell him so. What
becomes striking, then, is that Watson's most explicit evoca-
tion of McLuhan, in his major work *Let's Murder Clytemnestra
According to the Principles of Marshall McLuhan*, finds no place
in the vast landscape of the Watson/McLuhan letters. By the time
Watson had written it and, in November 1969, seen it produced,
his and McLuhan's steady exchange of letters had ceased.

For this chapter, I am drawing my material largely from
the vast archive of Wilfred Watson at the University of Alberta.
Although I am foregrounding Watson's letters, I look also to
entries in some of his many unpublished notebooks. Further, I
am drawing on mainly unpublished writing by McLuhan, starting
with his letters to Wilfred as well as Sheila Watson. In sections II
and III, I present most of what the two men wrote to each other
about Wilfred's respective plays and play fragments. In section
IV, I glance at Wilfred's and Marshall's (and Sheila's) expressions of "euphoria" in early 1968, when they were looking forward
to their year together in Toronto to finish their book. Section V
focuses on the breakdown in Wilfred and Marshall's relationship
in 1968–1969. In section VI, drawing on still-unpublished material at Library and Archives Canada, I depart from my emphasis
on Watson's perspective to take note of some of McLuhan's
responses—in letters to his New York publishers—to the breakdown. Section VII returns to Watson's reflections on the personal
and intellectual dynamics of 1968–1969, and his decision to
write *Let's Murder Clytemnestra According to the Principles of*

Marshall McLuhan. In sections VIII and IX, I offer an account of each man's gestures toward some degree of reconciliation.

Occasionally, I refer to my earlier essay, "'Shall I Say, It Is Necessary to Restore the Dialogue?': Wilfred Watson's Encounter with Marshall McLuhan, 1957–1988," a companion to the present study. There I foreground Watson's private thoughts about McLuhan as he expressed these in what was for him the liberating space of his notebooks, journals that he kept from the early 1950s on. By comparison, in this chapter, I move to his buoyantly conversational correspondence with McLuhan, with emphasis, as I have said, on his attention to his plays. I rely also, especially in sections V to IX, on each man's behind-the-scenes thoughts about the other.

Watson's letter writing with McLuhan during the nine-year period was fairly constant. If we include letters involving Sheila, their exchange came to well over 300 "dated" letters: 2 early letters in 1959, and then an average of almost a letter a week from the summer of 1960 to the summer of 1968. There are another 30 "undated" letters. Among the dated letters during those years, 86 are from Wilfred to Marshall, 107 from Marshall to Wilfred, and another 46 from Marshall to both Wilfred and Sheila. From Marshall to Sheila there are 56; from Sheila to Marshall, 31. Overall, only 14 of the hundreds of letters have been published, and those few—all from McLuhan—are in McLuhan's *Letters.*

The 1959–1968 Wilfred/Marshall letters are shaped by the pleasure and playfulness of intellectual insight, serious whimsy, and scholarly breakthroughs. They are filled with exploratory probes and erudite displays of wit and learning. Aware and wary always of the "archetype," they reveal the writers' boyish delight in imagining plots to vanquish their more conservative or orthodox "enemies"; in their roguishness they are notably keen on "overthrowing" the regime of Toronto English professor Northrop Frye (Flahiff, *Always* 245) whose theory of the archetype had appeared in his *Anatomy of Criticism* in 1957.

Watson and McLuhan's then still fledgling relationship was greatly strengthened in 1961 when they met for lunch in Montreal, where both men were presenting papers to the annual meeting of the Humanities Association of Canada. "I heard McLuhan's address," Wilfred wrote Sheila (who was in London working on her dissertation, which was on Wyndham Lewis). "It was excellent—the only thing worth hearing" (WW to SW, 15/06/61). Days later, in Toronto, they picked up their Montreal conversations, as well as conversations begun a couple years earlier when, along with Sheila, they had met in Toronto. In 1961 Sheila's five years in Toronto as a graduate student ended, and she moved to Edmonton to join Wilfred and take up a faculty position in the University of Alberta's English department.

Sheila, who was close to the McLuhan family from 1956 onward, could not, as her biographer Fred Flahiff suggests, "but have been delighted by Wilfred's involvement with McLuhan" (*Always* 245). In complicated and completely different ways, she was committed to both men, and each man (each born in 1911) must have held her view as critical to their own public and private postures within their man-to-man relationship. As we shall see, Sheila informed the men's relationship in varying degrees as time went by, but when things got complicated between them her reactions reflected her "capacity for fierce and protective loyalty" (Flahiff, *Always* 187) to her husband.

By the mid-1960s Wilfred's emerging links to McLuhan were becoming known here and there, and began to carry overtones not only of fame but also of notoriety. In 1965 the Canadian *Humanities Association Bulletin*, publishing his play, *Wail for Two Pedestals*, announced that he was "collaborating with Marshall McLuhan on a sequel to *Understanding Media, From Cliché to Archetype* to be published by Viking Press" (Editor's comment in Watson, "Wail" 63; see also Tiessen, "'Shall I Say'" 124). In his 1966 piece in *Canadian Literature*, "The Preface: On Radical Absurdity" (44), Watson, flying in the face of his Canadian literary colleagues' broadly shared consensus, explicitly declared what he perceived as McLuhan's greatness. To many of his contemporaries he seemed reckless. They tended to find McLuhan's probes and pronouncements about the future of media—including The Book—anxiety-producing. However,

Watson did not seem to share his colleagues' anxieties and, publically at least, cast his lot with McLuhan. When *LIFE* magazine mentioned that he was working with McLuhan, he jotted down in his notebook: "Consternation among my friends because my name appears in *Life* magazine in the article on McLuhan" (28/02/66; see also Tiessen, "'Shall I Say'" 124). Flahiff calls that period of Wilfred's attachment to Marshall "the glory days for Wilfred":

> [Those were the years of Wilfred's] collaborating with, being continually stimulated by "the only person at Toronto [he] ever got an idea from." His sense of himself and others' sense of him soared by virtue of his association with McLuhan. He let it be known that the phrase "cliché to archetype" was coined by him, that he was nurturing and working with, as well as following, the world's new bell-wether. (Flahiff, *Always* 245–46)

Given the good mood that imbued their correspondence about their *C/A* project, the disaster accompanying Watson and McLuhan's rendezvous in 1968–1969 seems all the more surprising. Personal affection and professional admiration became frustration and bare tolerance when Wilfred came to feel that the "camaraderie of the dialoguing days" had degenerated into what Marchand termed "'two monologues,' with Wilfred not certain whether Marshall had forgotten or simply chose to ignore what they had for so long discussed" (Flahiff, *Always* 249; see Marchand, *Marshall McLuhan* [1989] 219). Flahiff offers important insight into Wilfred's disillusionment that year:

> He found the restless, multi-notional nature of Marshall's interests and of his mind—stimulating and suggestive as these were for providing contexts for focused considerations of "C/A" in letters and in short, infrequent meetings— revealed their ongoing dialogue to be but a single facet of Marshall's prismatic enterprise. He had discovered, too,

> that teamwork and dialogue were for Marshall always a
> beginning of exploration, but seldom its end. (*Always*
> 253; see also Marchand, *Marshall McLuhan* [1989] 219)

But that year McLuhan, too, as we shall see, discovered in
the playwright someone he had not anticipated. Thus, in
retrospect, the playful choreography of their 1959–1968 correspondence seems all the more a bravura performance, even
if in its final test it led to their relationship coming apart.

By February 1969, that coming apart was felt keenly by Wilfred,
who had begun exploring the idea of their writing side-by-side
texts that would function as some kind of enforced dialogue in
their joint volume. In his notebook he recorded that he had run
out of ways to remain present within what had become Marshall's
creative process: "I feel for the first time no confidence that I shall
be able to keep my footing in the *C/A* book. // Every trace of my
style is being removed. If I can't win detail by detail, how can I
win the battle of the two halves of the book" (c. 26/02/69; see also
Tiessen, "'Shall I Say'" 126–27). Watson's assessment of his performance with McLuhan stands in distinct contrast to his assessment
of his performances with his theatre collaborators. Of course, the
1960s had been "glory days" for McLuhan, too, and, as is univer-
sally known, on an incredible scale. So there might have been some
inevitability—exacerbated by his brain operation in November
1967—in his drifting away from Watson. His fame as communication and media theorist expanded at a breathtaking pace, far
beyond anything Watson—indeed, perhaps McLuhan himself—
could have imagined when their relationship took root in 1959.

In some of his letters Watson hinted that he saw his playwriting
as his "putting on" an audience, if only a micro audience compared
to McLuhan's. In McLuhan he recognized the consummate global
performer who knew how to own his audience by "putting it on,"
"by appearing to know something they did not know about the very
things they were most certain they knew" (Marchand, *Marshall
McLuhan* [1989] 179–80; see also Willmott, *McLuhan* 45–46).

In his notebooks he alluded to "McLuhan's books as mimicry of audience": "He puts on the whole world...McLuhan invents an audience and writes his book by putting on this audience" (28/12/70). In writing to McLuhan about his plays, Watson, we come at times to feel, probably was, among other strategies, "putting on" McLuhan.

II

The first script Watson mentioned concerned his effort to adapt McLuhan's *The Mechanical Bride* (1951) for the stage. McLuhan, he later recalled in his notebook, had given him a copy of *The Mechanical Bride* at the end of the 1950s, inviting him to work with him on questions of technology and literature, media and culture (08/04/80). Sheila—to whom, as it happens, he had sent a copy of the book back in 1952 (Flahiff, *Always* 76)—suggested the adaptation project to him. McLuhan's book, short witty essays accompanying magazine advertisements, was an unlikely candidate for adaptation to the stage, and Wilfred may have taken it on to make plain his mettle as dramatist. Further, this project—a satire of McLuhan's satire—provided for him a gambit to enter his and Marshall's conversation in terms of his own making, but terms in which McLuhan would necessarily share a curiosity. Demonstrating to McLuhan that he had not only caught on to him, but also caught up with him, his project was an early testing of his potential identity within the still barely emerging outlines of their relationship.

In June 1960 Watson reported having completed forty pages of *The Mechanical Bride* playscript. He hoped Marshall would approve of his approach, and flattered him with comments on the original, which he felt was "not so much a study as a superb piece of idiosyncratic satire, with the best prose I've yet seen by a Canadian." He spelled out what he claimed as McLuhan's influence on him: "I came to realize that the whole problem of a satirist, when confronted by an indefinitely vast extent of the ludicrous, is one of focus: the drawing attention to some isolated point." Jauntily adding that Marshall should write up details about royalties, he quipped, "I don't foresee Cadillacs before

1966, at least" (WW to MM, 29/06/60). He developed the play, which remained a fragment, under the title "The Mechanical Bridegroom," slyly subverting McLuhan's position. Keeping his satire some steps removed from McLuhan's, he commented in his notebook: "The mechanical bride is merely a sardonic male view of the new electronic woman" (17/11/71; see Tiessen, "'Shall I Say'" 116–17; see also Gordon, *Escape* 248). Years later, in *Let's Murder Clytemnestra*, some characters from the "Mechanical Bridegroom" fragment—drawn from Aeschylus's *Oresteia* trilogy—reappeared. We do not know what Marshall thought of Wilfred's initiative, for he seems not to have replied in writing.

In the summer of 1960 Watson set the "Bridegroom" project aside so he could concentrate on *Cockcrow and the Gulls*, his first Studio Theatre production. Once the text of Cockcrow was established, he drew Marshall into a commodious and heady epistolary conversation about another possible adaptation: *The Apes of God*. The *Apes*, Wyndham Lewis's 1930 satire of the Sitwells and other London literati, was a novel that Sheila—with Marshall continuing to supervise her dissertation until its completion in 1965—was just then holding under close scrutiny. From the fall of 1961 until the spring of 1964 (the year that *Understanding Media* stormed into the world), the two men talked back and forth about Wilfred's imagined stage adaptation of *The Apes of God*, Marshall especially heartily, with a robust boldness dedicated to encouraging the milder and congenitally more timid Wilfred to go far with it. Driven by Marshall, who seems to have sought through the *Apes* project some degree of mastery over Wilfred's pursuits, this exchange became their longest and liveliest conversation about one of Wilfred's scripts.

Early on, in fantasizing about the *Apes*, McLuhan solicitously enquired about audience response to *Cockcrow and the Gulls* once it had been performed (over a five-night period in March and April 1962—the year *The Gutenberg Galaxy* appeared to international response): "We long to hear of how the play did go"; and days later: "we have had you and the play much in mind. Do drop us a word" (MM to SW and WW, 03/04/62 and "Palm Sunday" [1962]).

In the next letter, perhaps after a telephone conversation when he might have heard from the Watsons details of the Edmonton reception of the iconoclastic *Cockcrow and the Gulls*, Marshall sent a note of applause that matched something of what Wilfred or Sheila must have conveyed to him: "Our dear Wilfred and Sheila // You have been through much excitement and stress and must be a bit limp. // Just wanted to tell you how good it made us feel to hear that the play had really got past the guard of the percussed, the numb and the hollow" (MM to WW and SW, 01/05/[62]). McLuhan felt a kinship with Watson's "putting on" those—the percussed, the numb, and the hollow—who resisted his work.

But back to the dream of the *Apes*. In a letter not to Wilfred but to Sheila, Marshall expressed his hope that "Wilfred is able to complete the dramatization of the *Apes*." But surely McLuhan's ambitions on behalf of what he saw as Watson's stylistic opportunities were misplaced, and his emphasis on a particular kind of audience appeal—that the play should be "very acceptable"—was a miscalculation: "Done up in real strong period piece style, a Sitwell version of the Sitwells," he remarked, "it would be very acceptable" (MM to SW, [03/12/61]). Wilfred, inclined more toward Brecht or surrealism or the absurd than anything in "real strong period piece style," would have resisted such presuppositions about audience empathy. In August 1963, McLuhan suggested that he submit an excerpt of his *Apes* script to a literary magazine focusing on Lewis (MM to WW and SW, 11/08/63). Wilfred, intent on maintaining control over how he would position himself vis-à-vis not only his potential audience but also McLuhan, must have felt uneasy about being so much instructed and disciplined by Marshall. He preferred to write his own agenda.

Nonetheless, in September 1963, Wilfred, while assuring Marshall that he was throwing himself seriously into their *C/A* project, reported progress in adapting *The Apes of God* for stage: "some fifty (of a probable 75 or 80) pp. gone—an hour of playing time completed. I am enjoying myself immensely. I use as much of Lewis's phrase as possible. But I have had to introduce into the play a structure which I don't discover in the novel" (WW to MM, 03/09/[63]). His plan, he claimed, was to keep the length under two hours, and to finish in a week or two: "I will write you again when it is done. It goes directly in to stencils, so I will have copies available when it is finished" (WW to MM, 03/09/[63]). Sheila corroborated his news, referring as she did to the General Strike on which, it happened, she was then focusing in her dissertation, "Wyndham Lewis and Expressionism": "W. draws to the end of *The Apes*. It is I think an extraordinary translation. The house is strewed with General Strike papers etc. The dialogue goes over almost whole" (SW to MM, [06/09/63]). McLuhan responded to them both, embedding his brief comment concerning Wilfred's work within the ongoing discussion about the *Apes* that he and Sheila had underway: "Much looking forward to the *Apes*, naturally!" (MM to WW and SW, 17/09/63).

The next day Wilfred wrote Marshall that he had completed the play, but now he was concerned about copyright:

> *The Apes of God* is done into a playscript. It is on stencils, but not yet duplicated...I am worried—even anxious—about getting permission to use the Lewis text. Will Mrs. Lewis have the copyright? Or as Sheila suspects Methuen? The stage version should be enormously funny. In provenance, it is both very close to Lewis, and paradoxically, very far away from him.

Unable to curb his enthusiasm, he added as a postscript a quick snapshot of his emotional state: "P.S. I feel tremendously *elated* about finishing the *Apes*. I never thought it possible—for the book though magnificently visual & verbal, is not particularly dramatic. But it actually went easier than any other play I've done" (WW to MM, 18/09/63). A few days later, in her own letter to Marshall, Sheila was for some reason more detached: "*The Apes* as dramatized is I think self-explanatory" (SW to MM, 22/09/[63]).

Although McLuhan continued to portray himself as eager to hear news of Wilfred's playwriting he also, now,

PAUL **Tiessen**

expressed some impatience with his getting it to large audiences on the international stage. He responded effusively, but also a little urgently, to news of the finished draft:

> Dear Wilfred, / Word of the *Apes* is most inspiriting. Please do send it on as soon as you can. Really, it should be a top hit in London and New York. The time is propitious. It can be given full beatnik flavor, you know, like Shak. in modern dress. / Few books ever gave me as much fun as the *Apes*. Much could be done to provide the *MAD* magazine touch in the tableau. Surfboarding along on the snob wave of the creative process was what the boys and girls did in the '20s, i.e. the creative *image*. *Now* it has become less visual, more *involved*, the creative *posture*. / Don't think of the *Apes* as anything less than a major dramatic success. Should have been staged long ago. / Wish we could talk. / Marshall. (MM to WW, 27/09/63)

McLuhan eventually reported that he had written Mrs. Lewis on behalf of Wilfred concerning copyright (MM to WW and SW, 09/02/64). Wilfred responded immediately with thanks (WW to MM, 12/02/64). Then Marshall sent an update: "Mrs. Lewis writes that she owns dramatic rights in the *Apes* but that Penguin bought the novel! Says Bridson of BBC did a bit of *The Apes* and found it ideal. Was sure it could be a dramatic success. Have written Robt. Speaight [British writer and radio actor] for advice" (MM to WW and SW, Wed. February [1964]; also 19/02/64). Wilfred reiterated his thanks and added that, following advice from Gordon Peacock of the Studio Theatre, he might seek an agent: "I think I cd. do so with good prospects, and particularly with eye to American production of *Apes*" (WW to MM, 09/03/64). But amidst these vague notes of an "American production," the correspondence about the *Apes* adaptation—as also Wilfred's work on the play—ended, and the concerns about Lewis and copyright shifted from Wilfred's to Sheila's interests when she worked on what would become the 1967 Lewis issue of *artscanada*.

Another of Wilfred's plays of the early 1960s was *The Trial of Corporal Adam*, which advertising posters described as a "powerful, flamboyant play on the theme of Everyman—'a comedy in verse'—...[a] provocative and controversial new work." When this play went into production, Watson followed his practice of attending rehearsals, this time on McLuhan's turf in Toronto. In April 1963 he wrote McLuhan of his plan, funded by the Canada Council, to visit rehearsals and some of the May 1–12 performances of the play at Toronto's Coach House Theatre. In the same letter, he tossed out references to three other of his prospects: a festival play (*Is There an Elephant in the House?*); a television play; and "a rollicking satire, spoof, dry scoff on Genet's *The Maids*" (WW to MM, 03/04/63). He seems to have left a draft of the "festival play" with McLuhan, who thought it might speak to what he hoped would become the theme of a festival projected for Vancouver, "the extensions of man": "Surely the *Elephant in the House* is right on the old toe nail!" (MM to SW and WW, n.d., [Aug. 1963?]).

When *The Trial of Corporal Adam* opened, McLuhan and members of his family accompanied Watson to his play. Watson recalled the occasion warmly: "They—the McLuhan women[—] were more than an enthusiastic, they were a loving, audience. And Marshall, who had an incredible appetite to explain things[,] saw the performance as an instance of his theory that the modern mind is being re-medievalized by the electronic modalities" (WW, draft of a letter to Michael Tait, director of the performance, 29/05/90). McLuhan had "kidnapped" Watson from a hotel room and got him to stay with the McLuhans, where Watson and McLuhan agreed on the title for *From Cliché to Archetype*. After Watson had returned to Edmonton, McLuhan went to another performance of *The Trial of Corporal Adam*, hoping perhaps to figure out yet more fully what Watson was up to: "Tait as Death was too casual, not macabre, wore no beard or make-up. Mephistofiles was still apoplectic through-out. But we enjoyed it. Personally I found myself much more aware of the phrasing (and timing) and it gave much satisfaction" (MM to WW and SW, n.d.; see also Tiessen, "'Shall I Say'" 123).

Weeks later Wilfred was updating Marshall on yet another play: *Another Bloody Page from Plutarch*. Sheila wrote more than once to explain that Wilfred was hard at work on this play and much more; for example: "W. is finishing *Another Bloody Page*, and has multifarious activities afoot. He feels now that the *Page* is good, technical difficulties solved" (SW to MM, 25/06/63). Six weeks later, in a note that he attached to a letter from Sheila to Marshall, Wilfred stated that he had just finished the play (SW to MM, 07/08/63). Four days later, Marshall started his letter to Sheila and Wilfred by exulting at Wilfred's "great news." And in an undated letter to Sheila he said, "'Another Bloody Page from Plutarch' is a grand title." The play was never performed, but was published in Watson's *Plays at the Iron Bridge*.

In one of his many letters to McLuhan the following year, Watson included rollicking news about his newest play, *Wail for Two Pedestals*. It had just been performed at Edmonton's Yardbird Suite, a venue for experimental work. With the play's allusions to Beckett's *Waiting for Godot* and Odets's *Waiting for Lefty*, it was, he said, "a post-Beatnik farce about Godot and Lefty." With Martin Esslin's 1961 study *The Theatre of the Absurd* as his reference, he "put on" his audience by shaking off public expectations of where his work might stand. The "local punditry," he claimed, was "much dismayed by my rejection of the theatre of the absurd, which begins to be understood à la Esslin who is so much out of touch as to believe that modern language is in a decline." The English language, he consistently argued, remained a fertile field and an essential lifeline in a world favouring non-language technologies. He drew McLuhan's attention to his influences on this work, playing on the observation that the university itself was a "Gutenburging" force curbing response to what he was trying to achieve: "*Wail for II pedestals* was huge success in a grain of sand. Anyone whose sensibility had not advanced beyond that of an Albertan freshman (i.e. had not been Gutenburged) went wild about it" (WW to MM, 11/12/64).

He demonstrated further his attentiveness to McLuhan, weaving his reading of Marshall's most recent letter to him (written

December 3, 1964 concerning, among other topics, technology as the collective unconscious and the arts as the collective consciousness) into his stage experiment with *Wail for Two Pedestals*:

I like your idea about art as the consciousness, technology as the unconsciousness, of the age. / Part of success of *Wail for Two Peds* resided in fact that I'd recognized two emotional polarities possible in this age, nostalgia and wonder. Progress alienates and creates nostalgia and hence the proliferation of scads of nostalgia pieces—*The Waste Land*, etc. much of Joyce, as well as the continents of inverted nostalgia in Lewis. But Progress also generates an equal sense of wonder, which I take to be the emotion appropriate to the marvellous. In practice, the genuine wonder is actually tinged with nostalgia—it is wonder at the horror of...? [*sic*] / You will see that by contrasting these two basic emotions, I could get an almost brand new sense of the modernity of the times in the theatre. I set Godot up on one pedestal and Lefty (I took the liberty of changing the sex of Odets' communist) up on the other pedestal, and let them fall in love to the tune of Camusian lamentation for the hopeless transcendence of the age. / Other technical advances in Wail I hope to exploit. Chiefly the use of chorus. Much help from *Understanding Media*—I introduced acknowledgement in the climax of wail—at rehearsal I feared this might be a fatuity, but such is your renown in these parts that it seemed beautifully right and at one performance the audience responded with a peal of laughter—but what I sought was the medium-metaphor. Grasped at the chorus-theme as the conscience of mankind, and then went on to use other parts of theatre metaphor—including stage directions. / This chorus is wailing for you. Blessings, / Wilfred. (WW to MM, 11/12/64)

In his notebook, he gave more details about what he saw as the links between this play and McLuhan's work: "I am not concerned," he said, "with communication. I am concerned with display of medium" (18/11/64). A few months later, when the play was produced a second time, he gave a final report on the play to McLuhan—who in the preceding months had become absorbed with Sheila's submission of her Lewis dissertation: "We have had the Western Educational Theatre Conference here. They put on *Wail for Two Pedestals*. It went over reasonably well considering that it had an audience of theatre types hardest of all audiences" (WW to MM, 06/04/65).

Following the production of another work, a revue, at the Yardbird Suite, Wilfred shared with Marshall the simple pleasure that he took from it: "Congratulate me for having written a completely successful revue—*Chez Vous Comfortable Pew*," he declared, then hastened to add assurances of his headway on their *C/A* project (WW to MM, 01/06/65). He was giving an account of himself, clarifying for McLuhan that, even if *Chez Vous Comfortable Pew* was not explicitly furthering their joint cause, their *C/A* project was front of mind. At the same time, we do see in the extant letters that Watson certainly did not always mention his script writing and related theatre activities to McLuhan, perhaps concerned that McLuhan might come to regard them simply as distractions from their joint project. For example, in 1967 alone—which, as we shall see in section III, proved to be an especially important year for Wilfred's increasingly "McLuhanesque" theatre—he completed the scripts for the Edmonton performances of *Thing in Black* at the Yardbird Suite and *Two Teardrops Frozen in the Rearview Mirror* and *The Canadian Fact*, both at the Walterdale Playhouse. He avoided drawing attention to these three works in the correspondence; however, as we shall note, some six years later, McLuhan, with obvious pleasure, did read *The Canadian Fact*, a delightful two-hander—conversation involving a writer and a theatre director—published in the Winter 1972 issue of *White Pelican* (and reprinted in 2008 in Robin C. Whittaker's volume *Hot Thespian Action!*).

In 1967 Watson's eagerness to play—both sympathetically and iron-ically—with "McLuhan" topics and approaches became abundantly evident in his "Canadian centennial play," *O holy ghost dip your finger in the blood of Canada and write, I Love You*, directed at the Studio Theatre by Thomas Peacocke. Reviewing the play, Edmonton theatre critic Barry Westgate summarized the playwright's evolving program of the 1960s: "[Watson] sees the Canadian playwright of the future as a sort of Marshall McLuhan—'the same violence, the same intellectual bombardment of the senses'...He considers himself of the Peter Weiss school, the Theatre of Cruelty, of violence, and blood, and primitiveness" (see also Tiessen, "'Shall I Say'" 115). With this play Watson also seemed to be throwing out a challenge to McLuhan, eschewing or subverting any straightforward absorption or mimicry of McLuhan. McLuhan might not have been impressed.

Subtitling his play *flower power farce in 4 acts*, Watson later wrote in an Introduction to the published version:

> It succeeded as a poem about the "flower children,"
> about the northwestern sub-species of them which raced
> around me chanting anti-war slogans and plucked me
> aside to explain what Marshall McLuhan's famous pun
> meant, i.e., total theatre. I wanted to achieve it for them,
> but I knew it was an impossibility, and not even desir-
> able. I also sensed that they were doomed, and wanted
> to draw their portrait, so that some trace of them would
> persist, if not to be revived in the theatre, at least in the
> monumental space of a mise en page. (*Plays* [251])

His flower-children characters—or caricatures—figures who tried to accommodate themselves to a variant of McLuhan's global village were, he said, unable "to cope with the absolutism of the technologies and the media" (Watson, *Plays* [251]).

Meanwhile, Viking, with whom Watson and McLuhan had signed a contract in 1965, were eager to see the *C/A* manuscript.

In the spring of 1966, and again 1967—when he was at the peak of his international fame—McLuhan felt that they could wrap up the book with a few weeks of face-to-face dialogue in Toronto in the following summer (MM to WW, 25/03/66, 21/06/67). Through much of 1966–1967, with no book manuscript in hand, McLuhan kept putting Viking off, assuring them that the work was becoming more exciting, even though they were having trouble finishing it. In August 1967, as we learn from Watson's letter to Viking, McLuhan told Viking that he was pestering Watson to join him in New York, where he was spending 1967–1968 as visiting professor at Fordham, but that Watson was exceedingly busy with his "centennial play" (WW to Alan Williams, 04/11/67). Writing to McLuhan in mid-October, and aware of his expectations, Sheila—as defender of Wilfred—provided for him an alibi, conveying a tactile impression of his work in progress: "W's play has gone into the first stages of production. Feldman, the designer, and Tom Peacocke, the director, just interrupted my first successful attempt to write by calling to pick up a large model of Studio Theatre which has been part of the living room furniture for some time" (SW to MM, 13/10/67).

In late October, under pressure from Viking, McLuhan wrote from Fordham:

Dear Wilfred: / Allen [sic] Williams of Viking just talked to me. He says he has failed to elicit any response from you. / Right now he offers to advance you $1,000 on C-A, if you will come here to chat about the book. Wouldn't this serve to fly Sheila in here as well? / The largest C-A item of all is surely the new man-made environment around the planet which turns the planet into an archetype. It is another way of noting that the evolutionary process has shifted from biology to the man-made environment. / Hoping to hear from you soon. / Most cordially, / Marshall. (MM to WW, 24/10/67)

Were the Watsons to fly to New York, McLuhan was confident they could, with the help of Margaret Stewart, his secretary, finish the book within a week.

On November 4 Watson wrote Viking's Alan Williams, accepting the offer of an advance. He lamented having missed the opportunity to work with McLuhan during the summer of 1967. He now seemed to imply, however, that his own theatre work took precedence, distracting as it might be in relation to the Viking project. Yet he also tried to convince Williams that his method of producing material for the play would serve him well in shaping the *C/A* book:

The book however has never been out of my mind, because the project itself involved news magazine environments and I have now most of my graduate students working on various aspects of the "environmental" approach. / It would be very helpful if I could join Marshall, and I have written him asking about the most convenient time for my coming. Thank you for offering to advance me $1000 of my share of the royalties, which offer I do very gratefully accept. I am glad Viking believes in the book. After the theoretical basis was established, what bugged me most about it, was that it is many books in one, and it was difficult to know which to choose to work at—but Marshall I think has a most enviable sense of relevance. (WW to Alan Williams, 04/11/67)

On the same day, he wrote McLuhan, commenting on the links between his play and McLuhan's thought:

Dear Marshall, / It's good to hear from you. Mr Allen [*sic*] Williams of Viking's letter came right on the heels of yours. I have written to him accepting his offer of an advance. I'd very much like to see you about the *C/A* book. / I could get away for a brief visit at once. Or, for a longer one, after the 9th December. The Centennial play is now in rehearsal and will play for five nights starting December 5th. It has already been much talked about locally because of its title: O HOLY GHOST DIP YOUR FINGER IN THE BLOOD OF CANADA AND WRITE, *I love you*. The cast immediately reduced this to *Dip*. I shall have to be here for the week of Dec 5/9th. After that, I could get away for one week or two weeks or three weeks—if I remained for the Xmas vacation. Let me know specifically how long you think would be useful? / We wonder how you've been taking Fordham. I must be clairvoyant because just before your letter came I got a 3M copier with an eye to the documentation of *C/A*, etc. I wish you could be here for *Dip*. It owed an enormous amount to you. We take out all the seats and sit the audience on mats, wrestling mats. Then we have a Y-shaped stage at about shoulder height right in among the audience. My new theatre forms are working like a charm. / Love from us both, / Wilfred Watson. (WW to MM, 04/11/67)

McLuhan responded quickly. Rather than take up Watson's comment that *Dip* owed "an enormous amount" to his work, he replied: "I, too, must be clairvoyant, because I have kept all the time in December from the 9th onward absolutely clear, save for an occasional luncheon here at Fordham. Six weeks ago I made the resolution to avoid all out-of-town trips. I am beginning to reap the benefits thereof. // Corinne and I do very much hope that Sheila will be able to come along with you. We have ample space" (*Letters* 346).

In late November, however, McLuhan underwent surgery to remove a brain tumor and the planned meeting in New York was cancelled. He was fully out of commission from the end of November until December 12. Wilfred wrote shortly after that to tell Marshall about the stage production of *Dip* and, again, its relation to their work on the *C/A* project:

Glad to hear you are convalescing well. I am recovering from *O HOLY GHOST DIP YOUR FINGER IN THE BLOOD OF CANADA AND WRITE I LOVE YOU*. I suppose it was successful. We played seven nights [December 4–10] to capacity houses. I wish you cd. have seen it, since I deliberately tried to test some of the *C/A* theories. Principally I explored the MAKE LOVE NOT WAR cliché. I think we did capture some of the postures of the contemporary mind, if today can be said to have a mind. What was obvious was that when the fish does discover water, the water he discovers or rather the discovering itself becomes a new invisible environment. Thus art by discovering the modern world adds obscurity to obscurity. As Magritte said: I strive for mystery not clarity. (n.d. [latter half of December 1967])

In a postscript, Wilfred referred to the thousand-dollar advance that Viking had sent him: "Let me know when you are ready to consult about *C/A*. Viking sent me the cheque against that exigent."

When he referred to *Dip* one last time in his letters, Wilfred continued to overlay his stage experience with thoughts on how he and Marshall might finish their book and also launch it. He proposed that they link their joint project to events at the Electric Circus. When that venue had opened in New York in the summer of 1967, Jack Newfield described it in *The Village Voice* as a "total environment, McLuhanist discotheque." Now Watson proposed that he and Marshall think of *C/A* as a "happening/electric environment":

When we did *DIP* last year we researched the news magazine field and ended up with over 600 slides which we used as projections. / I enclose a sketch of the way I see our material [in our book] displaying itself, though I think it useful to hide the theory in lots of examples. It will be useful to play against the interest in war, protest and violence?... Why don't we publish the book, first of all, as a production, a happening, an electric environment in some co-operative art gallery?...The art gallery as the real, functional theatre? / Could we get Viking to produce the book as a happening/electric environment at some world fair? Theme of the book as electric circus? / A chap [here at the university], a computer expert, says that the new teaching machine is essentially a book which adapts itself to each reader. Why not write C/A as this sort of book? (WW to MM, 19/06/68)

McLuhan, however, might have had avant-garde plays such as Watson's *Dip* in mind when, "subjected" to "avant-garde, multiscreen works" during his year in New York, he reacted against them, rhetorically asking, "'What has this got to do with my work?'" (Gordon, *Escape* 231; Marchand, *Marshall McLuhan* [1989] 200).

IV

In the months following the brain surgery, McLuhan's plans to meet Wilfred and Sheila in New York for a week or two in December 1967 were transformed into plans for a year-long appointment for both Wilfred and Sheila as research associates at the Centre for Culture and Technology in Toronto in 1968–1969. As that year approached, Watson and McLuhan became increasingly giddy in their letters, the mood celebratory. Marshall, two months after the operation, put his excitement on display: "As for next year, my modest and conservative nature forbids that I explore the euphoria that I feel. Let's not lose our cool." Below his signature he added, "P.S. Naturally, anything I say to you about next year involves Sheila totally" (MM to WW, 21/02/68). Wilfred replied, "Dear Marshall, // The COOL you urge upon us is precarious in us, the EUPHORIA re next year enormous" (WW to MM, 22/03/68; see also Tiessen, "'Shall I Say'" 124). The same day Sheila chimed in, "Like you we have not yet explored our euphoria" (SW to MM, 22/03/68).

But in retrospect, Watson should perhaps have registered implicit warnings from McLuhan about how their long-awaited get-together might unfold. As early as November 1967 McLuhan started referring to "bundles of memos" he was waiting to use up, intimating that his voice and his method would be dominant in the project: "Am sure we can complete that book in ten days. Have bundles of memos, each one of which could become a chapter. We are going to find ourselves embarking on half a dozen more books while writing this one" (*Letters* 346). On December 15, 1967, only days after the operation, McLuhan precipitously—perhaps ominously, for Watson's prospect as co-writer—began proposing that they widen the writing team, citing both Sheila and his son Eric: "I know that when we get together (and I can see many advantages if Sheila will join us) that we can assemble the mosaic of the book very rapidly...Eric is quite prepared to rewrite the book at once" (*Letters* 347).

When Marshall sought—as he, unlike Wilfred, did repeatedly—to draw Sheila into the conversation, she always responded cautiously. For example, back in 1964 when he urged her to join them, she replied, "I am really on the periphery of the cliché-archetype dialogue" (SW to MM, letter dated only "Thursday," [early September 1964]). During the year at McLuhan's Centre she did, however, participate in his seminar. "In fact," says Marchand of that difficult post-surgery period, "Sheila Watson functioned...virtually as McLuhan's portable memory, directing his attention to passages he had forgotten from books he had once known by heart" (Marchand, *Marshall McLuhan* [1989] 295n3; see also Flahiff, *Always* 251–52).

Marshall was optimistic that *C/A* would continue the international momentum and success of *Understanding Media*. That was Wilfred's assumption too; in 1964 he had written Marshall about the "procedure" they might follow in blasting through their "Cliché/Arch" en route to what he blithely claimed would be his next academic book: "I suggest I do the chapter starts & that you extrude into them volcanically? I want to tear into this work with all speed, as I must do the genetic word play book as soon as possible" (WW to MM, 16/07/64). Watson, however, wanted to set an agenda different from what he understood as that of *The Gutenberg Galaxy* and *Understanding Media*; McLuhan, he feared, would want to preserve the status quo established by those works.

As it turns out, in the summer of 1968 the momentum of Wilfred and Marshall's incredible epistolary performance reached the end of the line. In the years that followed nothing was ever said by them, nor by Sheila, about their 1959–1968 feast of letter-writing. In his published articles about Marshall, Wilfred drew no attention to their long epistolary conversation; instead, with a somewhat jauntily struck note, he placed spirited emphasis on the apparently witty repartee in their face-to-face meetings. When the publisher of McLuhan's *Letters* enquired specifically about their correspondence, Watson responded, "I'm afraid I can't be as much help to you as I'd like to be, re your questions about MM's letters to me" (WW, draft of a letter to William Toye, 08/02/87). McLuhan also drew no public attention to the correspondence nor, for that matter, to his and Watson's year-long visit together. Watson, however, in his private writing, never stopped reflecting on the broader impact of McLuhan on his own thought and the world's.

V

Wilfred and Marshall's year of work together in 1968–1969 became an ordeal. McLuhan's fondly expressed hope that the year would launch them—along with Sheila—on to scintillating, new educational ground, offering "perceptual training programs of many kinds" to the "highest levels of business and politics," evaporated (MM to WW, 09/04/68; see Tiessen, "'Shall I Say'" 126–36 and Flahiff, *Always* 249–54). McLuhan biographer Terrence Gordon has noticed that Wilfred's jest to Marshall that he write his portion of *From Cliché to Archetype* on the left-hand pages, Marshall on the right, should have reminded McLuhan of his own observation, "that jests are based on grievances" (Gordon, *Escape* 248). Marchand has observed that during their year together "McLuhan seemed less and less tolerant of Watson's participation." In the presence of Margaret Stewart, "McLuhan did most of the dictating and ignored almost entirely every idea that had developed in the dialogues with Watson, reverting to his original thoughts on the subject" (Marchand, *Marshall McLuhan* [1989] 219).

Even the acknowledgement of their co-authorship—"Marshall McLuhan and Wilfred Watson"—did not survive when the book emerged. Instead, the title page bore the words, "Marshall McLuhan *with* Wilfred Watson," provoking Canadian scholar Stan Dragland to make this strong reaction:

"With." What does that mean? McLuhan has the whole reputation, even now...Who knows about Wilfred Watson, his poems, his plays, his stories? In the reputation sweepstakes,

just a few...I didn't set out to complain, but by God some-
body has to shout that **WILFRED WATSON'S WRITING
HASN'T ATTRACTED ENOUGH ATTENTION!**
(Dragland 5; see Tiessen, "'Shall I Say'" 143n64)

In his notebook Watson remarked, only partly sarcastically,
that Wilfred Watson *against* Marshall McLuhan might have
been more accurate. In meeting daily with McLuhan, he sought,
essentially, a fluid process resembling the kind of give and take
of the rehearsals he enjoyed with his Studio Theatre collaborators, or even the kind of cheerful exchanges represented by
the nine years of his and McLuhan's correspondence. By the
end of the decade, he was well along in his collaboration with
avant-garde audiences and artists—directors Gordon Peacock,
Bernhard Engel, Thomas Peacocke, artist and designer Norman
Yates—based in Edmonton's experimental theatre and art scene,
so his impasse with McLuhan felt especially discouraging.

Watson came to believe, too, that the rigid pressure of
contractual obligations created unmanageable stress for him and
Marshall, undercutting what might have been a fresh statement
on McLuhan's theories of anti-environment. To William Toye,
editor for Oxford University Press, he said, "I felt the publication
of what shd. have been a dictionary of definitions of his key-terms
was premature. But the temporal constraint, which is one of the
modalities, as you must know, of publishing, was inexorable"
(WW, draft of a letter to William Toye, 05/02/87; see also Tiessen,
"'Shall I Say'" 128). In *Let's Murder Clytemnestra* Watson's
character Electra—in a phrase parodying Eliot's Sweeney's "I've
gotta use words when I talk to you" (MM with WW, *From Cliché*
8)—seems to be articulating, or parodying, Watson's frustration
with the rushed job sans adequate face-to-face rehearsal time
when she sings, "He's gotta use words when he talks to me—//
He's gotta use feet when he walks to me" (Watson, *Plays* 369).

For Watson—who felt artists, as well as others, were respon-
sible for and capable of individual intervention in the face

of technologically determined action—their days together made visible differences in his and McLuhan's approaches to the artist. In his notebook he wrote,

> there was no space for me in MM's metaphysical imperium. His was a reader's view of things, esp. of the artist, who existed only as an historic fact, the result of a formal cause. Mine was a writer's view; I saw the artist with a possible role vis à vis the maelstrom of technological development. He wanted to find out how the buttons worked, to switch them off. I wanted to know how to do something about the finger pushing the button. I supposed the problem to be, primarily, a semantic one. MM's semantics—his collective wordplay—is ultimately non-productive. I believed it was possible to fine-tune semantics so that the button-finger, if it can't be absolutely could be partially controlled. (16/05/81)

Meanwhile, McLuhan was increasingly at home with international media and business. "More than any writer...McLuhan paid attention to his readers," Watson noted, his eye on the sheer magnitude of McLuhan's international readership; "They were the formal cause, he insisted, of what he wrote" (WW, typescript draft of "McLuhan's collective wordplay" 6). He felt that by 1968–1969 McLuhan's fame had gotten in the way of their relationship. Back in 1959 they were closer to being equals, in terms of international reputation, and it seemed then that they could remain somehow in sync with each other. But now, the McLuhan whom he had once known seemed absorbed into the maelstrom of McLuhanisms.

VI

That McLuhan was very uncomfortable with how Watson behaved during their year together has been noticed by his biographers. Marchand suggests that Marshall in his diary "perversely" blamed Wilfred for "derailing" their book (*Marshall McLuhan* [1989] 220; see also Gordon, *Escape* 251). However, in his letters to publishing personnel, McLuhan gestured toward forbearance and expressed a certain sympathy concerning Watson; yet these gestures soon gave way to impatience and anger. In April 1969 McLuhan told his New York literary agent, Claire Smith, that Watson was willing

> to come to New York to talk with Alan Williams about putting some pages on the left side of our "right-hand" pages. He is not too happy about many of the things that are in the folders, which would appear under both of our names; ergo he has written a group of pages of somewhat schematic and graphic pattern to counterpoint the present ones. I have barely seen them—certainly I haven't read them. Basically, Wilfred tends to conventional, classified procedures. He disapproves of probes and processes. It's just possible that his pages might have some real value by way of complementariness. (MM to Claire Smith, 02/04/69)

However, he did not leave the matter there. Drawing on his growing impatience with Watson, he added, "I shall be happy to leave the decision to Alan Williams. On the other hand, for the sake of speed, I hope that Alan will throw them [Watson's "left-hand" pages] in the waste-basket. Also, I have nearly killed myself this year trying to get Wilfred to do anything at all. At present, the relief of not working with him day after day has been colossal! Warm regards" (MM to Claire Smith, 02/04/69).

Writing McLuhan from Viking on April 30, Williams confirmed that Marshall's son, Eric, was helping clean up the manuscript, and wondered whether Marshall and Wilfred should both still be listed as co-authors or whether Wilfred might want his name removed altogether. Williams preferred the latter approach, suggesting that the book would have a greater impact if only Marshall's name appeared, and that, in any case, presumably only little of Wilfred's contribution remained. Their earlier agreement about royalty payments would remain intact, he said, unless a new contract was arranged. But McLuhan defended his partnership with Watson. He steadfastly reaffirmed that he valued Watson as poet and playwright; that he was important as a national and international figure; that he was important as a collaborator with McLuhan who, after all (as he reminded Williams), worked by "dialogue": "There is more Watson in the book than may appear, since I work by dialogue. So let his name stand as you suggest on the projected poster... // Apropos Wilfred, he is a well-known dramatist here in the Theatre of the Absurd. His *Friday's Child* is the only book of poems by a Canadian ever published by Faber & Faber" (MM to Alan Williams, 06/05/69). However, he added, "Eric is now back in New York, willing and able to help."

Continuing to assume that Watson's presence in the book was diminishing, Williams some months later impatiently insisted that McLuhan should send him an immediate and final decision about whether he was to be listed as an author at all and, if so, how (Alan Williams to MM, 02/10/69). McLuhan, in a sort of half-defence of Watson, replied, "Trust that you have not made Watson feel that he is not a participant in the enterprise" (MM to Alan Williams, 26/11/69).

In February 1970, Williams wrote Watson (with a copy to McLuhan): he apologized for not having answered a letter from Watson the preceding month; he indicated that Eric was on location in New York, helping to collate the final details of *From Cliché to Archetype*; and he hoped that there would be no change to the galleys—which he had put into Watson's hands—at this late date. Williams delicately asked, too, about the success of what he called the *Let's Murder Clytemnestra* play. (In his notebook Wilfred called this his "anti-McLuhan" play, for in it he addressed what he saw as failures in the development of McLuhan's thought [c. 09-10/01/71; Tiessen, "'Shall I Say'" 129–37].) With McLuhan copied in the correspondence, Williams discreetly avoided citing the remaining words of Watson's title: *According to the Principles of Marshall McLuhan* (Alan Williams to WW, 19/02/70).

Weeks later, in a stern letter to Williams about Watson's proof-reading of the galleys, McLuhan declared, "Should Watson drag his feet, which I feel certain he will do, I think we can proceed without him. Would it be feasible for you to give him a call?" McLuhan gave Watson's university and home telephone numbers to Williams, and insisted, "If he is in a great passion about this or that, try to ease him out of the project. If he says he can't get around to it for some time, urge him to let it go as is. // Now, back to proof-reading" (MM to Alan Williams, 14/04/70).

Williams wrote back quickly, agreeing in principle with McLuhan's sentiments, but suggesting that it might be best not to contact Watson at all. Watson might simply not return the galleys, and so be considered to have taken on a role of *"nolo contendre."* They would then proceed without him. McLuhan, still torn about what to make of Watson, replied with another protective nod on his behalf: "Herewith the galleys. We have incorporated most of Watson's additions. I think he will feel reasonably content." He added, "Eric has been of enormous aid in handling the whole process of the galleys" (MM to Alan Williams, 24/04/70). But later in 1970, in a letter to his son Eric, McLuhan confided, "The *Cliché to Archetype* thing could have been so much better if I had been able to do it alone"—that is, sans Watson (*Letters* 418).

VII

That same year, Watson summarized his own reaction to McLuhan's use of "dialogue," a view at odds with McLuhan's:

> The word itself exhausts me. We dialogued away all right. We did get finished *From Cliché to Archetype* the book we were working on, but I'm afraid it will be a rather unsat-isfactory affair because MM was afraid of the conclusions we were almost reaching. As it stands, it's a set of varia-tions on a bit of MM jargon, breakdown = breakthrough. This of course is the first new thing ever said about the cliché—that it is a good try that fails and that you don't pencil out clichés but try harder, that is, you go through breakdown to breakthrough. I don't think we ever got this

clearly enunciated, and never reached the point where
we could exploit the contexts of breakdown in which the
book was being written—the recent years of breakdown,
MM's own medical breakdown, and what I think was
happening, the breakdown of the basis of the *Gutenberg
Galaxy*[—]and see how the axiom we were exploring meant
that all these fracturings could have their breakthrough.
(WW, draft of a letter to Kay [Mathers?], 07/01/70)

Watson did not invite McLuhan to *Let's Murder Clytemnestra
According to the Principles of Marshall McLuhan*, which premiered
at Studio Theatre November 21 to 30, 1969, directed by Bernhard
Engel. In writing this "satire on technological utopianism" (n.d.,
[1969], folder 805), Watson worked through frustrations and
observations that had built up for him during the Toronto year.
He had felt trapped by McLuhan's definitions of "the artist": with
the play he broke with Marshall and defined himself on his own
terms, though without necessarily giving up on what he always felt
McLuhan offered. In the post-McLuhan age of the play, "we are
drilling wells upwards into the polluted sky to recover the wasted
minerals of the age of Marshall McLuhan" (Watson, *Plays* 372).

When Watson was in the midst of developing *Let's Murder
Clytemnestra*, a short piece by McLuhan called "Strike the Set"
in the May 1969 issue of his *DEW-Line* newsletter concerning
the usable garbage left behind by the most recent human environment became the trigger for a comment that Watson confided
to his notebook, differentiating himself from McLuhan:

MM's "strike the set" decides that all human environments are garbage, except the newest & latest one. This
is, currently, the one put around earth & moon by space
satellites. With it, the entire world becomes junk. / This
conclusion is really confession. MM is unable to understand
the modern world. / What has brought its most brilliant
interpreter to this impasse?... / What is at fault is MM's

description of media as extensions of the senses... / Instead
of thinking of the media as extensions of the senses, we
should regard them as new senses... / The development
of media supplies us with optional sensory equipment. /
Different men have different sets of senses. (25/06/69)

For Watson, McLuhan's "extensions" paradigm—with its garbage
production—had become unworkable. Thus, in his play, he satirized what he saw as the limits of McLuhan's dichotomous mode of
thinking, his use of equations between technologies and the senses
that, he felt, marked McLuhan's achievement with *Understanding
Media*, but which emerged as recycled material by the time of
books such as *The Medium is the Massage*. In a snide comment in
his notebook, Watson claimed that in *Let's Murder Clytemnestra*
he was adapting in new ways a method of McLuhan's: "We adopt
a principle or tactic of MM's in theatre...Instead of exposition,
which teaches, we have revelation, which creates ignorance...
This principle is used by the theatre of the absurd" (18/06/69).

Having felt abandoned and betrayed in Toronto, Watson
now, at the Studio Theatre, felt himself being re-absorbed
into the supportive production process of an "acting company
ensemble" with its generously functioning "laboratory of
the rehearsal" (Peacock [9]). Here he felt at home.

VIII

Following publication of *From Cliché to Archetype*, Marshall
corresponded with Sheila, not Wilfred. During the 1970s, he wrote
her about sixty letters. Seldom did he attempt any kind of accom-
modation with Wilfred. In the fall of 1971, when the University
of Alberta conferred on him an honorary degree, he did address
both Sheila and Wilfred, thanking them for their hospitality (MM
to SW, 09/12/71). Years later, in another letter, he asked whether
she—or Wilfred—might be interested in holding a chair in Canadian-
American studies at the University of Toronto for 1976–1977 (MM
to SW, 11/06/75). In another, having learned through Sheila of

Wilfred's retirement from the University of Alberta in 1976 (a year after her own retirement), he passed along his best wishes (*Letters* 524–25). Perhaps not insignificantly, in light of the special place of playscripts in the two men's earlier epistolary search for connectivity with one another, it was the publication of one of Watson's 1960s plays that sparked a generous, if still only indirect, overture from McLuhan, a reminder of friendship. As though residually resuming some of their earlier give and take about a work by Wilfred—in this case, the publication of *The Canadian Fact*, which, as I have noted, had been performed at the Walterdale Playhouse in 1967— McLuhan nodded in Wilfred's direction in a 1973 letter to Sheila. Catching up on his reading of *The White Pelican*, a literary magazine of which Sheila was the driving force, he wrote, "Have just been getting into The White Pelican (Winter, 1972) and got huge enjoyment from Wilfred's 'The Canadian Fact'" (MM to SW, 22/03/73).

It was not until the end of the 1970s, however, that Wilfred was ready to discuss his work for stage with Marshall once again, and to resume his efforts at projecting a sense of himself as productive and appreciated within a collaborative artistic environment. As usual, it was a daunting project, this time involving the theatrical performance of his newly invented category of poetry: "number grid verse." In what turned out to be the year before Marshall's death, the two men, now again attending to one of Wilfred's revolutionary experiments, hinted cautiously at something like a renewal of their high-spirited nine-year conversation. Sheila must have been keeping Marshall apprised of the thrust of Wilfred's current work, specifically of his first major publication of number grid verse, *I Begin with Counting*, launched by NeWest Press in Edmonton on November 29, 1978. After the performance of the new work, Marshall wrote Sheila, though not, even now, Wilfred: "Trust that the launching went well and hope that we shall be eligible for a copy of *I Begin With Counting*" (MM to SW, 07/12/78).

Upon reading Wilfred's new book, Marshall sent a very short, perhaps slightly distant, even curt, possibly ironic—or is it simply cautious, or jokey, or curious?—letter addressing

Wilfred: "Dear Wilfred: // I began by trying the poems on some computer programmers, and they thought that they might be able to decode them if they had a bit of time… // Will get on with decoding your coding… // Marshall" (MM to WW, 26/01/79).

In what turned out to be his final letter to Marshall, Wilfred responded at length, addressing Marshall and his work with a sudden burst of gusto, and positioning himself in relation to his work. He echoed the spirit of his letters that began twenty years before, in 1959. He acknowledged the lack of audience at the launch and explained his intention:

> The powers gave ear, etc. the performances were terrific, but almost no audience. / What surprised me was how well the contrapuntal verse worked. The actors had no trouble with rehearsing it. And it communicated much better than ordinary verse. Why—since contrapuntal use of language, with music, has been around since Chaucer's day, haven't we realized how effective language treated contrapuntally is—without music? / I hadn't set out to use language contrapuntally. My intention was to find an English equivalent for Japanese haiku. The seventeen-word grid I arrived at isn't 17-syllable Japanese haiku. But it is a radically new stanza form, dispensing with lines, but functioning like blank verse, similar vices, similar virtues.

Again, as during the 1960s, he lay claim to Marshall's inspiration, insisting that many of the poems in *I Begin with Counting* "[owe] so much to you," and describing them as "contrapuntal arrangements made possible by the notational device of stacking the number grids, one for each voice" (WW to MM, 05/02/79).

He concluded his embrace of McLuhan by pointing to an affinity between their literary styles: "I have a new theory about your prose. It's Meyerhold-ian. For explication (if necessary) see current issue of *October* which assesses the failure of Soviet art in terms of

Stanislavski (followed) and Meyerhold (rejected)." Stanislavski, he explained in a postscript, "tries to get into someone else's shoes, and speak like him." Meyerhold, he told McLuhan, "thinks in terms of *gesture* and *reaction* " (WW to MM, 05/02/79). He saw himself as a disciple of Meyerhold; he was against Stanislavski (see Tiessen, "'Shall I Say'" 120). I have not found a response by McLuhan to Watson's last letter. Perhaps he was content to avoid a new set of entanglements emerging from Watson's projection of himself as avant-garde playwright flourishing in a dialogic mode.

In *Mass on Cowback*, his 1981 book of number grid verse, Watson states that the "total poem," the "poetry" of his number grid verse, lay in its treatment neither of visual nor monumental space on the page, nor in its treatment of auditory space in its performance, but in its "*transformations* from its visual to its auditory forms" (xiv). This statement is, in effect, an echo of his experiments at Studio Theatre that, during the 1960s, had made possible for Watson "the visualization of acoustic space." He publically links his number grid verse to McLuhan's thought, while he simultaneously distances himself from it:

> The poem after each performance folds itself up into its
> original visual form. It can then be opened again in new
> performances. It is this re-opening of the visual form
> which proves its vitality. My thinking about space here
> owes much to Marshall McLuhan, but McLuhan supposed
> visual space to be the space men think in and auditory
> space to be the space we live in. I think of visual space
> as being the space into which we write, paint pictures,
> build monuments; and of auditory space as the space into
> which we perform—not quite the same as the space we
> live in, which I think of as the aggregate (in toto, virtu-
> ally unthinkable) of all the spaces we deal with. (xiv)

IX

In 1980 Wilfred Watson joined a group, led by Sheila Watson
and Fred Flahiff, in planning a collection of essays that would, in
its depth, breadth, and eclecticism, acknowledge and celebrate
McLuhan's achievement. If Wilfred was, as he thought of himself,
outside the "family" as defined by McLuhan, he still admired that
family and, from his position outside the circle, saw it with a considerable clarity and understanding. Recalling the wrenching failure
of the 1960s trajectory, as he understood it, he now wrote with
deep empathy in his notebook: "It wd be very difficult for those who
knew him only during the coach house phase [that is, from 1968 on]
of the centre [Centre for Culture and Technology], to understand
how profound a change MM's operation [in November 1967] had
on his career. Before, all had been exploratory & heuristic; after,
all was retrieval and defense" (19/11/80). Watson, in erudite and
appreciative essays such as "The Preface: On Radical Absurdity,"
"Education in the Tribal/Global Village," "Marshall McLuhan and
Multi-Consciousness: The Place Marie Dialogues," and "McLuhan's
Wordplay," had long protected and nurtured his public stance
concerning McLuhan the culture critic and intellectual. In his plays,
as we have seen, he reserved for himself an ironic, independent,
post-absurdist reading that was responsive to McLuhan as inspiration, yet simultaneously iconoclastic. But in the intellectually
capacious and private space of his notebooks, taking perhaps the
truest measure of McLuhan and of his relation to him, he tested
what seems like an infinite number of variations on these questions. By 1979–1980, and for some years following, he entered a
particularly mellow period of far-reaching assessments, identifying McLuhan's limitations and exploring his achievements.
The idea for the essay collection took shape in December 1980
during a "brain storming" around the Watsons' kitchen table after
they had moved from Edmonton to Nanaimo (Flahiff, *Always*
279–80). Flahiff proposed an early version of the idea, and the
Watsons both ran with and enlarged it, making the collection
a project "to document McLuhan's impact on artists, scholars,

and other public figures" (281). As it happened, McLuhan died later that month, but the proposed project continued.

Sheila, Fred, and Wilfred expanded their organizational team to include two younger Canadian scholars, Shirley Neuman and David Staines. For submissions they approached, or planned to approach, contributors such as

> Chris Chapman on film, Glenn Gould and Murray Schafer on music, bpNichol on poetry, Jane Jacobs on the city, Carl Berger on Marshall and Harold Innis, Donald Theall on Marshall's influence on communication studies in Canada, Pat Bruckmann on his influence on eighteenth-century literary studies. Even the then Prime Minister, Pierre Trudeau, was to be invited to write about McLuhan's impact on government. (Flahiff, *Always* 280)

"It was Wilfred," Flahiff notes, "who came up with a title for the volume—*Reconnaissance*" (280). As "Reconnaissance," that is, an "'examination of a territory to gain information of enemy troops, of the terrain, or of the resources,'" the project came to include, especially under Sheila's prompting, attention to the "'enemy'" camp: McLuhan's opponents in Canada during the 1960s and 1970s (S. Watson qtd. in Flahiff, *Always* 280).

In a series of notebook entries, Wilfred began sketching out a possible essay on "McLuhan and artistic form" for the collection, a reflection of his own concerns that emerged during the winter of 1968–1969: "when we debated about the shape & substance of the book form of *From C/A*. I frequently asked him about form. It wdnt be unfair to say he evaded my questions. He left me to find out what he thought of form from his practice as a writer" (08/06/82). From *Understanding Media* onward, he suggested in his notebook, McLuhan's strength lay in "texture"—the feel of surfaces—rather than in form (24/05/82). The project collapsed several years later, but Wilfred's attentiveness to Marshall did not. As Flahiff summarizes, "Marshall remained present to Wilfred...He had experienced with Marshall something of what others have observed in his relationship with Sheila—an interaction of minds and imaginations which stimulated at the same time it edified Wilfred, bringing out in him what was best in a human as well as in an intellectual sense" (Flahiff, *Always* 246).

I conclude by returning to Dragland's statement, however hyperbolic: "A few lucky readers know that Wilfred Watson could think and write circles around Marshall McLuhan—not that it makes sense to speak of thinking and writing so" (5). Indeed. Certainly we can take pleasure in Wilfred's many "McLuhan" entries in his notebooks during the late 1970s and early 1980s. They are testament to the elegance of his probes into McLuhan and his daring achievement. In them, an elegiac tone distances us from his early days of "putting on" McLuhan as epistolary correspondent. Excerpts from four entries give us the tone of Wilfred's voice, his speaking privately to himself and to his imagined archival readers, here bypassing McLuhan the interlocutor while offering tributes to him. These notes, with McLuhan as subject, are evidence of the kind of magnanimous intellectual gestures that might have informed Watson's contribution to the "Reconnaissance" collection:

> The greatness of Marshall McLuhan is that he enabled a whole age to discover itself. He seemed to be a man of many disciples...but in fact he himself was the greatest disciple of all, the disciple of the age he lived through. He prided himself on being the writer who better than any other understood the modern episteme. But it may be that greatness consists in misunderstanding the world that produces it more than in understanding it which turns a man into a devil, for misunderstanding creates, understanding destroys...It was an age of rationalism gone mad, through an obsessive belief in the magic of explanation. (16/01/78)

> Plato & Socrates, Kierkegaard & Ricoeur demonstrate the fallibility of man, vis à vis language. McLuhan shows us

man's fallibility, vis à vis technology. Addressing himself
to the optimistic liberalism of the sixties, he became
world-famous, for he seemed to know more about the media
explosion than anyone else. His rise was very sudden. His
fall from popular esteem was more gradual. It was accompanied by a growing respect for his ideas among the elite
who saw him as a follower of Innis. Innis spoke in crypto
one-liners. McLuhan used deliberate puns & irony, to show
that technology was an anti-Saviour. Thus he preached to
two sorts of people, those who were liberal utopians, and
those, like himself, who weren't. I became his student/
disciple when he gave me, in the years before *Understanding
Media & The Gutenberg Galaxy*, i.e. in the last quarter of
the nineteen-fifties, a copy of *The Mechanical Bride*. He
invited, urged me, to join his approach to literature—to
see it as an exploration of the technological [strains?] that
were brought about by man's attempt to exteriorize his
needs...My attachment to McLuhan, which was solem-
nized in the contract I made to write *From Cliché to
Archetype* with him, re-enforced the conversion my study
of Sterne's *Tristram Shandy* as a satire of mechanism had
begun. My career, from 1959 to 1970, was modified by my
de-colonization, as a student of the English tradition, and
my attempt to resist re-colonization by the U.S. (08/04/80)

As a saint MM was rather like the medieval, scholastic
saint, than like Mother Teresa. His sanctity arose out of
his learning. If saints have guardian angels, MM's angel
was St. Gabriel, the angel of annunciation. (11/01/81)

Marshall is dead now...He never wanted to know me,
and perhaps couldn't have done unless I'd died first. But
he did want me to know him. He thought I gave up the
attempt in the summer of 1969, when I decided to return
to Edmonton. But I didn't abandon the attempt, though

I wanted erroneously to change him into something he
wasn't...I don't believe he is dead, or rather, I know he
is dead, but don't know what the word "death" means,
any more than the whistling swan does, which lacks
the word but still keeps up the honking. (07/02/81)

Notes

1   Unless I indicate otherwise, I quote from manuscript materials—correspondence,
    notebooks—that are held in the Wilfred Watson archive at the University of
    Alberta in Edmonton. In section VI, my quotations from McLuhan's unpublished
    letters are from the Marshall McLuhan archive at Library and Archives Canada
    in Ottawa. When I quote from unpublished letters—by Wilfred Watson,
    Marshall McLuhan, or Sheila Watson—I annotate by referring to the writer, the
    recipient, and the date of the letter. I refer to the three principal letter writers
    and recipients as WW, MM, and SW, respectively. When I quote from Wilfred
    Watson's notebooks, which remain unpublished, I annotate by giving only the
    date (day/month/year) of the entry. Where dating is particularly difficult, I give
    a filing location (box/folder) in the archive. When I use two forward slashes (//)
    in quoted matter, I am indicating a paragraph or stanza break. I have placed titles
    of books and plays in italics, even when they are not so marked in the original.
    Note that in quotations making reference to McLuhan, he might be referred to
    as MM or M.M.

    My thanks to the estates of Wilfred Watson, Marshall McLuhan, and
    Sheila Watson, respectively, for permission to quote from hitherto unpublished
    material.

2   Diane Bessai provides a superb description and assessment of Watson, with
    extensive reference to his relationship with McLuhan, in her "Wilfred Watson."
    For information concerning Watson's extant playscripts that remain unpublished,
    consult the Wilfred Watson fonds Finding Aid, University of Alberta.

Marshall McLuhan, General Idea, and Me!

Philip Monk

WHAT WAS IT ABOUT WINNIPEG, because is this
not the initial connection between Marshall McLuhan, General
Idea, and me?[1] When, in 1968, I bought a pocket-book edition of
Understanding Media, attended architecture school in the wake
of Michael Tims (soon to become AA Bronson), and saw an exhibition of Ron Gabe's (soon to become Felix Partz) large-scale hand
paintings in some loft in downtown Winnipeg, what was it?—
because the McLuhanesque outlook of that time seems so foreign
to the insular surrealism that has dominated that city recently,
albeit in its rise to attention.[2] However, this is not a question of
Winnipeg but Toronto and the Toronto School: the Toronto School
of Communications, that is, which included Harold Innis, Eric
Havelock, and Marshall McLuhan—and, why not, General Idea?

Could these original bad boys of Canadian art ever belong to
a school—even a night school, the title of one of their 1989 exhibitions? Not that I am trying to get my foot in the door of such an
elite institution as the Toronto School by tagging along in the title.
Of course, by "me" I mean everybody. There is some trace in mine,
though, of Roland Barthes's initial title to his essay "Longtemps
je me suis couché de bonne heure," which was "Proust et moi"
("Longtemps"). But instead of a homosexual coupling of two, my
title is a ménage à trois (or a ménage à cinq). *Ménage à trois* is
also the name of a 1978 General Idea exhibition and publication.
There is a reason for maintaining *three* in my title, rather than two:
Marshall McLuhan and General Idea...or, again, General Idea and
me. "Two" is the number of rivalry—or mimicry (which are one
and the same). The number two ensures that we would talk here
of influence: the influence *of* Marshall McLuhan *on* General Idea.

The number two would give us our marching orders—one, two, one, two—to traditionally conceive influence, marching straight ahead, as unidirectional, which is often the case only of "mechanical matching" (McLuhan, *Gutenberg* 268), as McLuhan would say (rather than the possibility of the reverse: a posthumous queering of McLuhan, if that is at all possible—probably not!). On the other hand, and by saying this—that is, by saying "on the other hand"— we are already caught within the binary logic of handedness (one, two, left, right), the binding logic of either-or. Nonetheless, on the other hand, the number three complicates matters. It dispels influence in undermining one of the mainstays of its concept: that of authorship that a collective implicitly denies. Not that this passage from two to three is an *overturning*, which applies the same dualistic language, when we are concerned instead with the flipping or oscillating back and forth of ambiguity as it operates in General Idea's system, an ambiguity that is regulated instead by the contradictory logic of myth. General Idea materially realized this logic in the mirrored venetian blinds of their 1973 prototype *Luxon V.B.*

The numbers two and three underlie everything. They rule it since these numbers as well engender General Idea's system. This is easy to remember, not easy to see. One, two, three, a numeric cosmology rules General Idea's system.

Not the least concern in the passage from two to three is the anti-Oedipal nature of the transition, which renounces the father figure. I'll leave this question of renunciation and paternity suspended but it does touch upon, in the period between 1975 and 1977, what was abandoned in General Idea's system by arguably turning away, however unconsciously or ironically, from McLuhan. The *threesome*—becoming three—had something to do with this.

General Idea would have been the first to acknowledge the pervasive influence of Marshall McLuhan, as when, for instance, AA Bronson wrote in a text for the Art Gallery of Ontario's 1997 exhibition *The Search for the Spirit: General Idea 1968–1975*, "As children of the Summer of Love (1967) and spectators of the Paris riots (1968), we were well aware of the International Situationists and *Society of the Spectacle* on one hand, and of Marshall McLuhan, drug culture, digger houses, underground papers and free schools on the other" (Bronson, "Myth" 18). This is a complex "awareness" for a group that formed in 1969; but McLuhan, or the name McLuhan, could be taken *at the time* to sum them all up. And for at least AA Bronson, we know that McLuhan was a hero of sorts.

Turning to General Idea's work, one might think that it would make sense to examine McLuhan's influence on the artists through their *media* works, their brilliant television productions, such as *Pilot* (1977), *Test Tube* (1979), or *Shut the Fuck Up* (1985). Meant to be broadcast on television, these videos tended to deal with the mechanics not the medium itself—that is, when the artists were not directly talking back to the media, as in *Shut the Fuck Up*. *The 1984 Miss General Idea Pageant* performances (1970, 1971, 1975) were already "television," performed as if in television studios; they rehearsed both the performers and audience in their staged cues. They were ceremonies meant to parody the art system's methods of evaluation and elevation as seen through—or commented on by—the format of the beauty pageant. (In the end, they were all commentary, commentary being the linguistic basis of much of General Idea's fabrications.) Television was taken over as one other format to parody or plunder. Such nesting of contexts literalizes McLuhan's statement that "the 'content' of any medium is always another medium" (*Understanding Media* 23).

Rather than a specific medium—the television medium, for instance—we need to discover the immersive environment within which General Idea's own system operated, but not necessarily as the *visible* "anti-environments, or countersituations made by artists" as McLuhan called them, stressing the importance of artists in revealing the unconscious effects of new technology (*Medium* 68). When McLuhan wrote that "Environments are invisible. Their ground rules, pervasive structure, and overall patterns evade easy perception" (68), we might apply these comments word for word to General Idea's system itself, which likewise was invisible. Their system was the medium within which their work functioned.

Then again, we might look to *FILE Megazine*, General Idea's picture magazine in the guise of *LIFE* magazine, which began publishing in 1972, and find its source in McLuhan's *The Mechanical Bride: Folklore of Industrial Man*, first published in 1951 and reissued in soft cover in 1967 to capitalize on his fame—although by then, admittedly, the book was a bit dated. Yet General Idea always proved that the dated was fertile ground, indeed, camp ground; they took it as a principle of their work. Their retrospective futurity—creating an archaeology of the past's image of the future—based itself on the same type of images McLuhan used (in their case mainly drawn from *Fortune* magazine from the 1940s and 1950s), except these images were contemporary to McLuhan and retro for General Idea. Perhaps McLuhan gave General Idea licence to proceed with their own parody of the media in *FILE*, turning the media's devices against them, much the way McLuhan had done later when he stylistically adopted advertising lingo and techniques in his popular editions *The Medium is the Massage* (1967) and *War and Peace in the Global Village* (1968). By the way, *FILE* published from a Canadian point of view, which is its own special kind of irony, as we all know. It is important to remember that at a high point in Canadian nationalism, General Idea were nationalists, too, in spite of their international outlook (another McLuhanesque trait perhaps). Yet General Idea had an advantage over McLuhan in that their criticism was parasitical, not seemingly objective; it was produced from an artistic not academic point of view. It took place as an artwork mimicking the myth-making processes of advertising or popular culture but at a higher semiotic level. They "criticized" performatively, their operations taking place within the mechanisms they put on display. As Roland Barthes wrote in "Myth Today," an essay extremely influential on General Idea around 1974/1975, yet only offering a more sophisticated analytical language for what was already in their work,

It thus appears that it is extremely difficult to vanquish myth from the inside: for the very effort one makes in order to escape its stranglehold becomes in its turn the prey of myth: myth can always, as a last resort, signify the resistance which is brought to bear against it. Truth to tell, the best weapon against myth is perhaps to mythify it in its turn, and to produce an *artificial myth*; and this reconstituted myth will in fact be a mythology. Since myth robs language of something, why not rob myth? All that is needed is to use it as the departure point for a third semiological chain, to take its signification as the first term of a second myth. (135)

The latter proceeded from Barthes's observation of myth as a second order semiological system parasitical on a prior sign. General Idea's Glamour myth was a *third* order semiological system parasitical on a second order myth that it in turn cannibalized. While myth naturalizes, hiding its ideological construction, Glamour does the opposite: it artificializes. It's hard to imagine how an artificial myth can be produced except as an artwork, especially an artwork about artifice. Imagine Miss General Idea's shoes as a model of this artificiality: "They raise the Participant into an unnatural (hence cultured) position in which walking is rendered difficult (General Idea, "Glamour" n. pag.).

Not limited in their media analyses to McLuhan, General Idea were incredibly syncretic in amalgamating various influences within their fictional system. And being *mediumistic*, these influences extended, as well, to the Kabala and Mme. Blavatsky. In the real world, Guy Debord's *Society of the Spectacle* and Roland Barthes's *Mythologies* were equally important as McLuhan, not to mention the wild card of William Burroughs's provocative media speculations, which were more about radical media intervention breaking viral mind control than comfortable academic or ideological analyses of content. After outlining the mix of late 1960s influences cited earlier, AA Bronson went on to say, "Now we turned to the queer outsider methods of William Burroughs, for example, whose invented universe of sex-mad, body-snatcher espionage archetypes provided the ironic myth-making model we required" ("Myth" 18). Burroughs offered models, methods, and lingo, even to the advice to simulate a newsmagazine as here in his early 1960s novel *Nova Express*:

> "We need a peg to hang it on," he said. "Something really ugly like virus. Not for nothing do they come from a land without mirrors." So he takes over this newsmagazine.
>   "Now," he said, "I'll by God show them
> how ugly the Ugly American can be."
>   And he breaks out all the ugliest pictures in the image bank and puts it out on the subliminal so that one crisis piles up on another right on schedule. (Burroughs 11–12)

When you look at the ideas in this short dialogue—virus, the subliminal inhabitation of media (i.e., taking over formats such as a newsmagazine), mirrors (although the influence of Robert Smithson should be remarked here as well), and image banks—you realize how influential Burroughs was (not to mention his concept of cut-up) not just to General Idea but the whole correspondence network of mail artists.

But to keep our sight on McLuhan, consider this 1973 General Idea reference to McLuhan's *The Medium is the Massage*:

> Concerning the mechanics of vision it is necessary to see that a shift in realities is simply shifting seeing. It is necessary to realize the levels of vision, the split between naturalized and culturalized information and the manner in which culturized [*sic*] information may become ritual-ized as natural information to the point where it in turn may be absorbed by the cultural processes as raw mate-rial for further processing. The famous "Medium is the Massage" is simply this, media inversion and the raising of vision to additive levels and complexities. ("Pablum" 26)

Shifting seeing as shifting focus in order to look at the ways of seeing actually was more about the mapping of word lines on sightlines, a technique whereby the artists directed or, rather, controlled our vision. Both McLuhan's media inversion (the embedding of previous media as content of a new medium) and Barthes's second order semiological system could be seen to be the models here for how cultural information is ritualized, as if it was natural, and then taken to an additive level of parodic complexity by our artists. Yet the very mention of a nature/culture division should cue us to Claude Lévi-Strauss, whose writings on structural anthropology, strongly influential on early General Idea, also uncover the same mechanisms. Under the influence of Lévi-Strauss, General Idea saw themselves as anthropologists of contemporary myth. In fact, before the influence of Barthes's *Mythologies*, Lévi-Strauss's was General Idea's model of myth.

As an influence, McLuhan was only part of a mythic mix (a subversive mix, one might add). So I don't want to traditionally track down influences, which makes no sense in a body of work like this, but rather look at the relationship between McLuhan and General Idea in a more diffused way. For instance, listen to McLuhan's pronouncement from his 1968 book *Through the Vanishing Point*: "Perhaps the mere speed up of human events and the resulting increase of interfaces among men and institutions insure a multitude of innovations that upset all existing arrangements whatever" (xxiii). Increasing interfaces upsetting all existing arrangements perfectly describes the ethos and methodology of General Idea's early work, which was a radical collage aesthetic, but which owed as much or more to William Burroughs as it did to Marshall McLuhan, and which was shared amongst the short-lived correspondence art movement, and, moreover and significantly, which set up the long-term *systematic* framework within which General Idea's work developed (the *Pageant and Pavillion*)—which was a system of myth. In light of McLuhan's quotation above, consider this description from General Idea's May 1973 *FILE* article "Pablum for the Pablum Eaters":

When a junky when any junky when we art junkies gotta
get our fix we gotta make a connection we gotta get a fix we

need our correspondences...The logic of myth is the logic
of connections. Image making room for words. Naming
of partz, sensing the network working plugged into the
subliminal. The key to this logic is the borderline situation,
the neither one nor the other, camouflaged indifference,
mirror mirror on the wall. Flip flop. Lip flap....The logic
of myth is the moving territory of words, cut word lines,
shift linguals. The logic of myth is the sense of image upon
image image overdose the network causality affair with
ideas raining in the corner...Image trouble is no trouble
at all. Image overdose and suddenly snap you're out there
broken through the borderline floating on the dead edge
of nowhere with images diving in all directions, a sky full
of claws and feathers...Then there is jumbled jargon, lip
flap, loose vowels. Cut words lines shift linguals. (29)

As crazy as this sounds, in its increasing interfaces upsetting all existing arrangements, *all* General Idea is here, even if
we don't recognize their main themes. For, after all, we believe,
that as architecture, General Idea's is a stable system. But theirs
was a "system in motion" that was only temporarily stable,
or was only an illusion of stability based on alternatives:

In this article seeing art as a system of signs in motion
as an archive and indicator and stabilizer of culture
as a means of creating fetish objects as residence for
the field of imagery defining a culture, seeing all this
and more in many ways we have become aware of the
necessity of developing methods of generating realizing
stabilizing alternate myths alternate lifestyles. (20)

Taking seriously General Idea's early writing would allow us to shake
up our understanding of their work—upsetting all existing *interpretative* arrangements. What are the implications of a "system of
signs in motion" for interpreting a pre-existent body of artworks?

The problem with interpreting General Idea's work is that we take the artists at their word and at the same time we *don't* take them at their word. Their work was not just one big joke; it was a coherent system. Moreover, it was a coherent system that can be examined analytically with the period's interpretative tools, which General Idea used, significantly, as well to *construct* their work: Claude Lévi-Strauss's structural anthropology, Roland Barthes's semiology, Marshall McLuhan's media theory, amongst others. General Idea's work appeared as artworks—that is to say, visually—but its mode of appearing, or its *event* of appearing, one might say, was performative: it came into being through a language act; the *Pavillion* was erected through language—it did not exist otherwise. The *system* put the *Pavillion* in place (i.e., erected) and kept it standing (i.e., operating). As it was in their work, so it should be in our analyses: a priority given to language—in our case the close examination of their writing.

Twenty-one years after the end of General Idea, the systematic nature of their work needs to be addressed.[3] This is a difficult task because the system, in work that was all about presentation, did not show itself. In other words, in work that was all about articulation, the system could not articulate itself—but it was there in the telling, as the telling. While thus not appearing, nonetheless, this *total* system regulates all the operations of General Idea's enterprise, and, as in any system, all these operations are linked. The system's ruling term is Glamour. Glamour is a *concept* whose operations are achieved through the application of *techniques* produced by *strategies* and insinuated by tactics. Although there might be a number of sub-categories for each, there is only one concept: *Glamour*; one operation: *reversibility*; one technique: *cut-up*; one strategy: *theft*; one tactic: *camouflage*. (What is consequential for any interpretation of their work is that theirs was also a "system in motion.")

As a substitute for this discussion, here is a structuralist diagram of Glamour's operations, which explains the commutable system of reversibility of General Idea's work. I believe that everything in General Idea is expressed in this diagram.

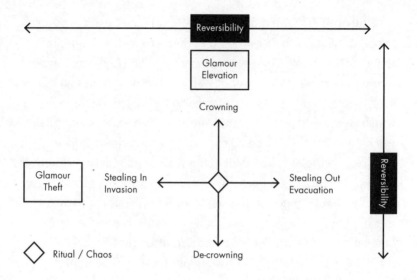

A diagram showing Glamour's operation of reversibility

So I want here briefly to uncover the early ground that instituted this system, the ground on which the *Pavillion* later stood, which rather was an abgrund: an ungrounding of system at the same time. The *Pavillion* was built on a fault line—a fault line that was both spatial and temporal. A recurring problem of critical interpretation is that we don't go back far enough in figuring out General Idea's work but tend to stop when it was consolidated in the period between 1975 and 1977: when the *Pavillion*—and its destruction—was most fully articulated. *Articulated.* General Idea were architect-advocates. Through their verbal advocacy, the *Pavillion* was erected. They were also advocates of their own program; their program was this advocacy, so why shouldn't we believe them? After all, they were persuasive: the *Pavillion* was built by persuasion, as the artists both directed our view of it and thus our understanding of their artistic program: "This is the story of General Idea," they said in 1975 ("Glamour" n. pag.). They told this story better than anyone else. And we have believed them. But, we also know that behind every story there is a backstory, even an underground story, or perhaps an ungrounding story.

Even when they were telling stories about others, it was still about themselves: for instance, the article "Pablum for the Pablum Eaters." Ostensibly, this was an article about Vancouver's Image Bank, which, in the process, was intended to describe the methodologies of the correspondence art movement. Without elaborating its complete thesis, which was about describing myth as a total system, what is important for our story here is the idea of alternatives ("alternate myths alternate lifestyles")— but not only hippie alternatives or the alternative myths that artists create through cannibalizing the detritus of commercial capitalistic culture. No, we are talking of the very concept of the alternative itself, the alternative in alternation with itself (what at about the same time in French philosophy began to be called *différance*): that is, a *perpetual* alternation of ideas, words, and images—a cut-up methodology where everything was in constant motion and in perpetual crisis. "Everything is permitted" was a Nietzschean slogan General Idea took from Burroughs.

To return by example to McLuhan, who wrote, "We actually live mythically and integrally, as it were, but we continue to think in the old, fragmented space and time patterns of the pre-electric age" (*Understanding Media* 20), General Idea's enterprise was a system of myth produced by the cut-up method. McLuhan's own method was collage-like—and his books were image banks of "what's happening." McLuhan called *The Medium is the Massage* "a collide-oscope of interfaced situations" (*Medium* 10), which is a perfect description of what General Idea were writing about. Even an academic book such as *The Gutenberg Galaxy* McLuhan called a collage event: "Thus the galaxy or constellation of events upon which the present study concentrates is itself a mosaic of perpetually interacting forms that have undergone kaleidoscopic transformation" (*Gutenberg* ii). This perfectly describes what the whole correspondence art movement was all about: image banks were individual myths, archives of like images obsessed upon by artists, which were solicited through the pages of *FILE* and submitted through the mail by fellow subliminal networkers to surface again sometimes in the same pages of *FILE*. Detached from their intended meaning or function within one context, they were perversely put into circulation in another. Belying their symbol of stability (that of a bank), image banks were systems of signs in motion composing varied cosmologies. "Pablum" continued: "Correspondences are the key to the mythical universe, the cosmology of moving bodies, images in collision, classification by jointing" (27). As image banks, not only *FILE*, but *The 1984 Miss General Idea Pavillion* itself were such precarious constructions.

Perpetually changing, constantly colliding, collage conjunctions were events that brought together, in continual cut-up, different alignments of words and images. Different classifications by jointing led to ever-new configurations. These were momentary events that were hardly visible, or at least visible only as after-images that offered the illusion of stability. Their conjunction was a vacillating borderline that was temporary.

The borderline (really, an interface) was a concept that General Idea shared with McLuhan, not surprisingly given that McLuhan posited it as part of the makeup of the Canadian persona (engendered vis-à-vis our relation to the United States).[4] An ambiguous model signifying between the domains of politics and psychology (as both the boundary between nations and a personality disorder, i.e., borderline personality), the borderline was a major operative concept for General Idea. In their September 1973 *FILE* article "General Idea's Borderline Cases," the artists wrote, "Ambiguity is not a symptom of a schizophrenic who travels back and forth across the line but a quality of the border dweller who performs in the stolen moments" (12). Borderlines came into existence every time there was a mirror insertion or collage cut. In fact, mirror, cut-up, and borderline were one and the same:

silent and invisible, yet engendering the verbosity of myth. ("The vacuum created by your invisibility has got to be filled with words," read a complementary article in the same issue ["Are You" 35]). Unlike the *Pavillion* or *Pageant*, which were containers or formats, the borderline was an operative concept by which and on which the *Pavillion* was erected through means of disguise and theft. The *Pavillion* was built on this unstable borderline where the border dweller (General Idea) performed in stolen moments.

This article was its own case of cut-up correspondence of words and images. The borderline cases were ten exercises in creating seeming symmetries between words and images. Between one and the other, between word and image, though, was the surreptitious insertion of a mirror. From the start, the mirror image, of course, always added up to two. Between one and the other, between the numbers one and two, were all the resources of mirroring, mimicry, and mockery as language clichés were married to banal images. Here is the text from the second case, titled "Imitation of Life (Mimicry)":

It's only natural to try to be part of our vision, our culture. Like chameleons at odds trying to be part of it all. Like letting our one hand know what the other is about. When one body is imitating one body lying down its life imitating life. This act of bodies rubbing is merely a shadow of things to come. Was meeting face to face the mother of invention of the looking glass? Was this prop-osal to end our singleness? There's safety in numbers and two can have a mind of its own. Our two hands applauded the engagement and came out dueling. In the crack of dawn a narcissus is blooming. All together now, one two, one two, one two. ("General Idea's Borderline Cases" 14)

Yet, the two, or the mirror image of two, did not mean equality or even actual symmetry. *One* brought forth the other (as if in a mirror), and engendering it gave it life, as simulacral as that life was since it was only mimicry. (Mimicry was viral:

indeed, a virus. The point of entry, the mirror act was a viral, replicating invasion.) One preceded two and that one was the word. That is, the word came first and did not merely caption an image after the fact. It took off from its invasion: serially, creating content in the process. Words, too, were mirrors.

Each case was an application: the application of a method through the insertion of a mirror. It was purely artificial. There was no given place to insert a mirror, however. No guideline. The borderline did not pre-exist. The *act* of mirror insertion created the borderline situation. Only the mirror preceded—as invisible as it was. As invisible as it was, it was an event, the instantiation of a case, an instance of now: a collage collision. It was the inaugurating act: the origin of *all* General Idea's work.

"The Great Divide was words," they said (20). Words made images secondary; in fact, they doubled them. Words split images. Or, the proliferation of words split images into mirror images of themselves. Here is case number three, "Self Conscious":

> Now that we've got our distance we look back over our shoulders. Could this be our skin? Still waters reflect our eyes reflecting still waters running deep. Let's keep this all on the surface. The surface of the silvered glass narcissus. Could this be our connection? Score one for us and chalk it up to experienced. Driving the wedge down deep through the centre and splitting the images in halves. There is two of us to contend with now. Two heads are better than one but it's really just one more mouth to feed on. Casting our image in the mirror revealed a cast of two. Our very own dialogue to talk to ourselves. We're not the one we used to be. (16)

Splitting in half was only a beginning that had no end. Words, like mirrors, were viral.

So in retrospect, when we read the statement from *FILE*'s first editorial ("Every image is a self image. Every image is a mirror" ["Some" 3]), we must now presume that *between* every image (that is, between every self-same image) is a borderline. This does not just make the image reflect itself (as if in a mirror) but is a fissure of words, indeed, of "cutting remarks" ("General Idea's Borderline Cases" 10). Words were a method of invasion, even of the image.

Identity, too, was viral. Identity—or role—was a mirror effect produced serially: one plus one plus one, which did not add up to three, however. Two was a precarious couple, not really the pillars of social and familial stability we think. As in a tripod, a motif in their late 1970s work, *three* was the stable number as when the 1977 *"Right Hand Man" Showcard* reads, "The three of them are all each others right-hand man but they aren't taking any chances. If one was lost on the job it would throw off the balance. They know that three's a crowd and a basic social unit and they'd hate to be reduced to a couple." General Idea were not always a threesome—the three men they became. A loose coalition at the beginning, General Idea did not *conceptually* consolidate themselves into a trio until 1975, when the first of their self-portraits began to appear: first as architects, then as their impersonations of babies, poodles, scholars, baby seals, etc. Is this fact significant? Yes. It is an intentional turn within their work, though not acknowledged: a crisis, you might say. And it pertains to the influence of McLuhan, which in 1975 ends, I would claim. The three-fold corporate stability could be argued as a turning away from both McLuhan *and* the principles of the collage-based correspondence movement, the origins of their early work that subsists throughout, nonetheless, in having set up the ground of their system.

The passage from two to three was a crisis indeed. Until this coup to the rule of three, the numbers one and two dominated in General Idea's system (as I've suggested by selecting the border-line cases cited earlier). Not even that many: the number *one* was above all. (Miss General Idea was the number one above all.) Two was only the effect of a mirror, engendered there as a simulacrum. But what an effect! Their whole system was sustained by it. But in 1975, henceforth the number three began to rule General Idea's work and it would have room for no others. This number, a troika, was all about control: controlling our vision, or, rather, constructing our vision in order to erect the *Pavillion* through these sightlines—and to elevate Miss General Idea at the same time. General Idea's corporate consolidation was consequential. Their fixed point of view, albeit established by a trio and not an individual, was a throwback. Paradoxically, it re-instituted the single-point perspectival system; "fixed relationships in pictorial space" were no longer images in collision (*Gutenberg* ii). "Fixed relationships in pictorial space," McLuhan claimed, with an accompanying fragmented private point of view, were key to establishing the concept of individual identity during the print epoch, and were at odds with a mythic vision brought about by today's "electric implosion" (*Understanding Media* 20). The latter was the mythic universe of correspondence and collage cut-up—"the cosmology of moving bodies, images in collision" with its collide-oscopic McLuhanesque overtones—that General Idea, having earlier participated in, seemingly gave up. For example, here is one of General Idea's guiding statements produced in that mid-1970s period that evokes their fixed point of view, accumulated, though, to excess:

> THE FRAME OF REFERENCE is basically this: a framing device within which we inhabit the role of the general public, the audience, the media. Mirrors mirroring mirrors expanding and contracting to the focal point of view and including the lines of perspective bisecting the successive frames to the vanishing point. The general public, the audience, the media playing the part of the sounding board, the comprehensive framework outlining whatever meets their eye. ("General Idea's Framing Devices" 12)

That the triadic turn of 1975 re-established identity—that is to say "authorship," even though of a collective nature—when the whole ethos of General Idea's early work was the flouting of copyright is one of the anomalies of this intriguing body of work— but, of course, it was then turned to ironic ends. This is no criticism on my part of the further development of General Idea's work, only a way of designating the end of McLuhan's influence. Not only can we not judge, we cannot argue with a *mythic* system such as General Idea's.

As a corporation General Idea had become what McLuhan had first written about in 1951 in *The Mechanical Bride*:

> Ours is the first age in which many thousands of the best-trained individual minds have made it a full-time business to get inside the collective public mind, [in the process creating a] folklore of industrial man, so much of which stems from the laboratory, the studio, and the advertising agencies. But amid the diversity of our inventions and abstract techniques of production and distribution there will be found a great degree of cohesion and unity. This consistency is not conscious in origin or effect and seems to arise from a sort of collective dream. (*Mechanical Bride* v)

General Idea were all three—a laboratory, a studio, and an advertising agency— and their collective dream was *The 1984 Miss General Idea Pavillion.*

Notes

1   A version of this article was first delivered as the McCready Lecture on Canadian Art, November 9, 2012, Art Gallery of Ontario, Toronto.

2   Formed in 1969, General Idea was Michael Tims, Ron Gabe, and Slobodan Saia-Levy, who respectively took the pseudonyms AA Bronson, Felix Partz, and Jorge Zontal.

3   This topic has now been addressed. See Monk, *Glamour Is Theft.*

4   See Marshall McLuhan, "Canada: The Borderline Case," in *The Canadian Imagination: Dimensions of a Literary Culture,* ed. David Staines (Cambridge, MA: Harvard UP, 1977), 226–48.

III

art and

ANTI-
ENVIRON
MENT

8

Sheila Watson, Wyndham Lewis, and Men without Art

Dean Irvine

Gestalt and Expressionist Aesthetics

EVEN BEFORE HER FAMOUS EXPLICATION of her 1959
novel *The Double Hook* as a work comprised of "figures in a
ground, from which they could not be separated," Sheila Watson
employed "a gestalt way of explaining the work of art" ("What
I'm" 183) in her 1965 doctoral thesis on Wyndham Lewis. "Lewis's
work," she writes, "however one responds to its total structure is
not...'a heap of splendid fragments,' but an organic whole which,
like any other organic structure, develops in a specific matrix
and is responsive to the conditions of its existence" (*Wyndham*
384). Without naming her source, she goes on to reiterate the first
proposition of a gestalt aesthetic by the late nineteenth-century
German philosopher Christian von Ehrenfels,[1] stating that, as an
ensemble, Lewis's drawings, paintings, and writings form "a whole
which is greater than the sum of its parts" (1). If, in the context of
her reading of *The Double Hook*, Watson intends only to describe
the relations between figures ("people," "objects," and "things")
and the *ground* in which they are suspended that serves as the
framework ("landscape" and "the other existences with which they
came in contact" ["What I'm" 183]), she conceives of the gestalt
as a synchronic, ahistorical structure, an organic whole whose
unity is articulated by the interdependencies of its internal parts.
This is not how she sees Lewis's oeuvre, however. By viewing the
whole of Lewis's texts and visual art in their historical contexts,
Watson accounts for the gestalt as a diachronic structure as well.

Among critics attentive to Watson's thesis and subsequent
essays on Lewis, Sherrill Grace and Angela Bowering have probed
the ways in which gestalt, expressionist, and vorticist aesthetics
inform Watson's fiction. Grace's argument is that the conjuncture

of expressionist and gestalt aesthetics in *The Double Hook* is
rearticulated in Watson's thesis. "If this thesis, completed more
than a decade after *The Double Hook*, is of interest here," Grace
writes, "it is because of the light it sheds on the subtlety and depth
of Watson's knowledge of Expressionism as a seminal modernist
aesthetic and style" (183). She goes on to say that "Watson articulates a vision of Lewis as abstract expressionist that reveals the
significant form of his oeuvre and provides us with a clear frame
of reference for her own work" (191). Bowering follows an analogous metacritical method, based not on the thesis but on the later
essays, that "Watson's reading of Lewis's art provides...[her] reader
with the instruction that is needed for a reading of her own" (3).
Watson's biographer F.T. Flahiff has documented the story behind
the writing of her thesis, which he links to *The Double Hook* and
her comments on its gestalt aesthetic (195). In particular, Flahiff
calls attention to the final section of the thesis, in which Watson
concludes that it "was not until he had explored the implications of
Expressionist theory...that Lewis realized fully the extent to which
men by a process of abstraction create outside themselves a reality
which dominates them like a fate" (*Wyndham* 272 qtd. in Flahiff,
Always 195). For Flahiff, Lewis's figural abstractions "prowling
and angling in London's Strand" find their correlatives in Watson's
"Coyote and old Mrs. Potter" (195). Gregory Betts positions his
interpretation of the vorticist aesthetics of *The Double Hook* in a
precise chronology based on Watson's Paris journals of 1955–1956 in
which she documents her reading of Lewis's books and simultaneous
revision of her novel manuscript (*Avant-Garde Canadian* 227).

Amid this revision process, Watson arrived at her earliest
articulation of *The Double Hook*'s signature gestalt in a journal
entry of April 21, 1956: "Now I ask myself if I have the power to
make it come whole—to fuse completely character, event, setting"
(Flahiff, *Always* 151). Even as she began to articulate this gestalt
of "character, event, setting" in her novel, Watson perceived it
in Lewis's typographic and visual art: "It seems to me that his
problem was the problem of an artist who used two media—that

he was primarily interested in gesture and gestalt—that is in a plastic medium—that he was interested in the architectural possibilities of the medium not the representative possibilities" (Letter to McLuhan, 20 July 1962). With her spatialized figuration of his intermedia aesthetic, Watson at once distances Lewis from the temporal gestalt and "time-cult" that he attacked in *Time and Western Man* (1927) and affiliates him with the concept of "spatial form," which Josef Frank introduced in 1945 to describe "the complete congruity of esthetic form in modern art with the form of modern literature" (Frank 651). Based on some of the German expressionist aesthetic theory—principally Wilhelm Worringer's *Abstraction and Empathy* (1908)—that Watson was reading for her thesis, Frank's influential theory of "spatial form" corresponds both with her intermedia interpretation of Lewis's gestalt and with her own creative configurations of "figures in a ground."[2]

While the correlation of Watson's fiction with her criticism is not without its methodological problems—namely, it follows a methodology that at times entails reading her early fiction retrospectively through her later criticism—and while it "remains unclear," as Flahiff puts it, "where or when or with whom she first encountered [Lewis's] work" (*Always* 194), the prevailing consensus among critics and her biographer should indicate the interpretive value that accrues to a bifocal perspective on her critical and creative practice.[3] My departure from others who have read Watson's fiction through the principles of gestalt and expressionist aesthetics is guided by her incisive and thorough critique of expressionism—at once in her thesis and subsequent essays on Lewis and in her novels and short fiction. For instance, when Donna Palmateer Pennee warns that Watson's interpolation of Anglo-American high modernist aesthetics in *The Double Hook* is symptomatic of her practice of a masculinist modernism, her reading is predicated on the novel's sanction of an expressionist *Weltanschauung*. Rather than assimilating expressionism wholesale into her aesthetic practice, Watson exhibits in her fiction a decisively censorious stance that foregrounds the failures of expressionism.

In doing so, her fiction accords with her critical assessment of Lewis's career. "Had not Lewis begun as an Expressionist he would not have understood the problems of Expressionism," she writes in a summation of her thesis, a study in which she anatomizes the troubled relationship between technology and the "human implications of an expressionist way of life" (*Wyndham* 265, 27).

Looking at the period immediately prior and contemporary to the visual and literary art movements of expressionism in Germany (circa 1910–1920) and vorticism in England (circa 1914–1919), Watson devotes the first half of her thesis to the impact of late nineteenth- and early twentieth-century Austrian-German aesthetic theory on Lewis. The structure that Watson constructs around Lewis situates him in an emergent field of gestalt and expressionist aesthetics, where Von Ehrenfels and other gestalt theorists are positioned alongside the principal aesthetic theorists of expressionism that influenced Lewis, including Konrad Fiedler, Alois Riegl, Wilhelm Worringer, Oswald Spengler, and Wassily Kandinsky.[4] Although he would have characteristically rebuked anyone who called him an expressionist, Lewis gathered with Ezra Pound, Henri Gaudier-Brzeska, and Jacob Epstein under the banner of vorticism, which they first advertised in the *Spectator* on June 13, 1914: "The Manifesto of the Vorticists. The English Parallel Movement to Cubism and Expressionism. Imagisme in Poetry. Death Blow to Impressionism and Futurism and all the Refuse of naïf science" (qtd. in Wees 162). While Lewis exhibits his early exposure to expressionism in his vorticist manifestos published in *Blast* (1914–1915) and in the essays of *The Caliph's Design: Architects! Where Is Your Vortex?* (1919), he simultaneously distances vorticism from certain manifestations of German expressionism. Watson recognizes that the aesthetic theories Lewis developed during his vorticist phase derive from Austrian and German theorists, but that after the appearance of Spengler's *The Decline of the West* (1918) Lewis denounces the appropriation of expressionist aesthetics to the formulation of the Spenglerian zeitgeist.

Spengler is the principal target of Watson's and Lewis's critique of the "expressionist *Zeitgeist*" (Watson, *Wyndham* 40).

According to Watson, Spengler's zeitgeist assimilates and distorts Kandinsky's formative expressionist treatise on "inner necessity" in *Concerning the Spiritual in Art* (1912) and Fiedler's theory of "form-language" (later popularized by the Bloomsbury art critic Clive Bell), which sees the work of art as the co-ordination of "inner necessity" and "significant form" (*Wyndham* 40). Of particular significance to Watson's and Lewis's critique is Spengler's deterministic interpretation of the gestalt or "form-language" of cultural history in the West—one that explicitly and ironically denies the expressionist artist's will to transcend the historical forces of modernity through the creation of abstract art forms—that compels her to reject his contradictory vision of artistic modernity in which the artist becomes the puppet of an expressionist zeitgeist (Lewis qtd. in Watson, *Wyndham* 79; Watson, "Artist-Ape" 117). These failures and contradictions of expressionism emerge in Watson's fiction as the object of prolonged inquiry—from her early fiction of the late 1930s and major novel of the 1950s through her short stories from the early 1950s to the early 1970s.

Men without Art

If Watson's thesis and essays on Lewis are of value beyond her formidable knowledge of modernist aesthetics, it is not only because they offer keen insights into her critique of expressionism. It is also because they evidence her long-standing interest in Lewis's theories and practice of satire. Given that his satire frequently takes expressionist art, aesthetics, and artist figures as objects of attack, it follows that Watson's fiction is similarly populated and that it regularly employs satiric modes. What I undertake here is to recontextualize her oeuvre through her signature statement on aesthetics in "What I'm Going to Do," but with a view to her critique of expressionist aesthetics and her practice of satire and metasatire. Taking her oeuvre as a gestalt, in a manner somewhat analogous to Watson's approach to Lewis, I reconstruct the sequence of her published fiction from "And the Four Animals" and *Deep Hollow Creek* (circa 1930s) through *The Double Hook* (1959) and *Four*

Stories (1979)—later expanded in *Five Stories* (1984). Each text in this reading is a part of a whole, a collection of increasingly critical portraits of expressionism. Her approach to expressionism emerges in her metasatiric picture of a Lewisian artist figure in *Deep Hollow Creek* and creator-artist figure in "And the Four Animals," evolves into her absurdist depiction of figures without art, ritual, or tradition in *The Double Hook*, and ends in her satiric portraiture of the failures of expressionism in her Oedipal story cycle. Watson's critique of expressionism in her thesis, essays, and fiction is, in this reading, an extension of Lewis's verbal assaults on dogmatic theories of expressionism in his own polemics and satires.

In "What I'm Going to Do," Watson reiterates the main points of Lewis's defence of his own mode of satire in his 1934 essay collection *Men Without Art*. When she describes the genesis of *The Double Hook* in her 1973 preamble, she says that she had intended to write "about how people are driven, how if they have no art, how if they have no tradition, how if they have no ritual, they are driven in one of two ways, either towards violence or towards insensibility—if they have no mediating rituals that manifest themselves in what I suppose we call art forms" ("What I'm Going" 183). Watson's community without "mediating rituals" contained in "art forms" is markedly similar to Lewis's world of "men without art." According to Lewis, "Art will die, perhaps. It can, however, paint us a picture of what life looks like without art. That will be, of course, a *satiric* picture. Indeed it *is* one" (*Men* 225). That Watson echoes Lewis's pronouncements on satire in *Men Without Art* is by no means unexpected. Suffice it to say that Lewis's signature statement on his own brand of satire in *Men Without Art* also concerns the relation of art to ritual:

> "Satire," as I have suggested the word should be used in this
> essay (applying to the art of the present time of any force at
> all) refers to an "'expressionist' universe" which is reeling
> a little, a little drunken with an overdose of the "ridicu-
> lous"—where everything is not only tipped but *steeped* in a

philosophic solution of the material, not of mirth, but of the intense and even painful sense of the absurd...And that is why, by stretching a point, no more, we can without exaggeration write *satire* for *art*—not the moralist satire directed at a given society, but a metaphysical satire occupied with mankind...Art in this respect is in the same class as ritual, as civilized behaviour, and all ceremonial forms and observances—a discipline, a symbolic discipline. (289, 291)

The satire that Lewis theorizes is "the type," he says, "no respectable lexicographer could ever envisage" (*Men* 48). As Fredric Jameson observes of Lewis, "Satire was not, in Lewis's mature aesthetic, one mode of discourse among others, but rather the very essence of art itself, vorticism or expressionism riding in the Trojan Horse of a generic designation, a style which is now in reality a whole world-view" (*Fables* 136). This tendency toward the universal allows Lewis to place satire in "the same class as ritual." It is a tendency that Robert C. Elliott describes in *The Power of Satire*, his study of satire as a literary mode originating in magical curses, sacrifices, and the ritual expulsion of the scapegoat; he posits that archaic satire was non-moral, and that its ritualistic and violent features are contained in the mode of literary satire that Lewis himself practiced (92). In view of these theories of satire, Lewis's hybrid of satire, art, and ritual no longer seems "the type no respectable lexicographer could ever envisage." More to the point, Watson's alignment of art and ritual takes as precedent the archaic, magical, and ritual origins of Lewis's theory of satire; for her, art forms function as mediating rituals to sublimate the drive towards either the barbarous violence or stuporous insensibility of men without art.

Watson's vision of a people without art and her correlation of art and ritual also find precursors in the early writings of her doctoral supervisor and fellow Lewis scholar, Marshall McLuhan. From her reading of *The Mechanical Bride: The Folklore of Industrial Man* when it came out in 1951 (Flahiff, *Always* 76) through her extensive correspondence with her supervisor during the writing of her thesis,

Watson witnessed and responded to the development of McLuhan's media theory in dialogue with Lewis throughout the 1950s and 1960s (Betts, *Avant-Garde Canadian* 220–25).[5] Among his publications on Lewis, McLuhan's 1944 essay "Wyndham Lewis: Lemuel in Lilliput" resonates strongly with Watson's commentary on *The Double Hook*. "Today," McLuhan writes, "the artist lives in a world which has no place for art." A society that is hostile to art, he adds, is the product of "the dehumanization of life by means of centralized methods of 'communication,' and by the lethal abstractionizing of the machine controlled by abstract greed" ("Wyndham Lewis: Lemuel" 180). McLuhan's inquiry into Lewis addresses the relationship between technology and art that Watson would further develop in her thesis and subsequent essays. Although his argument here is not principally concerned with Lewis's practice of satire, McLuhan's allusive figuration of Lewis as a Gulliver among the Lilliputians locates the society without art in a satiric context. McLuhan's 1953 essay "Wyndham Lewis: His Theory of Art and Communication" revisits Lewis's anti-art society, but in this instance one whose science-driven technology appropriates the traditional "magical" function of art. "We have," McLuhan concludes, "to consider that modern technology is itself mainly a product of art" (78). With insight gleaned from two decades of correspondence with his former student, supervision of her thesis, and her published essays on Lewis, McLuhan returns to well-travelled territory in his 1967 talk "Canada, the Borderline Case" in which he addresses, in the context of *The Double Hook*, the function of the artist in a "frontier" society without art. Anticipating Watson's 1973 commentary on her novel, McLuhan sees the people in *The Double Hook* "trying to create a sort of unity in their inner lives by forming images of social cohesion and communication," which he suggests "only the artist makes visible" (119). It is left to the artist to make a society without art visible to itself. In so describing the artist's function, then, McLuhan places Watson in a role that in his early essays he designated for Lewis.

In his correspondence with Watson, McLuhan cast himself in the role of media theorist as satirist. Writing to Watson on

August 6, 1974, McLuhan cites the distinction in *The Cankered Muse* (1959) that Alvin Kernan makes between formal and Menippean satire, positioning himself in the latter mode. Where the figure of the satirist is foregrounded in formal satire, the "scene is stressed and absorbs the satirist" in the Menippean mode. "I think this is very useful for Lewis who[se] satire [is] somewhere between these two modes," McLuhan offers. "I realize that my own work is extremely Menippean," he adds. "The satirist does not appear in person."[6] To say that McLuhan modelled his mode of satire on Lewis is also to acknowledge—in line with Gregory Betts (*Avant-Garde Canadian* 222), Glenn Willmott (*McLuhan* 40–45), and Richard Cavell (*McLuhan in Space* 9–12)—the profound influence that he exercised on McLuhan's early theorization of mass media.[7] That same model McLuhan in turn recommended to Watson for her thesis,[8] who had by that time already fashioned her own satiric mode, not in criticism but fiction. When, in reference to Lewis, McLuhan speaks of a satire between two modes—one in which the satirist's persona is prominent, the other in which the satirist disappears—he could have just as well been describing Watson's fiction, which oscillates between these modalities.

Metasatire and Ritual

When *Deep Hollow Creek* was published in 1992, its cover copy heralded the "second published novel by the acclaimed author of the beloved Canadian classic, *The Double Hook*." *Deep Hollow Creek* is, in fact, her first novel, written in the 1930s after her stint as a schoolteacher in the Cariboo region of British Columbia. Reviewing *Deep Hollow Creek* in 1993, George Bowering suggested that Watson's second published novel would be read as her secondary novel, that is, secondary to *The Double Hook*: "It is probably normal then that *Deep Hollow Creek* will be read in light cast by *The Double Hook*. Is this the ur-novel?" ("Narrative" 132). Bowering's rhetorical question restated what Shirley Neuman had already observed in 1988: that *The Double Hook* was preceded by "a quite different version of the novel written in the 1930s and titled *Deep Hollow Creek*" (iv). Reiterating the cover copy of *Deep Hollow Creek*, the generation of critics that conferred canonical status upon *The Double Hook* already read her first novel as an early version, a secondary variant of her canonized second novel. They situate *Deep Hollow Creek* as historically prior, but critically posterior, to their readings of *The Double Hook*.

Watson anticipated these critical tendencies in her own readings of *Deep Hollow Creek*. In 1976 she first made public her animosity toward it: "I wrote a novel before *The Double Hook* called *Deep Hollow Creek*...But it was wrong from the start really, I had to get rid of the narrator" ("Interview" 354). In 1984 she again isolated the problem of narration in *Deep Hollow Creek* in reference to Macmillan's rejection of the novel in the 1930s: "I realized then that there was something wrong with it and felt that somehow or other I had to get the authorial voice out of the novel" ("'It's What'" 158). As she explained in her last interview, conducted after the release of *Deep Hollow Creek* in 1992, "I had to do something to get the narrator out of it, so I killed the schoolteacher" (Barclay 13). Directed at the authorial voice, the narrator, and the schoolteacher figure in *Deep Hollow Creek*, Watson's public statements all call attention to the expulsion or symbolic death of this authorial-narratorial figure. Her autocritical readings of *Deep Hollow Creek* are carried out in the novel itself, an indication of how it may be read as a narrative about the expulsion or symbolic death of this figure.

These iterations of symbolic aggression haunt *Deep Hollow Creek* and mark the novel's metahistory with traces of satire that mediate its reception. Even in "What I'm Going to Do," which was occasioned by a reading from *The Double Hook*, Watson's backward glance in it—to the year 1934 and to her experience as a schoolteacher in the Cariboo (183–84)—invokes *Deep Hollow Creek*. This statement is not a reading of Watson's early novel; rather, it puts into question the possibility of writing that first novel at all: "I wanted to do something about the West, which wasn't a Western; and about Indians which wasn't about...

Indians...I wanted to take this place where I'd been put down as a stranger...I never had any intention of writing about it" (182). These repeated negations are indicative of Watson's persistent self-cancellation of that first narrativization of her Cariboo experience. That she rendered her experience in the self-reflexive mode of metasatire speaks to the ways in which both the novelistic and extra-novelistic discourses of *Deep Hollow Creek* are informed by a self-referential and autocritical practice.

Revisiting material first encountered in her master's thesis on Addison and Steele, Watson's 1967 essay "Swift and Ovid: The Development of Metasatire" provides a genealogy of satire that leads from Ovid through Addison and Swift to Lewis. For Watson, metasatire is a mode that involves the appropriation of satiric techniques from earlier satirists; its self-reflexivity is that of the "satirist satirized" (Elliott 237). Jameson considers the emergence of metasatire an inevitable result of the satirist, namely Lewis, turning away from moralist satire directed at a given society and turning toward satire itself, so that "the satirist becomes self-conscious about his own activity" (*Fables* 138). In her study of metasatire, Watson at once traces its practice through specific intertextual exchanges among satirists and identifies its incorporation of the "satirist satirized": "Swift, using Ovid as he does, becomes inevitably a satirist of the satirist. This sort of satire we can call metasatire and point to Swift's fullest realization of the mode in *Gulliver's Travels*. Ovidian transformation for satiric purposes is itself satirically transformed in the person of Gulliver" ("Swift and Ovid" 147). "Gulliver," as Watson says in her essay "Unaccommodated Man," is "the satirist malgré lui" (109). Watson arrives at her own practice of metasatire in *Deep Hollow Creek* by way of Swift and Lewis: from Swift she draws an Ovidian technique of metamorphosis, from Lewis a vorticist technique, which she calls "a way in which the whole of experience is dissolved in a vortex—a kind of metamorphosis" ("Interview" 357). In *Deep Hollow Creek*, "Ovidian transformation for satiric purposes is itself satirically transformed," not in the person of Gulliver, but in another of Swift's satiric figures, Stella.

Like Lewis and Swift, Watson is—in her own terms—a "satirist of the satirist" in *Deep Hollow Creek*; her central figure Stella is herself a vorticist-satirist and, in spite of herself, a satirist satirized. Thus following Lewis, Watson adopted his satirist mentor, Swift. Once questioned in interview about her early interest in Swift, Watson replied, "I reread Swift. I also had an interest in Wyndham Lewis. I was attracted to both of them because I am interested in satire" ("'It's What'" 163).[9] That Watson has selected the name Stella for the central figure of *Deep Hollow Creek* is by no means arbitrary, for it deliberately invokes Swiftian satire. Between September 1710 and June 1711, Swift composed a series of letters later collected as his *Journal to Stella*. The misnomer "journal" actually describes his letters to two women, Esther Johnson ("Stella") and her companion, Rebecca Dingley. Watson recasts their living arrangements through the figures of Stella, a schoolteacher, and Miriam Fairclough, a friend of Stella's who comes from the west coast to live with her in the fictional Cariboo community, Deep Hollow Creek.[10] The fact that Stella is the only character in the novel without a surname reinforces the link between Swift's and Watson's Stellas, and casts her as a conspicuously literary and metasatiric character. Allusions to Swiftian satire throughout the novel further develop Stella's metasatiric type.

Stella experiences life from the position of the satirist, the social and artistic outsider, and thereby distances herself from the things, animals, and people around her by virtue of her aesthetic detachment. She assimilates the vorticist's tendency toward "satiric detachment," to observe and analyze the chaos of fragments from a position at "the still centre of the vortex" (Dasenbrock 178, 54). From her detached point of view, she ceases to regard people as real, living beings and thinks of them instead as subjective patterns to be woven and stitched together according to her fancy. In Stella's interior monologues, Watson's style incorporates the Lewisian "way in which the whole of experience is dissolved in a vortex": the curious workings of Stella's fancy set in motion a vortex of story fragments, images, and allusions. That metamorphic style, according to Watson's study of the mode, is typical of metasatire.

Appropriate to her detachment, Stella adheres to Lewis's edict of an "externalist art in Satire" (*Men* 121) that Watson details in her thesis: "When Lewis explained his own technical approach to the problem of the image in satire in *Men Without Art*, he called attention to his preoccupation with the 'shells and pelts,' the 'cases and envelopes' which protect and extend within their bounding lines the human necessities which they clothe. The external approach, he held, could make an attractive companion of the grotesque" (*Wyndham* 252).[11] From the opening lines of *Deep Hollow Creek*, Stella contemplates the lifeless, hollow "shells and pelts" of people: "[Rose's] eyes, Stella thought, were the colour of Spanish mahogany, but they lacked the lustre of organic fibre. The soul had gone out of the wood, had dissipated" (7). It is the deadness of Rose's eyes upon which Stella fixates, deadness finely rendered as art. In her articulation of an "external approach" to the image in satire, Stella transforms people's bodies into the deadness of art. In the satiric words of Lewis's vorticist figure Tarr, "*deadness* is the first condition of art" (*Tarr* 277).

During an early interior monologue, Stella reflects upon her role as a satirist, meditating upon images of "broken fragments" and "pieces" of stories that she collects from the community and satirically transforms into art. What she contemplates is the deadness of people in the community, or to use Watson's word, their insensibility. They are, in Stella's opinion, people "who live by the body" (118); she believes they exist without the civilized "art forms" of those, like herself, who live by the mind. As a satirist concerned with deadness, she plays ironically with the idea of taking on the guise of Gulliver, who, upon leaving the land of the Houyhnhnms, flays the Yahoos in order to build himself a skin boat.[12] "Shall I set sail in a boat of yahoo skins or sit weaving a bracelet of bright hair[?]" (37) Stella asks herself, piecing together the Swift's yahoo skins and Donne's *memento mori*.[13] Living in a horse ranching community, Stella thinks herself a Gulliver living among Yahoos and Houyhnhnms; like him, she fancies herself a satirist. But after she satirizes the community, she queries, "why...must Swift conspire with Donne to mock my pen as it writes" (37)? As a self-conscious satirist, she senses the possibility of becoming a satirist satirized; she is aware that the failure of her own satire would make her vulnerable to satiric attack, that another satirist could satirize her.

Once she admits by the mid-point of the novel that her "mind has failed" (76), and that her satiric art has failed, Stella attempts to become one of those "who live by the body"; no longer a detached satirist, she unwittingly joins the satirized. She embraces what she perceives to be the only ritual of those "who live by the body," what she calls "the ritual of the horse." Stella herself purchases two horses under the influence of Bill Mockett's talk at his stopping house about Tom Paine (57): "At the moment a horse which she could ride when she chose stood for all the things implicit in Mockett's murmurings about freedom, equality, and the pursuit of happiness" (65). However, Stella is not liberated but indirectly mocked by "Mockett's talk." She, who once cursed Swift for mocking her pen as she writes, now attaches the epithet "Swift's buyer" (124) to the merchant and stable-operator Mockett for laughing at her as she rides her horse. She also uses the epithet "Mockett, the coyote" (129), so naming him as an avatar of the trickster figure—the "archetypal satirist" (Test 44) of indigenous tradition, the Shuswap trickster figure Coyote. In *Deep Hollow Creek*, Mockett serves as the human agent of the archetypal satirist Coyote. As she tries to mount her horse bareback in front of the stopping house, in the presence of Mockett and other members of the community, Stella revokes her belief in his liberalist talk of "freedom, equality, and the pursuit of happiness." As she tries, and fails, to mount her horse, Stella becomes an object of satire and exposes herself to public ridicule: "Even in the minute itself she contemplated the ridiculous tableau—the centaur inverted—Icarus under instead of above the earth" (119). Stella's reference to herself as a centaur (half-human, half-horse) and Icarus (half-human, half-bird) imagines the kind of metamorphosis typical of Ovidian and Swiftian satire. Her satiric transformation occurs in the larger vortex of Deep Hollow Creek itself, the topographical "centre" of which is occupied by the satirist-figure Mockett and his stopping house (19).[14] At that moment, she is no longer in a position of detachment as a satirist of those "who live by the body." Rather, she is a "ridiculous tableau," a satiric, grotesque figure; she is caught up in that modernist condition Lewis says "is reeling a little, a little drunken with an overdose of the 'ridiculous'—where everything is not only tipped but *steeped* in a philosophic solution of the material, not of mirth, but of the intense and even painful sense of the absurd." Stella's body, like the bodies of those around her, becomes part of the pattern of satiric art in *Deep Hollow Creek*: she is satirically transformed by Mockett's talk, figuratively rendered in terms of the deadness of art—that is, as "Icarus *under*...the earth." Mockett becomes the satirist of the satirist; Stella the satirist satirized.

Following her symbolic death, Stella experiences a scene of resurrection. It is staged by Coyote, whose "undulating voice" issues from the hills, crying, "Throw off the bands of custom, break down the barriers. Nature stirs deep within you. I am the primitive urge, out of the blastoderm endlessly rocking" (124). Coyote's thinly veiled allusion to Whitman's "Out of the Cradle Endlessly Rocking" mocks Stella, for it refers to the song of a mockingbird and, accordingly, mimics her allusive manner. In this same scene, Coyote plays upon her liberalist desires, incanting Latin and vernacular phrases in a ritualized voice and style, culminating in the ritual expression of the rebirth of "man" in *Deep Hollow Creek*. What Stella witnesses is Coyote's satiric ritual, a trickster's trick. Coyote's performance is a ruse, mimicry of her art and ritual; it exposes the artifice of her manner, her deadness rather than her rebirth. It is the moment at which the archetypal satirist, Coyote, ridicules the failed satirist, Stella—again representing her as a satirist satirized.

Readers of this scene are not privy to Stella's immediate reaction to Coyote's satiric ritual. Not until the closing scenes of the novel do we see her regress to that condition of insensibility of which Watson speaks in "What I'm Going to Do," that condition of one without art, without tradition, without ritual. Coyote's performance is integral to the narrative of Stella's departure from Deep Hollow Creek; it serves an archaic function of ritual satire—that is, the expulsion of the scapegoat from the community. For the scapegoat, that expulsion is a symbolic death. For Stella, it is a regression into a condition of insensibility, a kind of deadness, immediately followed by her exile from the community. Stella sinks into a madness akin to that of Gulliver before he leaves the Houyhnhnms. Like the misanthropic Gulliver conversing with his horses, Stella utters her last words in the novel to her dog Juno: "I don't know, she said to Juno, I really don't know who is mad. It is time for us to get out of here" (141).

Toward the close of "What I'm Going to Do," Watson says of *The Double Hook*, "I don't know now, if I rewrote it, whether I would use the Coyote figure." It seems that her ambivalence about Stella had been displaced by her ambivalence about Coyote. It is as difficult to imagine *The Double Hook* without Coyote as it is *Deep Hollow Creek* without Stella. Watson's signature statement in "What I'm Going to Do" makes the difficulty plain: "I would say that what I was concerned with was figures in a ground, from which they could not be separated" (183). Stella, however, is a figure already separated from that ground—a figure whose ground of art, tradition, and ritual is alien to the community. In a radically truncated version of *Deep Hollow Creek*, published in 1938 as a short story entitled "Rough Answer," an unnamed "girl"—who, like Stella and Watson herself, comes to teach in a ranching community—leaves because "She wasn't ready to meet herself yet" (180). The girl's rationalization for leaving speaks to Watson's decision to suppress "Rough Answer" from her later short-story collections and, quite possibly, her reason for withholding *Deep Hollow Creek* until 1992. In suppressing this abbreviated urtext, Watson first sacrificed her authorial voice, her narratorial figure, her schoolteacher self, and thereby initiated the narrative that she would rewrite in *Deep Hollow Creek*.

Ritual Words

The Double Hook opens with "the characteristic gesture of Expressionist art," as Watson says, "the clenched fist" (*Wyndham* 321n571; see Grace 194). James Potter is caught in the act of murdering his mother, "his hand half-raised" (13). The raised hand or clenched fist is typical of expressionist art in that it represents

what the German expressionists called *Aufbruch*, an awakening
from a repressed condition and a violent breaking free from the
past (Grace 195). The gesture also grasps the problematic of primitivism and modernity in expressionist art: the "hand half-raised"
is a ritualized gesture by which the young modern, the New Man,
sacrifices an older generation. It points further to the primitive and
violent tendencies of an expressionist aesthetic and way of life that
Watson, following Lewis, subjects to forceful critique. James carries
out a series of actions that call into question the subjective and
aggressive drive of the expressionist *Aufbruch*. In verbally attacking
and symbolically sacrificing his mother as a scapegoat, he performs a
ritualized act in self-interest and not in the interests of the community. "This is my day," he says (13). Neither his actions nor his words
perform the traditional communal function of ritual; by committing
matricide, he performs a false ritual, a violent parody severed from
the ground of tradition.[15] James's descent into violence is indicative
of a man without tradition, without mediating rituals, without art.

Altogether devoid of communal values, James moves toward
extreme aggression, committing matricide, impregnating and
abandoning Lenchen, blinding Kip with a bullwhip, and then finally
breaking away from the community entirely. The depth of James's
fall is most poignantly dramatized by the fallenness of his language
during his period of exile in town. This fallen condition is articulated
through his exchanges and transactions, his engagement with the
reified world of commodities. For a brief while James acts the part
of "a man filthy rich, leastwise by some men's reckoning" (89) after
he withdraws all of his savings from the bank. When he leaves the
valley for town he abandons one set of values and rituals, only to
encounter a whole new set of values and rituals in town. These are
the rituals of business. Around town he goes about his business—at
the bank, at the store, at the bar, at the prostitute Felicia's house—
but in every case the rituals of business, of monetary exchange,
fail to establish for James an authentic sense of community.

At the centre of one of these rituals is the parrot. Parodying the
humans, the parrot underscores the mindless absurdity of their

rote repetition of clichés. There is no distinctive human feature to the language of cliché that is not imitated by the parrot. When the parrot says, "Drinks all round" (92), it initiates the social ritual of men drinking in a bar. It is, however, a reified language appropriate to the routinized rituals of strangers gathered in a bar as an ersatz community. At his nadir of abjection, James's hollow rationalization of his mother's death ("She was old" [92]) to the parrot is indicative of his utter alienation. No expenditure of cash, no round of beer, is going to bring about his redemption, especially not among a community of strangers in town whose only real interest in him is for his business. Absurdly and darkly comic, he speaks to, pours beer into the tin cup of, and later leaves money to buy beer for a parrot whose only response is to repeat "Drinks all round" (94).

After he is through with the rituals of business, after the prostitute Lily lifts his wallet in the hotel room, he abandons his dealings in cash to discover a new means of social and economic relations. In this way, James's redemption comes about after his complete expenditure and loss of cash. He is forced to go into debt, and thus secure new communal relations: "Write it down, he said. I'll pay when I'm next in town. There are times when a man spends more than he has and must go one credit…Unless a man defaults, he said, a debt is a sort of bond" (121). The rearticulation of social relations necessitated by the exchange of commodities is the first sign of James's reintegration into society. The commodity forces James into a recognition of the sociality of his existence. Having reached a point of complete psychic and economic expenditure, he is ready to return to the community in search of redemption.

Just as James performs a parodic ritual act through which he vents his violent aggression, so too Felix Prosper parodies verbal and gestural rituals as he descends into a regressive state of insensibility. The inverse relationship between James and Felix is represented through mirrored images of their ritualized hand gestures. The image of James's "hand half-raised" against his mother is later repeated in Felix's gesture toward Lenchen (who comes to him pregnant with James's child) in the opening scene of the second part of the novel:

I've got no words to clear a woman off my bench. No words
except: Keep moving, scatter, get-the-hell-out.

His mind sifted ritual phrases. Some half-forgotten.
You're welcome. Put your horse in. Pull up. *Ave Maria.*
Benedictus fructus ventris. Introibo.

Introibo. The beginning. The whole thing to live
again. Words said over and over here by the stove. His
father knowing them by heart. God's servants. The priest's
servants. The cup lifting. The bread breaking. *Domine no*
sum dignus. Words coming. The last words.

He rolled from his chair. Stood barefoot. His hands raised.
Pax vobiscum, he said...
Go in peace, he said. (38)

Like James's actions and words, Felix's ritual phrases and gesture
of benediction are not only detached from any tradition of spiritual
meaning or communal function but they are also performatives
of the breakdown of social rituals and speech in their fragmented
form. In juxtaposition to clichéd forms of quotidian speech and
habitual acts, these archetypal forms of benediction function instead
as verbal and gestural clichés. Writing of an analogous condition
of language in Lewis's satire, Jameson posits the fall of archetype
into cliché: "the truth is that what we have called gestural archetypes are in reality nothing but clichés also; only they are clichés
before the fall" (*Fables* 80). Jameson does not specify what the
fall is, but implies a descent from mythic and ritualized discourse
into the commonplace languages of modernity. Contrary to the
verbal or gestural archetype that returns in the process of eternal
repetition of some original mythic event or image, the cliché is a
reified form of expression that has expended its original, creative,
and often redemptive power in the process of repetition.

Building on Barbara Godard's analysis of *The Double Hook*
as "an inventory of ritual ways of expression detached from their
original emotional and spiritual meaning" and "hardened into
cliché in the modern world" (153), Margaret Turner argues that

"the clichés that saved both face and time when common meanings were understood now damn: they obstruct human communication and drive people further into themselves and silence" (74). So the original redemptive function of the priest's address to the congregation, "*Pax vobiscum*" or "Go in peace," now only serves Felix as a cliché with which to damn Lenchen. In effect, he delivers a message of social and spiritual damnation to which her curse, "What the *hell*" (38), is a parodically *apropos* response. As forms of verbal aggression, their mutual exchange of clichés actually resembles an agon, originally a mode of ritual satire; and since the agon is rooted in ritual practice, their clichés retain the performativity of ritualized curses. Because Watson presents the cliché as reified language, the performative power of Felix's and Lenchen's clichés brings about the complete inversion of the meanings and functions of ritual expression. As expressive forms of modernity's fallen discourse, Watson's clichés work as probes into reified forms of ritual expression that no longer obtain.

According to Marshall McLuhan and Wilfred Watson in *From Cliché to Archetype*, the fall of language from archetype to cliché is a kind of *felix culpa*, in so far as the cliché foregrounds the need for redemption of expended expressions in art. In their words, "Make it new is a mere necessity of art today" (59). In *The Double Hook* this need for redemption obtains in the "urge to abstraction" manifest in the novel; this compulsion to abstraction is a signature of both Worringer's aesthetics (which were foundational for both expressionism and vorticism) and Lewis's vorticist manifestos. In Worringer's view, the artist's will to abstraction is one and the same with the redemption of the object from the outer world. By abstracting objects from what Worringer calls "the entangled inter-relationship and flux of phenomena of the outer world," the artist seizes upon "the possibility of taking the individual thing out of its arbitrariness and seeming fortuituousness, of eternalizing by approximation to abstract forms and, in this manner, of finding a point of tranquility and a refuge from appearances" (16). This key statement of Worringer's expressionist aesthetics holds true not only for Lewis's vorticist artist but also for Watson's artist figure, the fiddler Felix.

Consider Felix holding his coffee cup at the still centre of a vortex, with memories of rain and his wife whorling around his cabin:

> The cup which Angel had put into his hand, her bitter going, he'd left untouched. Left standing. A something set down. No constraint to make him drink. No struggle against the drinking. No let-it-pass. No it-is-done. Simply redeemed. Claiming before death a share of his inheritance.
>
> The cup he reached for was not the ironware lined with the etch of tea and coffee. It was the knobbed glass moulded to the size of his content. Pleasure in the light of it. The knowing how much to drink. The rough knobbed heat of it...
>
> The remembrance of event and slash of rain merged. Time annihilated in the concurrence. The present contracted into the sweet hot cup he fondled. (25)

Felix has two cups: one a reified object, another an abstracted object. The first is associated with ritual phrases, clichés, indicative of the gestures of an arbitrary, unnecessary routine of daily life. It is not a mimetic object, not an unmediated representation of an ironware cup, but a defamiliarized one. Its significations and functions are inversions of customary ones; rather than a communal exchange between husband and wife, the cup Angel gives to Felix signifies a lack of communication. Its function as a mediating ritual object is apparent in the phrase "simply redeemed": it is an object he takes from her hand, recovers it and along with it memories of Angel, but it is also an object he automatically associates with the ritual of the communion cup. Angel, at the moment she abandons him, dispossesses him of grace, leaves him with an inheritance of sin. Felix's second cup, the knobbed glass, is an abstracted object: it affords its viewer what Worringer calls the "tranquilizing consciousness" (41) of its pleasure and enjoyment. It is a redeemed object, a point of tranquility, a still point at the centre of the vortex, abstracted from the flux of phenomena and time. With "time annihilated," Felix holds the "present contracted into the sweet hot cup" (25).

If, with Lukács, I were to stage a critique of Felix's embodiment of an expressionist-vorticist aesthetic, I need look no further than William's response to Heinrich's statement that "Felix sits there like the round world all centred in on himself" (129). Felix's physical, emotional, and spiritual detachment from the community simulates an experience of aesthetic detachment or, in Worringer's words, "the need for self-alienation" in all aesthetic experience, "an urge to seek deliverance...in the contemplation of something necessary" (24). Meditation on his coffee cup is at once a spiritual act of self-redemption made possible by taking himself into a state of "tranquilizing consciousness" through an aesthetic act of redeeming the object of his contemplation by abstracting it, rendering it as the still point of the vortex. William, however, thoroughly debunks Felix's spiritual and aesthetic posture: "He drinks coffee like the rest of us, William said. Though, he said, I'd be hard pressed to know how he comes by the money to pay for it. If you think of it, he said, this case of Felix is a standing lesson for someone to think twice. A man who drinks coffee is dependent on something outside of himself" (129). Although Watson by no means endorses Lukács's claim that only realism as an aesthetic practice transcends reification, penetrates appearances to the real relations among people and objects as social phenomena, there is little doubt that William's critique of Felix proceeds from an analysis of coffee as commodity determined by its exchange value to an understanding that it is a sign of social exchange between and interdependence among people. In Lukács's view expressionism's failure lies in its inability to dereify social phenomena through abstraction: it is not "a penetration of the social roots of phenomena, but rather an abstracting from them" (Lukács 107). Abstraction engages in "the destruction of all connections" (102), the matrix of which is precisely what makes up the material and social relations among people and objects. William, too, articulates the need for connections between Felix and the world beyond the circumference of his coffee cup. Detached from communal relations, Felix regresses into a condition of insensibility. By showing how Felix actually exists in relation to the community, William points to the authentic means of Felix's redemption (which is brought about by the convergence of the community in his cabin to deliver baby Felix, and which is at least nominally a sign of his namesake's redemption). If Felix's fall into insensibility is predicated on the failure of expressionism as a means of self-redemption, it does so with an echo of the fortunate fall from archetype to cliché and the need for the redemption of an expended mode of artistic expression.

Once James returns to the cabin and lifts up baby Felix "in his two hands" (134), with a final gesture markedly reminiscent of his "hand half-raised" toward his mother and Felix's "hands raised" toward Lenchen, we bear momentary witness to the redemption of not just individual members of the community but "the rebirth of *communitas*" in the valley (Grace 195). Given that both James and Felix embody different but related failures of expressionism, one its descent into violence and the other its decline into insensibility, their emergence from extreme states of self-interestedness or, as Lukács puts it, "subjectivism that borders on solipsism" (109) facilitates not just individual but communal redemption. It would be mistaken, however, to allow their redemption to overshadow the novel's final lines, where Coyote separates baby Felix from the community and thus positions him as a figure alienated from the ground of tradition and ritual: "I have set his feet on soft ground; / I have set his feet on the sloping shoulders of the world" (134). A figure detached from his ground, baby Felix stands as the archetype of a fallen world, an emblem of alienation and unredeemed modernity. This is the final trick of Watson's archetypal satirist, the Shuswap trickster-god Coyote,[16] who by abstracting baby Felix from the community positions him atop the earth in the what appears to be the ascendant pose of an expressionist New Man, but in doing so sets his feet astride the symbolically fallen ("sloping") shoulders of the world. Coyote's last trick is a sign of the community's return to fallenness, a portent embodied by the figural abstraction of baby Felix as an archetype, as Jameson puts it, *"before the fall"* (*Fables* 80).

Mythic Cycles

Analogous to her compendium of reified ritual forms of expression in *The Double Hook*, Watson's *Four Stories* is an inventory of myths, archetypes, and rituals translated into the language of modernity. "Brother Oedipus," "The Black Farm," "Antigone," and "The Rumble Seat" collectively inscribe what Watson calls a "mythic cycle" ("Myth" 125)—that is, a story cycle analogous to the Sophoclean myth of Oedipus recorded in his Theban cycle, *Oedipus Rex, Oedipus at Colonus,* and *Antigone.* Watson's Oedipal cycle is inhabited by characters bearing the names of figures from classical Greek myth, but cast in the roles of the modern bourgeois and enacting what Roland Barthes names an "artificial myth" or, alternately, a "bourgeois myth" (*Mythologies* 147). In this context, myth functions as a gestalt: in Greek myth, mythical figures exist in relation to the ground of tradition, religion, ritual, and mythology; in "bourgeois myth," Watson's mythical bourgeois are figures alienated from that ground. As such, her Oedipal cycle reconstitutes the figures of Greek myth in a satiric and expressionist exploration of the familial, psychiatric, and religious institutions of Western bourgeois society in the mid-twentieth century.

While her short stories bear the unmistakeable markings of "expressionist anti-middle classness" (Lukács 87), the true objects of Watson's satire (both in her Oedipal cycle and in "And the Four Animals") are most often the expressionist New Man, the expressionist artist figure, and the Spenglerian ape of the "expressionist *Zeitgeist,*" the "crowd-master" (Watson, *Wyndham* 40; "Artist-Ape" 115). Not so distant from their historical German expressionist predecessors, who saw themselves "mired in the *petit bourgeois* life of middle-class acquisitiveness and repressive social structures" and who were "so often the disaffected sons of the despised *bürgerliche* fathers who still supported them" (Grace 18, 19), the expressionist figures in Watson's Oedipal cycle are members of a "mythic middle class" (Watson, "Myth" 122). Just as the expressionist pattern of *Aufbruch* and violent action in *The Double Hook* cannot bring about the redemption of the community from the alienated and fragmented

conditions of modernity, the figures in her Oedipal cycle always fail
in their attempts to break free from "middle-classness" and repressive social institutions. In writing her "bourgeois myth" as a satire
of expressionist figures, Watson rehearses the role that she later
assigns to Lewis, "the mythographer of the age" (*Wyndham* xix).

Watson's earliest story in the Oedipal cycle, "Brother Oedipus,"
immediately signifies as an "artificial myth" insofar as its title
breaks with the referent of classical myth: Oedipus neither *has*
a brother nor is he a brother in either the classical or Freudian
myths (though he is the half-brother of his own children). Brother
Oedipus is a figure detached from the ground of Greek myth:
his identity is artificially constructed within the institution of
the middle-class family. In satirizing the middle class, Watson
presents the unnamed narrator and his brother Oedipus as expressionist middle-class rebels who were inspired in their youth by
Thorstein Veblen's critique of the "leisure class": "Puss [Oedipus]
and I had read Veblen together. We had hidden the book under
the mattress and read it in the toilet behind locked doors...We
foreswore our heritage, played commuters, hobnobbed with the
gardener and the cook, and damned the family dog as one of
the symbols of our class" (12). Neither Oedipus nor the narrator
seem to learn anything from Veblen, for they spend their lives
offering psychoanalytic critiques of the symbols of their class;
their clichéd Freudian and Jungian psychobabble is patently
absurd and merely serves to underscore Watson's satirization of
these middle-class rebels. Even as they wander between house
and garden in middle-class suburbia, these disaffected sons of the
bourgeois dramatize the repressive institution of the middle-class
family; they mimic the expressionists' break with their heritage
and criticism of bourgeois institutions, symbols, and values; they
embody the self-contradiction of the anti-bourgeois bourgeois.

The story centres around a willow tree rooted in the mother's
drain system. After much debate back and forth between Oedipus,
his mother, and his wife over taxes, loss of privacy and property
value, and hiring a tree surgeon, the inebriated Oedipus takes it

upon himself to chop down the willow tree with an axe. Oedipus's violent action is akin to the expressionist *Aufbruch*, since he acts out against what he perceives to be the repressive authority of his mother and wife. As he wields the axe Oedipus shouts, "The world... is a vast amphitheatre. We are all actors in a rite. My sensible brother here is a mere spectator" (20). But his ritual action and moment of violent liberation is, in a manner of speaking, cut short: "Oedipus chipped away at the bark. Then he laid down the axe and rooted for the bottle" (20). Like James, also given to *Aufbruch*, Oedipus is ultimately an individual without ritual: he swings between extremes of violence and drunken stupor of insensibility.

Watson's second story in the collection, "The Black Farm," introduces an extended Oedipal family. Uncle Daedalus and his sister Europa join Oedipus and his clan. Daedalus and Europa are not entirely foreign to the Theban cycle of Greek myths: Europa is the brother of Cadmus, the founder of Thebes, and, after she is taken to Crete by Zeus, who is disguised as a bull, she becomes the mother of Minos by Zeus; Daedalus is the craftsman and inventor for the House of Minos. Of course, the identities and genealogies of Greek myth break down in Watson's fiction. Europa is the old maid—domestic and pastoral, living in Edenic hills; Daedalus is the modern bourgeois—inventor, entrepreneur, and land developer, buying up the hills around her. They are, in short, Lewisian abstractions, "walking clichés" (Lewis, *Time* 93). They are, however, delineated not as satiric types but as expressionist projections of "soul-states"; these "figures in a ground," to borrow from Grace, "like the characters in so many expressionist plays, are types, are embodiments of larger forces" (197). If this is satire, then it is one of Watson's blackest satires. Narrated by Oedipus's unnamed brother, the narrative shifts between his meditations on the death of Daedalus and his record of the events leading up to the typically expressionist apocalyptic ending of the story. Daedalus, as an artist figure, embodies the "human implications of an expressionist way of life" (Watson, *Wyndham* 27).

The Black Farm is Daedalus's monumental art work, literally a life work. After a visit to Europa and Daedalus, Oedipus describes his uncle's project: "He talks wildly about building some sort of show-place on his property, some monument for posterity—something unusual and striking—the house black, all the fittings black, black flowers in the garden, black hens on the roost, herds of black cattle, black dogs on the lawn, and, in contrast, everything reserved for the master gold so that he may shine like a wrought monogram on a rich velvet ground" (35). What begins as the developer's desire to build a show home on his consolidated holdings of land in the hills surrounding Europa's house soon turns into an artist's obsession with "blackness in all its manifestations" (36). Daedalus undergoes a process of regression from his life as a modern bourgeois, becoming increasingly primitive (though his exploitation of primitivism is but a manifestation of what Veblen calls the "predatory variant" or "conservation of the barbarian temperament" [162] in the modern bourgeois). The man who once marketed "barbaric masks and patterned prayer rugs" (32) now "imported servants from Haiti and the heart of dark Africa" to serve and tutor him in "black magic" (37). In a virtual citation of Worringer's description of primitive man's desire to abstract objects from nature as evidence of his "instinct for the thing-in-itself" (18), Daedalus's urgent search for an absolute blackness leads him to say, "Colour...can't be rubbed on. It's the thing itself" (36). His desire for "a natural uniformity" (37) and "eternal verities" (34) again echoes Worringer's call for the regularity and absolutes produced by the urge to abstraction. Daedalus is driven to abstract blackness, "to purify it of all its dependence on life" (Worringer 17), even to renounce the values of life itself.

In the end, Daedalus comes to believe that he is chosen to worship "Ghede," "the eternal figure in black" (38): "[Ghede] is, said Oedipus, death at the crossroads. He stands at the inter-section of time and eternity. He is corpse and phallus, king and clown. He introduces men to their own devil. He is the last day of the week and the cross in every cemetery. He sings the song of the gravedigger" (39). Like Coyote, Ghede is a trickster figure: he is both creator and destroyer of life (Test 41).[17] Not unlike Conrad's Kurtz, Watson's Daedalus goes mad following Ghede into the heart of darkest Canada. In his final letter to Oedipus,

Daedalus writes of Ghede's deadly trick in white ink on black photo album paper: *"The god of the abyss has spoken. All black is white. There are no eternal verities"* (46). And, like Greta in *The Double Hook*, in his final apocalyptic act, Daedalus immolates himself and his Black Farm, so blackening himself and his monument to expressionism. Daedalus ends his life without ritual, without art: shifting from one extreme of primitive regression to aggression, his last act of violence is left unredeemed.

After her exploration of an extreme form of expressionism in "The Black Farm," Watson recontains the explosive energies of her art in the institutional environment of "Antigone." Where "Brother Oedipus" recasts the generation of Oedipus himself and "The Black Farm" his invented ancestors, "Antigone" turns to his children now living in his twentieth-century legacy, the psychiatric institution. "Antigone" begins on the grounds of an institution surrounded by gardens where Watson's father was superintendent of the Provincial Hospital for the Insane in New Westminster, British Columbia. The cover of *Four Stories* actually bears an image of the hospital, which, as Watson says, is a coloured "bronze tint of the mental hospital taken about the time I was born, with the gardener I remember raking the garden" ("'It's What'" 165). The realism of the cover, however, undergoes significant distortion and abstraction in the story itself: the landscape and architecture are symbolic, the characters and narrative mythic. Yet the story is carefully balanced, to use Worringer's terms, between Haemon's tendency to abstraction in his narration and the realism reserved for Antigone's dialogue and actions.

In the Sophoclean version of the Antigone myth, Haemon is betrothed to Antigone, the daughter of Oedipus, who is condemned by Creon, the father of Haemon and ruler of Thebes, to be buried alive as punishment for giving her brother, Polynices, a forbidden burial (by throwing three handfuls of dust over his corpse). In Watson's version, Creon's kingdom is the psychiatric institution; together, Haemon and Antigone perform the ritual burial of a sparrow in the institution lawn (54). The seemingly insignificant "six

inches" (54) of ground broken for the burial of the sparrow mark
the site of a fissure in the order of the psychiatric institution—
that is, the institution symbolizing "the massive structures of
bourgeois society and its values" (Foucault 274). Antigone is
fascinated with such breakages in institutional and architectural
structures: she tells Haemon the story of a man who escaped
from the penitentiary on the right bank, "who scorned any kind of
bridge" (48), and who crossed the river ice to live "forever on the
far side of the river in the Alaska tea and bulrushes" (46). From
the far side of the river, "the wilderness" (45), Antigone carries the
dead bird over the bridge and inters it in "The habitable world…
on the right bank of the river" (46). Antigone thus introduces
the disorder of the wilderness into the ordered world of the right
bank—the site of the suburbs, the convent, the churches, the
penitentiary, and the asylum (47). She devises an artificial ritual,
and selects for her rite a sparrow of special providence, so named
in the Book of Matthew, "for not one of them will fall to the ground
without your Father's will" (10.29). Yet Antigone's sparrow falls
in the wilderness, beyond the will and order of the father, Creon.

The burial at the close of the story is performed as a ritual, a
parody of Christian burial, and the various attendants view the
rites in different ways. Kallisto, one of the inmates, brings "Pink
fish sandwiches," as she says, "For the party" (50). Haemon, who
plays the role of the chorus, opens the ceremony with a garbled
quotation (which Antigone corrects) from Revelations: "Between
four trumpeting angels at the four corners of the earth a bride
stands before the altar in a gown as white as snow" (50). Antigone
insists to both Kallisto and Haemon that it is neither a party, nor
a wedding, "It's a funeral" (50, 51). Then Antigone repeats, three
different times, "It's *my* funeral" (50, 52, emphasis added). In their
choric roles, both Kallisto and Haemon interject "ritual words"
(52) from the burial service in the Book of Common Prayer and
from Revelations (52, 53). Antigone admonishes and then ignores
them; they utter (and repeatedly misquote) ritual phrases that hold
no meaning for her. Haemon and Kallisto speak a language tied to

the institution of the church, and Antigone will have no truck with institutional rituals as such. There is a communication breakdown between Haemon's and Kallisto's ritual forms of expression and Antigone's actual performance of the funerary rite, that is, a fissure signalled by the rapid paragraph breaks between dialogue and narration. "Antigone does not seem to hear me," Haemon says (53). He and Kallisto repeat reified ritual expressions amputated from their traditional meanings. Antigone resists conventional forms of expression; she invents a new form of expression, an artificial ritual that incorporates the Christian burial into *her* funeral, though not as a sign of her death, but as an affirmation of her life.

While the figure of Antigone and her defiant ritual has garnered much critical attention,[18] the figure of Haemon has remained an enigma. As the narrator of the story, he is commonly identified as a chorus figure; but his role is greater than the sum of his narrations. Haemon, in the enactment of the ritual, is the embodiment of the expressionist New Man, the "voice of a people" (52). Speaking in the apocalyptic voice of St. John, Haemon dons the mask of the New Man: he is the only figure who, after the grave is sealed, hears "the sparrow twittering in the box" (53)—that is, the surrogate victim, the symbolic substitution for Antigone, buried and resurrected at the hour of judgement. Haemon believes that, through his part in the ritual, he bears witness to the rebirth and transfiguration of his father's kingdom. But Haemon's *Aufbruch*, his awakening from the repressed conditions of his father's institution, is not followed by a typically violent and liberating break from the past. Rather, Haemon incants a litany of fears: "If I could see with Kallisto's eyes I wouldn't be afraid of death, or punishment, or the penitentiary guards. I wouldn't be afraid of my father's belt or his honing strap or his bedroom slipper. I wouldn't be afraid of falling into the river through a knot-hole in the bridge" (53). It is Kallisto's, Haemon's choric double, not Antigone's eyes through which he would see his father's world anew. Antigone "defies what she sees with a defiance which is almost denial" (48). Haemon, like Kallisto, does not deny his father's power to discipline and punish. Where Antigone confronts his father, Haemon regresses into a condition of fear and silence before him. So the expressionist New Man appears in a moment of revelation, but in the final judgement cowers at the sight of his father, the judge of the bourgeois institution. The failure of the New Man is, at least here, tantamount to the failure of expressionism as a means for liberation from repressive social institutions.

Watson returns once more to institutional structures in her final story in the Oedipal cycle, "The Rumble Seat." Through the figure of Oedipus, Watson re-enters the bourgeois psychiatric institution, and through the popular historian and icon of Canadian television, Pierre Berton, she explores both bourgeois religious and mass media institutions. In a satirical renaming of Berton's *The Comfortable Pew: A Critical Look at Christianity and the Religious Establishment in the New Age* (1965), "The Rumble Seat" gives the author a rough ride in a satiric television interview with Oedipus. By placing him in interview with the mythological figure Oedipus, Watson satirizes the mythologization of Berton as a mass media figure: the myth both figures share is a "bourgeois myth," a myth perpetuated not by tradition but by technology.

Responding to the introduction of new technology into the homes of her "mythic middle class," Watson's story develops out of the interface between print and television media. McLuhan's contemporary vision of the coexistence of typographic and electric technologies in a television age is an obvious influence on the form of Watson's story. The first half of the story passes through fragmented networks of human communication: the rapid shifts between languages (mostly English and French, and some German, Italian, and Latin); the accelerated trialogue (among interviewer, interviewee, and viewer); the clipped syntax and incomplete sentences; and the incorporation of multiple kinds of discourse (scientific jargon, statistics, etymologies, and popular songs). Both form and content serve to create a chaotic text, that is, not an orderly, rule-governed, non-random gestalt, but an arbitrary, random, and unstructured mode of expression. The chaos of Watson's typographic media thus reflects the evolution and impact of electronic media in the mid-twentieth century. Here Watson assumes yet another role she ascribes to Lewis: "It is the role of the artist as artist in a world which is being transformed by technological magic" (*Wyndham* xvii).

Watson claims that the role of the modern artist is to be aware of "a world in which expressionist doctrine had been translated into the language of technological power" and to chart "the appearance of those temporal absolutes which masqueraded as the significant forms of the Zeitgeist's creative will or the age's inner necessity" (*Wyndham* xviii–xix, xviii). In "The Rumble Seat," she presents Berton's "religious establishment in the New Age" as one manifestation of a "temporal absolute," the institution of mass television media as another. Just as Lewis in *The Childermass* (1928) satirizes the control of wireless radio by demagogic apes of the expressionist zeitgeist, so Watson not only satirizes mass television media as another way in which the expressionist theory of significant form has been "translated into the language of technological power" but also creates Berton as the satiric type that, in Lewis's satires, she names the crowd-master. Berton gains technological power in his capacity as crowd-master, that is, the self-appointed prophet of "a new kind of church" (65); the creed of his church in the technological new age is *The Comfortable Pew*.

The crowd-master, Watson explains, is the satiric figure who "masks himself in some cliché or in some pastiche of images taken from a common stock" ("Artist-Ape" 115). The pastiche that Watson makes of Berton is drawn from *The Comfortable Pew*. Through his incoherent attempts to express his creed of the church in the "new age," Watson satirically exposes Berton as the crowd-master, the "type [that] represents embodiments which lacking instruments for self-expression substitute a simulacrum of self-expression" (115). With obvious satiric irony, in naming the central premise of *The Comfortable Pew*, Berton says to Oedipus, "We must...demythologize,"[19] to which Oedipus replies, "I have already become a complex, for others a thematic design like the sphere, the cylinder, and the cube," and to which the television viewer

Daedalus adds, looking at Berton, "The point, the line and the square" (61). Reduced to geometrical abstractions (perhaps reminiscent of Kandinsky), Oedipus and Berton are rendered here as significant forms, expressionist simulacra, pure abstractions. As demythologized figures, Oedipus and Berton are here cut "free from the clinging undergrowth of myth" (Berton 120), but at the cost of becoming meaningless abstractions "taken from a common stock."

In the course of the interview, Berton loses verbal coherence and control over the medium over which he is supposed to be master, while Oedipus gains coherence through self-expression in his anecdote that concludes the story and so acquires mastery over the medium. In his anecdote, Oedipus masks himself in a pastiche of bourgeois clichés, recounting to Berton the history of his childhood spent living inside the walls of a mental hospital (62) and going to the parish church (63). The anecdote obviously parodies the Freudian method of returning to the sources of phobias, neuroses, and complexes in childhood. Oedipus's anecdote about the bourgeois child's pleasure taken in sitting on the cushions of a comfortable pew, rather than the hard boards of the pew their father rents for them (66), leaves Berton completely silent, defeated, insensible. In effect, Berton's critique of bourgeois religious institutions in *The Comfortable Pew* is satirically transformed into Oedipus's clichéd bourgeois memoir. Having displaced and silenced Berton by the end of his anecdote, Oedipus then usurps technological power and controlling role of the crowd-master.

Lapsarian Expressionism

Originally written in the late 1930s (under the title "The Black Dogs" [Flahiff, *Always* 48]) but first circulated in 1980 as a Coach House Press manuscript of works in progress and later collected in 1984 with the Oedipal cycle in *Five Stories*, Watson's story "And the Four Animals" is uniquely positioned among her published works. Its delayed publication not only provides a point of retrospection on her expressionist vision of an age without art or ritual in *The Double Hook* and *Four Stories* but also marks an even earlier return to her formative critique of expressionism in her early fiction of the 1930s. Read as the final story in the sequence of *Five Stories*, "And the Four Animals" picks up where "The Rumble Seat" leaves off and presents a final installment of her satire of the expressionist artist as crowd-master. But read in its historical context, "And the Four Animals" returns us to the originary period of her mythographic fiction, a kind of cyclic return to the moment at which she first delineates the mythic dimensions of a fallen world of men without art. Two decades before the Oedipal cycle and *The Double Hook*, Watson already inhabits a Lewisian role as the mythographer of her age; her early story not only envisions the engendering moment of the work of art as a creation myth but also describes the fall of myth into history and the annihilating moment of apocalypse. Yet her mythic narrative of the creation and destruction of the work of art is surely not identical with her own creative method: her myth is a projection of the expressionist artist's vision shot through with her signature black humour and satire. As well as its early satiric perspective on expressionism, her mythic narrative introduces an extended gloss on gestalt aesthetics, one that long precedes her own late articulation of "figures in a ground" and McLuhan's late turn to gestalt configurations in his media theory. It is with "And the Four Animals" that her conception of figures alienated from their ground begins, and it is to that same gestalt structure that her fiction returns throughout her career.

"And the Four Animals" envisions three stages of a creation myth: it is an animistic vision, concerned with the relation of figure to ground, and composed principally of primary pigments, yellow, blue, and red, as well as "fugitive green" (73). Black is reserved for the animals. Similar to the figure-and-ground patterns and primary pigments of Lewis's Creation Myth paintings (1912–1942)—such as *The Mind of the Artist, About to Make a Picture* (1942)—Watson's story is about an artist-creator figure making a work of art. In the first stage, three black dogs come "around the curve of the hill, or out of the hill itself" (73). A "watching eye" (73) observes the dogs advance and climb the hill "until they stood as if freed from the land against the flat blue of the sky" (74). In the second stage, after the "eye closed and the dogs sank back into their proper darkness," the dogs enter into the eye itself, where they "could be observed clearly" (74). At this point the narrator describes a gestalt aesthetic and provides a history of the dogs, now domesticated Labrador retrievers: "The dogs were against the eye and in the eye. They were in the land but not of it. They were of Coyote's house, but became aristocrats in time which had now yielded them up to the timeless hills. They, too, were gods, but civil gods made tractable by use and custom" (74). The eye then opens and closes twice, and the three dogs twice repeat the action of climbing the hill until they are exhausted. In the third stage, the eye opens and there are four dogs and a man. The man is the landscape itself, his eye staring from "the hill of his head along the slope of his arm on which the four dogs lay" (75). He proceeds to dismember the dogs, feeding their bodies, eyes, and bones to each other, "until only one tooth remained and this he hid in his own belly" (76).

As with any myth, its layers of meaning are manifold. In the first stage, the black dogs seem to emerge out of the hills as "figures in a ground," as Watson says: "they're interacting with the landscape, and the landscape is interacting with them" ("What I'm" 183). She uses the conditional tense to illuminate the contingency of their existence: "Had the dogs worn the colour of the hills...the eye *might have recognized* a congruence between them and the land" (73–74, emphasis added); similarly, "Here Coyote...*might have walked* since the dawn of creation" (74, emphasis added). The implication is that the dogs are *not* figures in a ground, nor is Coyote present in the landscape. These dogs are ultimately separated from the landscape, "freed from the land," abstracted from the hills. They are, as we come to discover in the second stage, "aliens in this spot or exiles returned as if they had never been" (75). Like Watson's Stella in *Deep Hollow Creek*, or her whole community in *The Double Hook*, they are figures alienated from their ground. In the second stage, the reasons for the dogs' alienation are delineated: they are descendants of the god Coyote, but now inhabit a class structure owing to their domestication by their master; they are "in the land but not of it" because they obey the law of custom (*nomos*), not of nature (*physis*); they are what Lewis would call the apes of gods, "shaped by their master's will" (74). One suspects that the palindromic relation of "dog" and "god" also comes into play here; the master's expressive will tends toward dogma, and his creation of the dogs as inferior gods embodies the popular palindrome "dogma I am god."

To a similar end, the cannibalization of the dogs in the third stage is aptly described in Stephen Scobie's commentary on the story's black humour: "even here, we should allow for the possible presence of Watson's dry and quiet sense of humour—so quiet that it is all too often ignored, or simply not noticed. This story may be myth, but it is also a quietly humorous literalization of the cliché 'dog eat dog'" (285–86). Though Scobie's suggestion of the personalization of Watson's humour seems out of place in the context of a story about a depersonalized artist-creator as "master," such a reading is still provocative for its insight into Watson's mode of satire in a Lewisian absurdist, expressionist world. Rather than Watson's personality, the impersonality of her narrator provides a buffer between the master's art and hers: like all of her artist figures, the master is subject to her satire. So the master is, in the end, Watson's creation of the expressionist artist as the object of satire: his "subjectivism that borders on solipsism" (Lukács 109), his projection of the dogs as images "which he had whistled up from his own depths" (Watson, *Five* 75), and his violence are all symptomatic of the expressionist artist. The reduction of his art to a cliché therefore exposes the failure of the master's expressionist art. In Watson's "dog eat dog" world, her vision of the master is what, in Lewis's satires, she calls the artist-ape of god as crowd-master; or rather, in her satire, the portrait of the artist-ape of god as dog-master. "That the artist [is] always in danger of assuming the ape-like mask of the crowd-master," Watson is, as was Lewis, "constantly aware" ("Artist-Ape" 118); her blackly humorous satirization of the master exhibits her keen awareness of his expressionist ape-of-god type.

Watson's late recovery of her satire of a Lewisian artist-ape in one of her earliest extant works of fiction presents, as I have already suggested, an opportunity for retrospection on her anatomization of expressionist figures and types. The culmination of her critique of the expressionist artist-ape is the aggressive satire of the crowd-masters Berton and Oedipus in "The Rumble Seat." Looking back to *Deep Hollow Creek*, however, her satire of Stella as a failed artist figure is but mockery in comparison to the violent intensities captured in her early and middle period apocalyptic portraits of the master in "And the Four Animals" and Daedalus in "The Black Farm" as failed expressionist artist figures. And not so different from the impotent *Aufbruch* of Oedipus in "Brother Oedipus" and of Haemon in "Antigone," the master's final gesture in "And the Four Animals" is one that signifies the failure of expressionism. Akin to James's and Antigone's ritual gestures, the master's ritual sacrifice is an individual act, not a service performed in the interests of the community as a whole. The master is not a figure in a ground, but simply the ground itself, a pure abstraction: so by destroying his art through a ritual sacrifice, the master becomes not redeemed but a kind of wasteland in himself. After Watson's vision of the "rebirth of *communitas*" (Grace 95) in *The Double Hook*, the isolation of the master in "And the Four Animals" adumbrates her subsequent conception of the need for community as the means of redeeming a world without art and ritual, which she initially represents through the master's violence and the dogs' insensibility.

Having reached the end of the body of work that Watson published during her lifetime, her reader may be faced with an uncomfortable realization that her sustained critique of expressionist art and aesthetics, and of the expressionist New Man, crowd-master, and artist figure, does not offer resolution. Analogous to Lewis's satire of modernity in his trilogy *The Human Age* (1928–1955), Watson's unintended trilogy of *Deep Hollow Creek*, *The Double Hook*, and *Five Stories* does not offer an eschatological vision of a redeemed humanity in the modern age. There are no wholly positive inscriptions of expressionism in Watson's oeuvre, only metacritical and satiric reinscriptions of its aesthetic. Without choosing positive examples of expressionism upon which to build,

Watson carries on the satiric project that Lewis started a generation before her, repeatedly targeting the dogmas and failures of
expressionism and, in doing so, exhausting its aesthetic even as
she uses it. Like Lewis, Watson creates an expressionist universe
full of unresolved problems, but only because she has problema-
tized expressionism and so laid bare its aesthetic. If we can carry
away an understanding of the whole of Watson's published work,
it must acknowledge the dogged persistence of her critique of
expressionism. And if one reads only a part of the whole, what is
lost is its recurrent patterns, its insistent return to expressionism
as an object of critique. Because expressionism desires yet always
fails to yield the expressive forms necessary, in Watson's view, to
redemption, the language she employs in her fiction is a fallen one,
an unredeemed discourse of reified abstraction. It follows that
her fiction is replete with unredeemed figures, especially expressionist ones, who speak in the fallen tongue of clichés and act out
exhausted rituals. Because the gestalt of Watson's oeuvre cannot
ultimately fulfill the expressionist desire for redemption through
abstraction but instead rearticulates it as modernity's tendency to
reification, it remains unfinished and unredeemed. The irony of
a whole that is inevitably incomplete is the corollary to Watson's
unresolved agon with expressionism: to view only the sum of the
parts, Watson's oeuvre simply articulates an aesthetic of satire and
metasatire; but to see the whole that is greater than the sum of the
parts, it reveals the absence of the means of redemption from her
aesthetic and her art. Structured as a gestalt without redemption,
Watson's satiric oeuvre reinscribes the metanarrative of expressionism and its aesthetic mediations of the reified technological,
social, and spiritual conditions of modernity as a fall without end.

Notes

1   See Von Ehrenfels, "On 'Gestalt Qualities'" (1890): "The whole is greater than the sum of its parts" (qtd. in Kanizsa 59). On the history of gestalt aesthetics and psychology in German culture, see Ash, *Gestalt Psychology in German Culture*.

2   Watson lists Frank's 1945 essay on spatial form in the bibliography of her dissertation (376), but she does not refer to it directly.

3   Based on her personal interview with Watson in the mid-1970s, Grace situates the novels in relation to Watson's encounter with Lewis and expressionist aesthetics as early as her undergraduate studies at the University of British Columbia in the early 1930s (188). In his preface to the 2003 publication of her thesis, Flahiff conjectures that she likely discussed Lewis with Norman Endicott, a professor in the Department of English at the University of Toronto, with whom she took a graduate course in the 1940s when she and her husband, Wilfred, were living in Toronto for his doctoral studies; he adds, in confirmation of Grace's hypothesis, that Watson "might well have read [Lewis] as a student at UBC" (Preface n. pag.).

4   That vorticism emerged as a parallel movement to both official and unofficial German expressionism Watson attributes to three lines of transmission, which she traces through the concepts of inner necessity and significant form: (1) that the Austrian art historian Alois Riegl directly influenced official German expressionist aesthetics with his concepts will to form and inner necessity in *Spätrömische Kunstindustrie* (1901), which Worringer rechristens as *Kunstwollen* or artistic volition in *Abstraction and Empathy* (1908); (2) that both Lewis and Pound attended T.E. Hulme's January 1914 Modern Art and Its Philosophy lecture in London, which applied Worringer's aesthetics to contemporary English art; and (3) that, in the first issue of the vorticist magazine *Blast* (June 1914), Lewis published Edward Wadsworth's translations of and commentary on extracts from Kandinsky's unofficial German expressionist tract, *Concerning the Spiritual in Art*, which, as Peter Selz notes, probably derived from Fiedler's theories of inner necessity and significant form (5).

5   Watson lists all of McLuhan's early publications on Lewis in the bibliography of her dissertation (348), but she does not quote from or cite any of them.

6   On McLuhan's satiric modes and persona, see Chrystall, "The New American Vortex," esp. 447–57.

7   As McLuhan admitted in a letter to Lewis after the publication of *The Mechanical Bride*, "the book owes much to you" (*Letters* 241)—a tacit nod to his book's imitation of Lewis's "A Gallery of Exhibits" in *The Doom of Youth* (1932), which consists of newspaper headlines and clippings, together with commentary (*Letters* 271n5).

8   In a letter from the fall of 1961, McLuhan instructed Watson to adopt a similar strategy, exhorting her to model the section headers in her thesis after the headlines in Lewis's *The Art of Being Ruled* (1926)—a design that McLuhan himself implemented in collaboration with typographer Harold Kurschenska for *The Gutenberg Galaxy: The Making of Typographic Man* (1962) (Flahiff, *Always* 236). As it happens, McLuhan confused *The Art of Being Ruled* with *The Doom of Youth* (see n7).

9   While we know that her interest in Lewis coincides with her reading of Swift during her study at the University of British Columbia with W.L. MacDonald, who supervised her 1933 master's thesis (Flahiff, *Always* 31), there is as yet no precise way of knowing which works by Lewis she was reading or ascertaining exact dates of contact. Even if chronologies prove difficult to substantiate irrefragably, there is little doubt that Lewis's satires *Tarr* (1918; rev. 1928), *The Wild Body* (1927), and *The Apes of God* (1930) and his polemic *Men Without Art* must be considered among the principal influences on *Deep Hollow Creek*.

10   Watson also implicates Miriam in her mode of metasatire. While many of the dialogues between Stella and Miriam constitute satiric agons, one in particular is explicitly metasatiric: "You should become a contemporary Boswell, Stella remarked. You have enough opportunity to. You could turn your observation to account. I don't know that I won't, said Miriam" (96). In some ways, James Boswell's *Journal of a Tour to the Hebrides* (1785) and *The Life of Samuel Johnson, LL.D.* (1791) are apposite analogues to *Deep Hollow Creek*: the former documents the experiences of Johnson and Boswell amid the primitive, sparsely populated regions and peoples of Scotland's Highlands and Hebrides, not so unlike the experiences of Stella and Miriam in the Cariboo. The latter is a biography of a satirist in which the biographer appears as a character: if Stella plays Johnson, then she is the satirist; and if Miriam plays a contemporary Boswell, then she is the biographer of the satirist.

11   See also Watson, "Interview," in which she speaks of writing about her time in Dog Creek: "I had the experience of living with people who felt intensely but who were not particularly articulate—in any conventional or predictable way. I learned things from them and I wanted to create a language for what I learned. I could have done it the Lewis way—from external detail simply—the hides and pelts" (356). Here Watson is speaking of *The Double Hook*, but it can be inferred that the "Lewis way" to which she refers may well be the method she adopted for her earlier novel.

12   Gulliver's final predicament is taken up by Watson in her essay on Swift's satire, "Power: Nude or Naked": "The conviction that his clothing is a false covering is Gulliver's final step towards misanthropy and total madness. For him the physiological truth of the Yahoo becomes a naked iconoclastic truth which finally transforms the world into a *peau de chagrin*" (152).

13   That is, "the bracelet of bright hair about the bone" in Donne's satiric love poem, "The Relic" (76).

14   On the topographical orientation of the narrative around Mockett's stopping house, see Willmott, "The Nature of Modernism" 35–36, 40–43.

15   By falsely assuming the role of the ritual satirist in verbally attacking and sacrificing his mother, James is subsequently recast in the role of the satirist satirized. Constance Rooke has suggested that James's murder of his mother in the opening section and Mrs. Potter's reappearance in the second and thereafter can be thought of as a kind of trick, black comedy inspired by Coyote (85). If this satiric trick played upon James is, as Rooke says, inspired by Coyote, it is because Coyote is the archetypal trickster-satirist.

16   George Bowering's Afterword to his influential 1978 collection *Sheila Watson and The Double Hook* goes so far as to argue that Watson herself assumes Coyote's role as trickster, a position echoed by Robert Kroetsch in "Death Is a Happy Ending: A Dialogue in Thirteen Parts" (209–10). Any reading of Watson as a Coyote figure should proceed cautiously, since it ignores the corollary of identifying the author herself or even her narrator with the character of Coyote: the trickster figure is always in danger of being tricked himself, which is not a risk that Watson takes as a satirist. Her satire may be inspired by Coyote, but she does not arrogate herself to his role (albeit precarious) as trickster. Among the most recent scholarship on the trickster figure in *The Double Hook*, see Morra, "The Anti-Trickster"; Radu, "'More Like a Devil'"; and Willmott, "Sheila."

17   For a brief account of the parallels between Ghede and Coyote, see Monkman 65.

18   For other scholarship on "Antigone," see Scobie, *Sheila Watson and Her Works*; J. Miller, "Rummaging in the Sewing Basket of the Gods"; Legge, "Sheila Watson's 'Antigone'"; Kuester, "Myth and the Postmodernist Turn in Canadian Short Fiction" and Kuester, "(Post-)modern Bricolage."

19   Watson briefly entertains the concept of "demythologizing" in her essay "Myth and Counter-Myth," "in the sense in which the word has been used in certain theological circles," but then cautions, "how much this demythologizing is strategic, only those who have given sufficient attention to Bultmann's polemic are competent to judge" (120). Rudolf Bultmann's coinage of the term "demythologizing" in *Jesus Christ and Mythology* boils down to the question of whether there is a need to translate the symbols and images of myth out of a mythological world view, though not into a modern scientific world view, but into a language "freed from any world view produced by man's thought, whether mythological or scientific" (83).

9

Artist as Catalytic Agent
and the Counter-Environment in
Sheila Watson's The Double Hook

"His Name Is Felix"

Linda M. Morra

Communication, in the conventional sense, is difficult under any conditions. People prefer *rapport* through smoking or drinking together. There is more communication there than there ever is by verbal means. We can share environments, we can share weather, we can share all sorts of cultural factors together but communication takes place only inadequately and is very seldom understood...Actually, [it] is an exceedingly difficult activity. In the sense of a mere point-to-point correspondence between what is said, done and thought and felt between people—this is the rarest thing in the world. If there is the slightest tangential area of touch, agreement, and so on among people, *that* is communication in a big way...Most people have the idea of communication as something matching between what is said and what is understood. In actual fact, communication is *making*. The person who sees or heeds or hears is engaged in making a response to a situation, which is mostly of his own fictional invention.

—Marshall McLuhan, interview with Gerald E. Stearn

LINDA M. **Morra**

BY MARSHALL MCLUHAN'S DEFINITION, what others would readily perceive as communication has little correspondence with what it actually is or when it transpires. By his terms, it occurs with difficulty and either through "rapport," that is, through a shared understanding produced by mutual engagement with an activity, or as a response to a situation, even if the latter has been "invented" or manufactured by the person who "perceives" the event. Yet, by the same definition, McLuhan virtually excludes the catalytic agent, and, in so doing, would seem to characterize the communication process as somewhat passive. He absents the agent who engenders its "making"—that is, the person who, in effect, lights the match so that people might smoke together, or who pours the coffee so that people might drink together. Even about his perhaps most well-known formulation, "the medium is the message," he notes that "I suppress the fact that the user or audience or cognitive agent is both the 'content' and maker of the experience in order to highlight the *effects* of the medium, or the hidden environment or ground of the experience" (italics in original, qtd. in Gordon, *Escape* 176). In other words, he privileges the medium over the maker.

However he might suppress the cognitive agent as an integral part of the communication process in these theoretical formulations, he elsewhere notes that it is, in fact, often the artist figure—if not the arts itself—who is a decisive catalyst behind shifts from what he described as "environments" towards "anti-environments," or "counter-environments." These latter terms are also pivotal to his critical lexicon related to communication. McLuhan, for example, holds that "a new technology" might enjoy "a brief reign as an anti-environment" before becoming "environmental in turn" (*Letters* 315);[1] language, as a technology, might serve as both environment and anti-environment. He regards new environments as shaped by old ones; so he argues that the "content of the new environment is always the old one" and that "one environment creates another" (*Letters* 309).[2] Even cliché, that which reifies elements of an old environment, has potential: "new cliché, new technology retrieves unexpected archetypes from the rag-and-bone shop" (*From Cliché* 46). Significantly, McLuhan also asserts that counter-environments are often created by the artist, who "raises these hidden environments to the level of conscious appreciation" (77). If he sees the artist figure as drawing attention to or in possession of a heightened awareness of the environment, he also believes that the artist pushes beyond the current environment through the use of cliché "into a new dimension of experience" (58).[3] The arts as a whole are central, he argues, in their provision of "anti-environments that represent efforts at environmental control"; however, he adds, even if "art as anti-environment awakens perception of the environment," it may be that the anti-environments might yet "prove inadequate," in which case "we resort in desperation to technological innovation and change as an attempt to control the environmental effects of earlier technologies" (*Letters* 315).[4] Art usually remediates our experience of the environment by revitalizing our perception of that environment successfully, but, when art fails to do so, artists must resort to other forms of technological innovation to stimulate communication.

By contrast, Sheila Watson, McLuhan's doctoral student between 1957 and 1965, maintains that violence—rather than a desperate turn to technological innovation—is one of two responses of those for whom communication has failed. So she notes about her experimental novel, *The Double Hook* (1959), "there was something I wanted to say: about how people are driven, how if they have no art, how if they have no tradition, how if they have no ritual, they are driven in one of two ways, either towards violence or towards insensibility—if they have no mediating rituals which manifest themselves in what I suppose we call art forms" ("What I'm" 183). Indeed, *The Double Hook* might be seen as an exploration of communication, of its attendant failures, and of the repercussions for a group of people whose environment is no longer a source of mutual understanding and for whom the current "technology"—language, art, and mediating rituals, the vehicles for communication—does not function. Within the confines of her novel, the dissonances and struggle for comprehension eventually find greater coherence and resolution because of one character who serves as the vector for change: Felix Prosper. As the artist figure of the novel, Felix is driven towards neither violence nor insensibility, but towards positive action that effects change and generates communication. The conferring of Felix's very name upon the baby born in the community, the final gesture of the novel, suggests that what McLuhan would call a new environment, or counter-environment, has been established.

Watson herself does not employ such terms as "environments" or "anti-environments," not simply because the novel appeared several years before she completed her dissertation under McLuhan's supervision; she later resisted doing so, although McLuhan urged her.[5] Instead, she makes several critical remarks about the "ground" from which the characters operated in *The Double Hook*. In one instance, she notes, "I was concerned with figures in a ground, from which they could not be separated" ("What I'm" 183). In "'It's What You Say,'" she remarks again that her intention in the writing of *The Double Hook* was "to get away from any idea of setting. Here the voices came from somewhere else. Place was important only in its relationship to them as ground" (159). Initially, Watson's sense of "ground" in which the characters operate might seem to bear similarity to McLuhan's approach to environments; however, the latter term is both more abstract and much broader in application. In fact, McLuhan's use of "environment"—by which he means the effects of a technology, such as language, which allows for the unconscious habitation of space—bears closer resemblance to her use of the term "myth." In her lecture on Wyndham Lewis, "Myth and Counter-Myth," she characterizes myth using the work of Lewis to suggest how it generates or appropriates "ritual patterns and protective coverings" (120), and how it is reformulated over and over from its original content—just as McLuhan argues "anti-environments" are generated from "environments." In effect, McLuhan's definition of environment would have been translated in more precise terms by Watson as mediating art, language, and rituals. As her novel highlights, she was far more interested not only in mediating art and

LINDA M. **Morra**

rituals, but also in *those people* upon whom the environment had an impact rather than the environment itself. She thus wanted to write "about a number of people who had no ability to communicate because they had found little to replace the myths and rituals which might have bound them together" ("'It's What'" 159).

Whatever their differences in terms of emphasis and terminology, what she and McLuhan share is a conception about the integral function of the artist as an agent for change; they would subscribe to Ezra Pound's sense that the artist operates as the "antennae" of a people. As already noted, McLuhan characterizes the artist as in possession of a developed or heightened consciousness about "environments"—what Watson would identify as "mythic patterns"—and is therefore able to alert others to their presence. Watson argued along similar lines. In a lecture, for example, she characterizes Lewis, as "concerned with surveying ground-patterns and with training his eyes, and the eyes of others, to read the arbitrary signs by which mythic objects thrust into the foreground of life, habituate themselves there and generate" those ritual patterns ("Myth and Counter-Myth" 120). Lewis, as artist, could train others to read such "arbitrary signs" only because he had trained his own eyes first. That McLuhan and Watson both approach the role of the artist figure as of singular importance is thus especially relevant when considering the characterization of Felix and the means by which communication is at last generated in *The Double Hook*.

There is no better place, then, to observe the ideological affinities between McLuhan and Watson than in the characterization of the artist figure, Felix, in Watson's novel. An assessment of his character reveals that he is the artist figure, the key person who sees, heeds, and hears and forms a response to situations. He works beyond the community's dissonances because his heightened perception allows him to recognize their needs. His artistic endeavours (specifically, the playing of his fiddle), his ability to use and push beyond fragments of clichéd speech and Catholic liturgy, and his own benevolent actions eventually produce mutual engagement by members of the community—rather than violence.

By the end of the novel, the characters move towards greater coherence, as initiated by Felix, and are compelled by him into organized forms of responding to others.[6] Ultimately, Watson shows that productive communication, as McLuhan would also suggest, is generated from one's heightened awareness to a situation to which others then react; in other words, it is only when Felix recognizes and then responds to the needs of the community and to the situation at hand that communication is effected.

Critical consensus about Sheila Watson's *The Double Hook* would seem to corroborate the assessment that communication is indeed "the rarest thing in world"—although such criticism has also neglected Felix's pivotal mediations of the novel's action and resolution.[7] Whatever discrepancies exist among the interpretive perspectives that have accumulated around Watson's 1959 novel, one facet of her book seems largely to have secured critical agreement (Pennee 248; Nesbitt 167; Deer 36): little communication between the characters transpires throughout the course of the narrative. As Watson once remarked in a 1976 interview published in the *Capilano Review*, the novel had emerged from her "experience of living closely with people who felt intensely but who were not particularly articulate—in any conventional or predictable way" ("Interview" 356). In "'It's What You Say,'" she noted that "I was thinking rather of a cry of voices...voices crying out in the wilderness...I was thinking of a group of bodies that were virtually inarticulate and I had to make them articulate without making them *faux-semblants* so to speak" (158). I take this to mean that Watson is interested in presenting characters that struggled to communicate, even if they were able to speak.[8]

Indeed, communication in the novel may be characterized initially and largely by its very negation. Most characters in *The Double Hook* primarily work against the process of communication; their tendencies are instead either to reject attempts at understanding, or to eschew responding to situations or engaging with others. They are, at turns, "suspended in silence" (29), preoccupied with waiting (see, for example, how the "Widow Wagner waited all day" [106]), or driven outdoors and off their respective properties.[9]

When characters do speak, they employ cliché, are misapprehended, or use speech to reject communication outright—that is, they do so for the paradoxical purpose of refusing such interactions with others. Thus, for example, Greta declares, "I don't want you coming, Ara. I don't want anything from William" (27), as she simultaneously turns Ara and Angel away from her house. Other characters distance themselves from or refuse a sense of responsibility for their actions. If the "making" of understanding is undermined by those who repudiate interaction—and, for that matter, calls to action—that repudiation is then compounded by the means by which these themselves form a direct act in which they would otherwise be implicated.[10] Watson reinforces this sense from the novel's outset when, for example, she writes that it is his "will" and his "hand" that engender the death of Mrs. Potter—not James himself. One interpretive approach to this moment, as Glenn Deer suggests, is to observe how "the act...hovers unattached to an agent" (27).[11] Even then, these actions do not seem immediately to take effect. Little "tangential area of touch, or agreement" exists about what he has done and what other members of the community observe. Instead, members of the community continue to engage in what might be described as visual cliché: they see Mrs. Potter fishing in various parts of the creek well after she has died. To use McLuhan's terminology, they are not conscious of their environment or the changes that have already been rendered. Readers thus may have their own assessment of the situation at the novel's outset also denied them. They may assume Mrs. Potter was killed, but, as critic Yinglin Ji notes, that assessment "is constantly challenged and naturally seesaws between affirmation and denial" (353). A second interpretive approach to this moment involves suggesting what Watson posits elsewhere: violence is the recourse for those for whom all other forms of communication have failed.

When critics do suggest that the characters are working successfully towards meaningful exchanges in this novel, they focus on how other characters—rather than Felix—participate in its making. In her article, "Messages and Messengers in *The Double Hook*," Dawn Rae Downton privileges only three figures as significant messengers:

William, Kip, and Heinrich. She excludes Felix from this assessment. Whereas she argues that the "careers" of the three are involved in the "birth of language," I would suggest that these careers highlight communal dissonances. Messages are improperly articulated, undelivered, or dismissed outright. Each of the characters Downton names is consistently distinguished by an inability to communicate or, in Kip's case, by violence. Kip, for example, is referred to as "nothing but a go-between for James and his women" (67). He fails, however, to do just that bit of "nothingness": deliver Lenchen's message to James. So Lenchen is compelled to ask, "Did Kip bring my message? Did Kip tell you I was waiting?" (46). As Downton herself observes, "Kip chooses to withhold or alter the messages with which he is entrusted at will, so that the community is to a great extent culpable in the breakdowns [in understanding] which occur, having placed its faith in an untrustworthy courier" (144). Instead, he imposes a kind of violence upon Lenchen when he aggressively attempts to seduce her. Later, he denies personal responsibility for his assault upon her: "The old white moon had me by the hair" (107).

Communal discord is also featured in the frustrated attempts at communication by the other "messenger" figures, William and Heinrich, who fare no better. William speaks in meaningless clichés that he does not push beyond, or makes trivial observations that have no effect, except perhaps to create an ironic divide between the dramatic event and his failure to understand its complexity. His penultimate assertion in the novel is exemplary, especially given the remarkable events that have transpired by this point in the novel: "it's going to be another scorcher" (121). He is a man who, as Watson insinuates, "only felt, but he always felt he knew" (5). When Ara, his wife, at long last confronts him directly about her fears of his infidelity, he has little to say—indeed almost refuses to "say"—and apparently is confused by her straightforward honesty: "It doesn't make sense in your mouth somehow" (64). "What do you want me to tell you?" is his response to Ara's questions, and this remark is followed by his bewilderment at her sudden loquaciousness: "I don't know what's the matter with you, Ara. You've never talked like this before" (64). Heinrich is as bewildered and frustrated. He observes that "I should have been able to tell Lenchen something" (70), but what that "something" is remains unclear. When he arrives at the Potter household, he flounders in accounting for his presence there before making the not-so-profound (and unsubstantiated) observation, "your Ma's out in the storm" (31). For the rest of the novel, moreover, he conjectures about his sister's whereabouts and well-being. Ultimately, he fails to ask or do anything meaningful by way of her discovery, as he laments, "everyone in the creek must know and no one has turned a hand to help. I don't know what to do" (72).

But someone has turned a hand to help: Felix. He recognizes, assumes responsibility for, and attends to the needs of others; in so doing, he becomes the vector for change. He unleashes a chain of events that is integral to "making a response" to the situation at hand, and that eventually creates a counter-environment. If we were to accept other characters' assessment of Felix, we might be tempted to concur that he is capable of little beyond his seeming indolence. Margaret Morriss, for example, characterizes Felix as apathetic (56). Within the novel, therefore, "no one [thinks] of Felix" when trying to discover to whom the expectant Lenchen has turned for help. Most revealing, perhaps, is William's assessment: "He drinks coffee like the rest of us...Though, he said, I'd be hard pressed to know how he comes by the money to pay for it. If you think of it, he said, this case of Felix is a standing lesson for someone to think twice. A man who drinks coffee is dependent on something outside himself. But I myself doubt that he'd be much help to a person in trouble" (121). Felix and his tendencies are indeed a "standing lesson" to think twice about, but not for the derogatory reasons William suggests. However questionable the means by which he is able to obtain his coffee (and there is no indication within the novel of how he does so), Felix's actions suggest that he is establishing the *rapport* that McLuhan identified as generating real communication: he is the catalytic agent, the person who willingly shares his coffee with others. In this capacity, he fosters, not a capitalist economy, but a gift economy, in which reciprocity is neither expected nor purchased.[12] In this instance, Watson avoids the "capital-technological dimension of human culture," not by "erasing" it (Betts, "Media, McLuhan" 275), but rather by showing how capital exchanges are circumvented through Felix's benevolent actions.

William impugns Felix, however, for a three-fold reason. He also sees him as both dependent on others and offering little to the community. To this he adds that Felix allows his "troubles" to "lie on another man's doorstep" and "spends all his days lying round like a dog in a strip of sunlight taking warmth where he finds it" (121). In other words, William regards Felix as a freeloading, irresponsible, and slothful human being. He fails to recognize that he, like Felix, is dependent on something outside himself because, like all other community members, he also drinks coffee. Most critics have acknowledged, however, how many characters like William are also plagued by lack of sight and insight, such that their assessment or vision of Felix cannot be depended upon: they cannot "see"; or, as in Ara's case, they see "in flashes" (64); or they "shoo" out what settles in their eye (42); or, as in the Widow's case, they deliberately keep their "eyes shut" and "see nothing" at all (69 and 44; see also Godard 156). But Felix is the artist figure who is in possession of a heightened consciousness. The other characters' incapacity to appreciate him, his kindly gestures, and his imaginative gifts, therefore, should not impede our understanding of this character, but rather should be taken as an indicator of their inherent failings or, at least, as an assessment of a community and of an environment of which they are unconscious.

Felix introduces that new technology that renders others conscious of the plight of their neighbours and of their environment, and not solely by going beyond cliché, as McLuhan would suggest, to "break through into a new dimension of experience" (*From Cliché* 58). As would be typical of the artist figure, he is awakened to the needs of others, which becomes a trigger for his own actions; the latter are thus marked by a peculiar understanding about, sensitivity to, and compassion for the whole environment he inhabits. Watson's early draft shows that the characterization of Felix was altered to showcase these attributes more consistently. Professor

Frederick M. Salter, a professor who also taught creative writing at the University of Alberta and Watson's editor, suggested to her that "an incident be removed: in Draft I, Felix teases his dogs before giving them the fish leavings to eat, cruel behavior that Salter [saw] as out of character for the passive but well-intentioned Felix" (qtd. in Morriss 58). Watson agreed. Her decision to remove this scene suggests a more coherent sense of Felix as sympathetic: he is consistently capable of feeling so for others, for his environment as a whole, even in his seemingly more trivial actions. Thus, when Kip arrives with his eyes seared by the violence James has wrought upon him, Felix puts "down his fiddle," and, in a gesture of empathy, he "reach[es] for Kip's arm" (60). Whereas other characters, especially Greta, turn people away from their homes, Felix takes him in and sits Kip upon his own bed; then, in what I consider one of more kindly actions in the novel, he makes him coffee and, in so doing, generates the rapport that McLuhan perceived as generating "more communication" than "by verbal means" ("Interview" 292). This response is in marked contrast with the opening scene of the novel, wherein Greta reaches for coffee beans with which she is "grinding away James's voice" (14). Her gesture suggests the annihilation of a human attempt at expression and connection, rather than rapport.[13]

The dissonances by which Felix is confronted are not easily overcome, yet he persists by responding to others and working through the challenges inherent in the clichéd language, or the environment, that is part of the community's legacy. He thus quickly responds to Kip's arrival at Felix's doorstep, his injuries, and his need for attention, and he thereafter draws many of the community members together by appealing to them about Kip's physical well-being. He immediately sets on the road to search for Angel, residing with Theophil. On the journey there, he acknowledges there is an impasse in verbal communication: "What could he say...All the way up the road he'd been trying to form the words" (67). At this point in the novel, he is embroiled in the same plight as the other characters within the novel: they grapple with the means to express themselves, or with finding ways to engender meaningful communication.

Neither his appearance at her door, therefore, nor his first words to Angel induce her to come with him or to act in the way Felix requires: indeed, she spins "round like a flame on the wide boards of the floor. Behind Theophil" (67). He then significantly invokes remnants of the Catholic liturgy, "the legacy of priests" (Flahiff, Afterword 129): "Peace be with you" and "Forgive us our trespasses" (67).

Theophil's initial response to these important declarations contrasts with that of Felix, while highlighting the existing failures in communication. He asserts that the "priest taught me the same way he taught you," while curling his fingers in "the palms of his hands" (67). As Watson suggests is characteristic of those who have no art and no ritual, Theophil turns to destructive action. He does not, moreover, see the world as Felix's language would compel him (67); that is, if a language "teaches its users a way of seeing and feeling the world, and of acting in the world, that is quite unique," then Theophil does not understand that Felix is compelling him to shift beyond cliché and to work with decontextualized ritual in order to break through unresponsive indifference into "a new dimension of experience" (McLuhan, *From Cliché* 58). Certainly, Theophil has not learned how to conduct himself in the world as the priestly language would enjoin him. Felix, however, has.[14] The latter demonstrates, moreover, that he understands that in certain contexts or in the forging of a counter-environment, language comes to serve another purpose and loses its clichéd status. He takes ritual forms of expression that are of use in cultivating new forms of expression. Yet, if "language and ritual in Watson's novels emerge as tools of human interaction," as "technologies that extend isolated individuals beyond themselves, enable communication, and make possible the creation of community" (Betts, "Media, McLuhan" 255), these technologies still have limited immediate use. Thus, whereas Felix includes himself in "our trespasses," Theophil is quick to point out those of others and to respond with unthinking violence.[15] Still, it is important that Felix is the only character here and elsewhere in the novel who invokes Catholic ritual: at least he recognizes its importance to communicating with others and as a resource for developing that facility.

But it is what Felix does that eventually demonstrates that he is the catalytic agent who initiates the communication process. At long last, he turns to Angel and adds one of the most definitive and explicit statements in the novel: "Angel...I need you" (68). Felix thus announces, as William would argue, that he is dependent on others—as are the others who have not yet recognized their need for each other. This plea follows only a few pages after Theophil declares to Angel, "I sure *don't need you* and your kids round here showing me how miserable a person can be" (62, italics mine). Felix's open, communal, and striking appeal to Angel is more successful, however, after he announces he is there on an altruistic mission:

> It's Kip, he said.
> Angel shoved past Theophil and beat her hands against Felix's bib. What's the matter? she cried. Don't stand there like a lump of meat. What's happened?

If Angel remarks upon Felix's bellowing out her name and claims she "never in my life heard you call on anyone," he has only done so—on someone else's behalf (68). He is also successful by *how* he demands her assistance: the gesture of crying out has almost as great an impact as his pronouncement that "it's Kip." Angel is thus compelled into action. He seeks her out, moreover, not because he is dependent, as William would have it, but because he has the inner spiritual resources to become conscious of the environment he inhabits and answer to the contingencies of the community.

Felix has this capacity to respond both in word and deed to the immediacy of such situations, to understand that he cannot approach or respond to such situations in isolation, and to appreciate the richness of both language and musical expression as a means of enjoining others. As McLuhan notes in *Understanding Media*, language is "an extension or uttering (outering) of our senses at once," and, as such, it is "held to be man's richest art form, that which distinguishes from the animal creation" (83). Felix, however, has access to another rich art form or "mediating ritual":

music (Watson, "What I'm" 83). He plays the fiddle, which invokes the acoustic mode to which characters such as Kip and Lenchen are responsive. His art, as McLuhan would argue, awakens their "perception of the environment" (*Letters* 315). Kip, for example, blinded by this point in the novel, "raise[s] himself on his elbow to listen" (109). His blindness subsequently allows him to be ushered into an auditory space in which he can pay heed to Felix's artistic expression. In employing art and ritual to foster communication and connection, Felix demonstrates that he is not driven, like other characters, towards violence, if not insensibility.[16] By contrast, James Potter is most strikingly engaged in a "series of violent acts": he kills his mother, he blinds Kip, he whips Lenchen and Greta (Godard 156).[17] If James is driven by a lack of art and tradition towards violence, Felix uses cliché, ritual, and art to generate community.

Informed by his upbringing in the Catholic Church, Felix's imagination and, at least, memory of Church liturgy offer a specific mediating ritual, a striking contrast with the spiritual aridity and inertia of the community. In his invocation of Catholic rituals, Felix thus becomes a necessary disruptive element in the existing media ecology rather than insisting upon the "cultural environment that most of its inhabitants take for granted" (Heise 157); that is, he provides a means by which to communicate that heightens awareness of the language the characters use and beyond the disparate and disconnected lives led by the characters. So he literally and figuratively opens his door to other characters, both Kip and Lenchen, who seek out shelter under his roof. Initially, it would seem, he desires to turn Lenchen away. He considers that he has "no words to clear a woman off my bench. No words except: Keep moving, scatter, get-the-hell-out" (37). His ruminations directly thereafter also indicate another impulse:

His mind sifted ritual phrases. Some half forgotten.
You're welcome. Put your horse in. Pull up.
Ave Maria. Benedictus fructus ventris. Introibo.
He rolled from his chair. Stood barefoot. His hands raised.
Pax vobiscum, he said...
What the hell, she said.
Go in peace, he said...
The girl looked at him.
I got no place to go, she said. (38)

Felix clearly knows and understands the existing environment,
demonstrated in the fact that he considers several expressions in
the vernacular: "keep moving, scatter, get-the-hell-out." However,
he decides that these words are not appropriate, not sufficiently
precise for his immediate purpose, or are no longer the appropriate medium. Barbara Godard argues that Felix "has no words,
that all is silence" (156), but Felix has options aside from the bits
of Catholic liturgy he invokes. Elsewhere, he also works through
poetic ruminations that suggest his capacity and role as artist:
"Can your joy be bound by a glass river? Is death a fishbone in
your hand?" (62). As Watson notes, he "has some pity for the girl,"
which is why "he resorts to fragments of the mass, perhaps trying
remember the *ite* of the *ite, missa est*" ("'It's What'" 159). He finally
settles on "*Pax vobiscum*," the greeting of the Angel who announces
Christ's birth to Mary, but, in contrast to Godard's sense that the
problem of language has not been resolved, I think it serves its
purpose—for Lenchen *does* understand him: "I got no place to go."
If he had been working with (instead of beyond) cliché, he would
not have elicited Lenchen's surprise ("What the hell").[18] His turn
to Latin suggests he has invoked an aural mode, as it also suggests
the confrontation of an environment and anti-environment[19]—an
important confrontation that eventually allows for the community to be spiritually charged and changed. When he does settle
into silence, a "break in the uniformity and continuity of space,"
because he had "come to the end of his saying," it may suggest

the limits of speech (Cavell, "McLuhan in Space" 180; Watson, *Double Hook* 38); however, from this point forward, Felix acts. He accepts those who show up at his door, he seeks the assistance of others, and he learns to take care of Lenchen when she returns to him. By contrast, Lenchen also tells Greta that she has "no place to go," but, unlike Felix, Greta adamantly refuses to allow her into her home. She stands in the doorway and insists: "Go away" (54). Having no place to go, Lenchen returns to Felix's house.

Ultimately, Felix's own struggle with language demonstrates the inadequacies of the current environment, the need to take existing clichés and push them, until they are "scrapped in favour of a new cliché, which may be the revival of an old one" (McLuhan, *From Cliché* 51). Simultaneously, he demonstrates non-violent alternatives, which stimulates communal reintegration and forges a counter-environment in which he is understood. So he himself turns to altruistic action. He calls upon Angel for help; he takes care of Kip; and he single-handedly delivers Lenchen's baby, such that even Angel feels compelled to observe, "[he] didn't do bad for a man" (132). Thereafter, he makes sure all are nourished: "When a house is full of women and children, Felix said, a man has to get something for their mouths" (133).[20] As evidence of this animation, the members of the community have not changed the kind of language they use (which are clearly still clichés), but altered their conduct towards one another and the context from which they operate: almost every character responds with a heightened awareness of their environment and of the situation at hand. They respond to the needs of Lenchen and Kip, and are involved in "turning a hand to help," what Heinrich lamented that the community had earlier refused.

In this counter-environment, communication has been produced by both Watson's and McLuhan's terms, since the characters see, hear, and heed each other; they respond to the situation of which Felix has made them all aware. There is a "tangential area of touch" and "agreement," which is evidenced in the fact that, by the novel's conclusion, the action has shifted from the characters' isolation "under the jaw of the roof" of Mrs. Potter's house to their collective regrouping at the foot of Felix's bed, where Lenchen's baby is born. For the purposes of the conclusion, Salter had "suggested en elaborate *coda* complete with Coyote, the double hook, fear and glory, and a Latin tag from the Mass" (Flahiff, Afterword 122). Watson, however, decided to "add one detail": "His name is Felix" (Flahiff 122). The naming of the baby suggests that material has been appropriated from the previous environment—Felix's own name—to create the existing one. For the first time in the novel, most of the characters are brought together harmoniously in a conjoining of word and action: the naming of the baby. That gesture is characterized by benevolence and altruism, stimulated by Felix's reintegrative actions and by his successful remediation of their environment; these actions thus generate a new context, the counter-environment the characters come to occupy.

Notes

1   Marshall McLuhan to Jonathan Miller, 8 January 1965.

2   Marshall McLuhan to John Culkin, 17 September 1964.

3   It is, appropriately, the use of cliché as a form of communication in *The Double Hook* that several critics have commented upon. Barbara Godard, one such critic, has argued that the characters therein are sufficiently alienated so that "they only have fragments of experience left, fragments that have hardened into cliché" (150). Godard thus argues that Watson is endeavouring to "develop a universal language from a number of different modes of discourse, all of which, however, are ritual forms of speech...detached from their original emotional and spiritual meaning" (153). The result is that these fragments of expression are little understood by the characters that use them

4   Marshall McLuhan to Jonathan Miller, 8 January 1965.

5   During this period, as her supervisor, McLuhan proposed that she adopt the terminology about environments in her dissertation on Wyndham Lewis. She "assured McLuhan that she was giving his ideas much thought," although her integration of his terminology was very limited at best (Tiessen, "'I Want'" 385).

6   Of note are the "resonances," defined by McLuhan as a "break in the uniformity and continuity of space," which include gaps in dialogue, and which contribute to this form of communication (as qtd. in Cavell 180); they suggest the limits of a speech form as well as the means by which to communicate beyond those limits and beyond the disparate and disconnected lives led by the characters.

7 See Godard (156–57) as one exception and Deer (34) as another exception to this critical consensus.

8 See also Sheila Watson's conversation with Daphne Marlatt in the *Capilano Review*:

> DM: But the various characters have very special questions they need to ask each other.
> SW: Yes. And often don't ask each other.
> DM: Yes. Or often don't get the answer.
> SW: Don't get the answer they want. ("Interview" 358)

9 That is, some characters forcibly enjoin others into one form of action or another; see, as one example, Greta telling Ara and Heinrich to "go home" (32).

10 See Glenn Deer's article for his analysis of cause and effect (or the lack thereof) in the novel (33).

11 In the scene in which James whips Greta and Lenchen, James is described as lifting the whip, but "it" reaches "out towards her, tearing through the flowers of her housecoat" (54). As another example, Greta claims about the catalogue, "There are things one needs from time to time. There are things people think other people have no need of. There are things that other people think people need that no one needs at all" (27). Later William notes, "A man needs living things about him," to which Heinrich responds, "Perhaps no living man can do just that."

12 See Lewis Hyde, *The Gift*. Gregory Betts, on this subject, notes that "capitalist ideology, ironically, produces in the novel an economic dependency that enables and demands social commitment and participation but only after James overcomes fragmentation and isolation and the influence of his mother" ("Media, McLuhan" 268).

13 Richard Cavell, for example, expands upon McLuhan's ideas to suggest how he regarded space, and particularly acoustic space, as the medium of communication, which becomes a catalyst for change rather than as a simple modality or paradigm that entailed a sender-receiver dualism.

14 Instead, Theophil's violence also marks what Betts has identified as characteristic of "Western expansionist values": it is figured in characters, such as Theophil or James, that tend to "cling to their sense of themselves as detached individuals" (Betts, "Media, McLuhan" 257). The violence, however, is counterbalanced by "more humanistic, Western values" (257), as represented by those positive gestures made by Felix.

15 Theophil's name, which means love of God, is evidently ironic.

16 They are engaged in various forms of destruction, the very negation of communication or the denial of human contact—a pattern that, some critics observe, eventually shifts in the course of the novel "from isolation to community" (Morriss 55).

17 Yinglin Ji observes that "he kills his mother as a defiance and rejection of her all-pervasive tyranny that has held him in thrall; he blinds Kip, whose probing insight makes him restless and apprehensive; in a rage he also, before fleeing to the distant town, whips the girl Lenchen, who is pregnant with his baby, and his sister Greta, who subsequently commits fiery suicide" (349). James's action, which precipitate a sequence of events in the novel, is "involved in the matricide...lumped together into a circumstantial whole" (351).

18 Godard suggests that "he also speaks the language of catholicity, an earlier universal language...now reduced to cliché" (156).

19 McLuhan argued that the shift to the vernacular in the Catholic mass was a means of interrelating with the private life: he observed that the "Latin world... held print at bay" (*Gutenberg* 224).

20 As Godard notes, his name "suggests the 'felix culpa' or happy fall that led to Christ's presence in the world" and therefore he becomes "the vehicle for the Christian message of love and action that eventually animates the community" (156).

10

Sheila Watson and Marshall McLuhan's
Dialogue on Photography

Magic, Monstrosity, "the and Mechanization of Death"

Kristine Smitka

THIS CHAPTER ANALYZES the ways in which Canadian
modernist writer Sheila Watson customized the terminology of
her dissertation supervisor, Marshall McLuhan, through an investigation of their correspondence on the medium of photography.
Its goals are twofold: to build on an emerging conversation about
"Watson's little known media interests" (Tiessen, "'I Want'" 264),
and to apply these findings to her short story "The Rumble Seat."
In situating Watson in a media discourse for which she is little
known, this chapter demonstrates Watson's ongoing exploration
of the relationship between technology and power. It also situates
"The Rumble Seat" in the context of Watson's academic writing,
to render visible the ways in which this seemingly anomalous
short story is rather part of her ongoing interrogation of technological innovation and its effects on the human condition.

An investigation of the relationship between Watson and
McLuhan has been made possible by the confluence of two
initiatives: (1) the republication of Watson's dissertation
on Wyndham Lewis in 2003, prepared for the press by Paul
Tiessen and introduced by Fred Flahiff, and (2) the official
opening of the Watson archives in 2009 at St. Michael's College,
University of Toronto. Prior to this, Watson criticism has been
primarily dominated by close readings of *The Double Hook*
(A. Bowering; Grube) and a desire to situate her work in relation to expressionism and/or modernism more broadly (Grace;
Scobie). Her dialogue with McLuhan and her interests in media
have been, until recently, mostly buried in the archive.

Watson worked from 1956 to 1965 on her dissertation
Wyndham Lewis and Expressionism, under the supervision of
McLuhan (Flahiff, *Always* 176). Her dissertation work began in

Toronto, where she lived until the last four years of her doctoral program, which she spent in Edmonton with her husband, Wilfred Watson (246). This move, combined with McLuhan's propensity for travel, resulted in correspondence between supervisee and supervisor that engages with Lewis's work and poses questions about technology more broadly. Chronologically, this conversation occurred after Watson had already written the majority of her creative work: *Deep Hollow Creek, The Double Hook,*[1] "Rough Answer," "Brother Oedipus," and "The Black Farm." Nevertheless, her dialogue with McLuhan is an important resource for reading her academic articles in *White Pelican* and her later short story, "The Rumble Seat." While it would be easy to misread McLuhan and Watson's supervisor-supervisee relationship as one of influence, in fact, the relationship is far more complex. Watson was older than McLuhan when he accepted her as his student (Flahiff, *Always* 177), and their letters demonstrate a collegiality of mutual respect. They also prove Watson's ability to discuss, debate, and, at times, resist McLuhan's points of view. She brought to their conversation her own preoccupations, specifically the relationship between technology and power. With a focus on their dialogue on photography, I will show how Watson politicized McLuhan's term "extension" and wrote with a sense of aesthetic mortality.

McLuhan's friendship and professional relationship with Lewis made him uniquely qualified to supervise her work. Written as a pastiche of observations about Lewis's philosophy, Watson's dissertation outlines Lewis's impression of the "role of the artist in a world which is being transformed by technological magic" (Watson, *Wyndham Lewis* xvii). Lewis's view that both art and the machine are moving away from local settings towards international networks charts the political implications of these expansive systems that "provided unequal and unexpected extensions and amputations of power" (xviii). This relationship between mechanical reproduction and fascism became an ongoing fascination for Watson, visible in her letters, as well as her academic and creative work.

Two years before the publication of McLuhan's *Understanding Media* (1964), Watson wrote to McLuhan on July 20, 1962 and offered a lengthy analysis of her opinion on Gertrude Stein's technique. Through an analysis of form language, she then links Stein and photography. Of significance is the way in which Watson's voice rises to the surface of her analysis and reveals her position in relation to both Lewis and McLuhan. Watson closes the letter with an extended exposition on language, photography, typography, and gestalt aesthetics. Here she responds to a letter McLuhan wrote two days earlier, where he argues that the "photo is [a] substitute for language," because it "enables things to say themselves automatically" (McLuhan qtd. in Tiessen, "'I Want'" 271). Writers such as Stein accept "gesture and gestalt" as replacements for language (271). However, Lewis decried these writers as "enemies of language," for failing to analyze "the process in question" (271).

In response, Watson rejects McLuhan's assertion that the photograph is a "statement without syntax" (Shelia Watson fonds [SWF] box 21, file 352, folder 2); rather, she asserts that the photograph

> records light, obstruction to light, reflections of light, and relations of light and shade—all in relation to an accidental or arbitrary position of the chemically treated plate which determines the final image—moreover it sees things with one eye. People say themselves in their gestures in their responses, in their smile I suppose...and the camera eye is a rough net which records something of this saying—a photograph is a limitation not an extension of the person—though it may extend the person[']s power[—]a recording is not the extension of a voice or an instrument but a limitation of it—the more abstract and limited the more range or operation in time but the less intensity of being. At least this is Lewis[']s point. (H. Marshall McLuhan Papers [HMMP], vol. 40, box 28)

As Paul Tiessen has noted in ""I Want My Story Told": The Sheila Watson Archive, the Reader, and the Search for Voice," Watson's response shifts "attention from McLuhan's photograph-as-process to Lewis's camera-as-machine" (272). In so doing, she defines the photograph as a representational medium incapable of arresting nature in its totality, a slippery technique of chemical reactions where stereoscopic depth is lost in the monocular perspective of the camera. From this position, Watson rejects McLuhan's term "extension" and instead argues that the camera limits the "intensity of being" of the subject (HMMP, vol. 40, box 28). In so doing, she distinguishes "between extension and power" (Tiessen, "'I Want'" 272). Similar to Benjamin's work on the loss of the aura in works of mechanical reproduction, Watson argues that the photographic image circulates to extend the range of the subject, but the essence of the person is absent from the document.[2]

In this same letter, she also takes issue with McLuhan's use of the term "language": "You say Stein etc. were for Lewis enemies of language. The word 'language' is misleading in the context of Lewis' work" (HMMP, vol. 40, box 28). Watson clarifies that Lewis is drawing on the work of German philosopher and art collector Konrad Fiedler. In this context, Lewis employs the term "language" to designate "form language," which is constituted by the relationship between "significant form" and "inner necessity." Each medium or art has its own form language, its own tradition of enunciation, which arises from a combination of compulsion and technique. The result of this analysis was Fiedler's belief that "it is not possible to distinguish between form and content in any work of art'" (Lewis qtd. in Watson, *Wyndham Lewis* 42).

Watson's definition of inner necessity draws on Lewis's publication of Wassily Kandinsky's work in *Blast* and asserts that the artist is driven by three needs: (1) to express himself; (2) to express his epoch; and (3) to serve his art form or to express what is unique about art (37). It is "a progressive expression of the eternally objective within the temporarily subjective" (Kandinsky 120). Kandinsky's contribution to the term (as opposed to the way Fiedler employed it) moves from speaking of intuitive consciousness to an "insistence on the value of one's feelings as the only authentic impulse" (Lewis, *Blast* 125). The emotional compulsion to create is harnessed in the significant form of composition.[3] Watson, in keeping with Lewis, works from Fiedler's original definition of *sinnvollste gliederung* or "significant articulation." This definition is more concerned with the architectural possibilities of an art form.

Watson's quarrel with McLuhan's use of the term "language" hinges on her understanding of Lewis's use of the term "form language." As she writes in her thesis, "Gertrude Stein affirmed that her technique of beginning again and again developed only after she became interested in visual images and noticed that the motion picture film produces the illusion of life by joining to one picture another 'just that much different from the one before'" (Lewis qtd. in Watson, *Wyndham Lewis* 46). Stein's style draws from the mechanized quality of the photographic revolution, which culminated in the motion picture. For Lewis, Stein lacked the potential of the artist capable of transforming the city and was to be distrusted for her fidelity to the form language of photography. In drawing her influence from the minimal changes in each frame of film, Stein creates an "illusion of life" (46) that should be distrusted, because while the camera purports to reflect without alteration, it really deceives with its "built in perspective" and "its accidental or mechanical distortions" (HMMP, vol. 40, box 28). For both Lewis and Watson, Stein's style is not so much distasteful, as it is something to be distrusted, for its form of repetition illuminates aspects of the world without an attempt to transform it. Watson and Lewis alike offer versions of the argument put forth by Fiedler that "imitative pictures, technical drawings, photography, and death masks only fix and explain objects. Imitation always takes us back to the original, and reproduces something already present in our consciousness. Art, on the other hand, gives form to something that cannot be expressed otherwise" (Selz 4). While interested in the idea of an objective science of art, Fiedler maintains a focus on the individual artist over aesthetic traditions by separating art from the idea of natural beauty. In arresting nature, the camera fails to rise above the natural world, "for art is nothing else but a means by which man conquers reality" (Fiedler qtd. in Selz 5). Lewis's belief in the architectural capabilities of art mirrors this analysis. He urges artists not to ape god in a reiteration of the natural world but to sculpt a new future in the plastic arts.

Two years after their correspondence on photography, McLuhan published *Understanding Media: The Extensions of Man* (1964), which includes a chapter entitled "The Photograph: The Brothel-without-Walls." In this chapter he argues that "both the monocle and camera tend to turn people into things, and the photograph extends and multiplies the human image to the proportions of mass-produced merchandise" (170). Here McLuhan echoes Watson's observation that the camera sees its subject with "only one eye" (HMMP, vol. 40, box 28), yet he does not condemn the photograph. Rather, he argues that it signifies the transition from the age of Typographic Man to the age of Graphic Man. Turning to Joyce, as he so often does, McLuhan admits that the camera usurps the word, but posits that if "there is indeed a terrible nihilism in the photo and a substitution of shadows for substance, then we are surely not the worse for knowing it" (*Understanding* 193). Rather, photography restores the world of gesture that was destroyed with the invention of the written word (193), leading to the motion picture, which frees man from the semantic universe and reunites the body and orality. Both Freud and Jung, McLuhan argues, were able to build on the gestalt, or language of gestures, captured in the photo to build a better understanding of the collective. In shifting from the temporality of gestures towards a sempiternal theory of movement, these thinkers moved away from the isolated aspect of each photo and towards theories pertaining to archetypal gestures.

In his later work *From Cliché to Archetype* (1970), which McLuhan co-authored with Watson's husband Wilfred Watson, McLuhan and Wilfred Watson argue that the repetition and development of archetypal images leads to their inevitable state of redundancy; "the most masterful images, when complete, are tossed aside and the process begins anew" (20). Thus, the fall of language into cliché is not a cause for concern, but rather the impetus to create new modes of expression. The fact that the "human city is a waste land of abandoned images" (20) is nothing more than the perpetual call for artistic action. McLuhan saw the photograph as the tool for emancipation from the typographic environment because it marked a return to embodied voice. Alongside this return was a heightened awareness, a self-reflective stance, become newly possible through human ingenuity.

Watson resists McLuhan's reading; for her, the form language of photography does not empower the artist to shape his or her subject. This tension is visible in the contrast between her dissertation chapter title, "The Dead Hand of the Nineteenth-Century Robot: The Camera Eye" (97) and the title of McLuhan's chapter "The Photograph: The Brothel-without-Walls" (*Understanding Media* 169). Her title is "apocalyptic, sober, cryptic; his, playful, teasing, audacious" (Tiessen, "'I Want'" 271). Tiessen argues that in the following years, Watson started "drawing away" from McLuhan, believing that they were "operating within different registers, drawing on different frames of thought" (274). To clarify, while Watson drew away from McLuhan's assertions regarding the role of photography, she continued to engage with the theorists and themes on which she and McLuhan were coming to disagree. In fact, she was so deeply invested in this conversation that almost a decade later she published an academic article on the subject.

In "Michael Ondaatje: The Mechanization of Death" (1972) Watson continues her thinking on developments in the photographic process, expanding on the relationship between power and mechanization. She focuses on the horror of human ingenuity, while responding to Ondaatje's long poem *The Collected Works of Billy the Kid* (1970). It begins, "Michael Ondaatje was born in 1943. Two years before that Sigfried Giedion published *Space, Time and Architecture, the Growth of a New Tradition*" (158). While Ondaatje's text references open-range photographer L.A. Huffman and uses Eadweard Muybridge's photography in its cover design, Watson turns to Giedion as a key figure for analyzing Ondaatje's work. She further emphasizes this point in quoting Giedion in the subtitle for her article: "The Mechanization of Death." Although Watson's essay uses Ondaatje's engagement with photography as the centre from which to analyze the monstrosity of efficiency, Ondaatje is really a springboard for her to talk about the work of Giedion. In addition to these two writers, Watson introduces the writings of Wyndham Lewis, Upton Sinclair, and Kurt Vonnegut.

Watson connects these writers through their mutual interest in how mechanization has penetrated man and the abominations that this has made possible. In so doing, she links the assembly line of *The Jungle* with the banality of evil that ran the efficient trains of the Holocaust. Ondaatje's method, she writes, "is paratactic and explosive. He does not speak of the slaughterhouse. However, the centre of which the trains, the telegraph, and the refrigerated cars are extensions makes itself felt in phrase after phrase" (63). Here, Watson customizes McLuhan's term "extensions" to signify an extension of power. In listing the telegraph after the (death) trains, Watson argues that communications technology spread fascist ideology and made the Holocaust possible. Of course, it was not the telegraph, but modern communication technology, such as film, radio, and photography, that the Nazi state employed to distribute its propaganda. Both transportation and communication technology extend the horror that is Hitler. Aligning her thinking with Lewis's, she highlights the ways in which technology amplifies inequalities of power and extends those inequalities over increasing territory.

In Ondaatje's work, Watson sees a similar concern with mechanization (increasing from *The Dainty Monsters* and *The Man with Seven Toes* to *The Collected Works of Billy the Kid*), as technology comes to haunt every aspect of organic life. To characterize this transition, Watson borrows Giedion's phrase "'the mechanization of death,'" which Watson defines as "death in its 'biological nakedness'...'the sudden, incalculable destruction of organic creatures'" (61). Watson turns to Giedion, just as McLuhan had a decade earlier in *The Gutenberg Galaxy* (1962),[4] for an explanation of the technological developments that opened the doors for this preoccupation with efficiency. In *Space, Time and Architecture* (1941) Giedion analyzes the rupture of thought and feeling. In *Mechanization Takes Command: A Contribution to Anonymous History* (1948) he expands on his previous work, positing mechanization as the cause of this rupture. In a sweeping historical synopsis, Giedion claims that the rise of rationalism resulted in a marginalization of feelings through an investment in productivity and a belief in the "perfectibility of man" (*Mechanization* 30). The nineteenth century (c. 1860) saw the culmination of this desire in its efforts to capture movement in graphic form, to literally learn "to feel the pulse of nature" (17). For Giedion, the nineteenth century's desire to perfect the human form is best exemplified by the work of Étienne-Jules Marey, inventor of the sphygmograph, which rendered visible the human pulse. Marey's photography (he is perhaps most famous for his invention of the photogun) captured what escapes the human eye. His experiments harnessed animals and sought to chart the movement of a wing or the gait of a leg. These photos traced trajectories; the specters of these movements were rendered visible in the "luminous trails" (28) they left behind. Marey notes that these stereoscopic images "might be called the language of the phenomena themselves" (20). For Marey, his photos had "an impressiveness that needs no further explanation" (22), rendering linguistic representation obsolete. Note here the similarity to McLuhan's assertion that the photograph is "a statement without syntax" (SWF, box 21, file 352, folder 2). For Marey, the language that emerges from the movement of the organism replaces the need for verbal communication. He rendered visible an honesty of movement, and his images are haunting for reading the body back to the viewer, parsing everyday activities to the point of defamiliarization.[5]

While both Ondaatje and Giedion are interested in mechanization (in *Billy the Kid* and *Mechanization Takes Command* both authors show particular attention to the innovations of the 1860s through to the 1890s), the main point of connection between these two thinkers is their interest in photography. It is Giedion's work on Marey and Muybridge that strikes Watson as particularly relevant to her analysis of Ondaatje: both Marey and Muybridge were interested in how the technology of photography could capture organic processes in the name of scientific investigation. Muybridge used a series of cameras, where as Marey crystallized successive phases of movement on a single film, but both photographers' experiments render visible nuances of movement. In so doing, they created the opportunity for quantitative measurements of fluid processes. Motion can be parsed into a series of steps and analyzed in terms of a measurable cadence, for example, how many times a bird may flap its wings over a demarcated space. Granted, the work of Marey may have translated movement to the world, but the language of organisms began to change with the "malady" (58) of technology. Documenting movement opened the possibility of perfecting these actions.

While Marey's experiments helped expose the patterns of the human form, Giedeon argues that the body is actually ill-suited to automation. Isolating the hand as the symbolic limb, he explains that organic forms repeat movements with variability, yet automation strives to make movement consistent. The industrial revolution strove towards standardization and interchangeability: the mechanization of movement aims to transform the "pushing, pulling, pressing of the hand into continuous rotation" (47). The nuances of the fist—sewing the handicraft, kneading the bread, and working the soil—have been replaced by the synchronous efficiency of the assembly line. It is through this tension between the wheel and the hand that Watson links Giedion to Ondaatje.

Ondaatje's anthropomorphic descriptions fascinate Watson: the way Billy's hand churns "within itself, each finger circling alternately like a train wheel" (Ondaatje qtd. in Watson, "Michael" 57). She writes, "Ondaatje's monsters are flesh and like all flesh are grass but they are also machines. They fly with the precision of watches and arch their feet like compasses" (59). In Ondaatje, the blend of the biological and the technological blurs the boundaries between the human and the industrial. Whereas Giedion argues that the hand will never roll like a wheel and therefore must be replaced by a machine, Ondaatje describes a hybridized body that echoes McLuhan's observation that technologies are "extensions of man."

While Watson describes Ondaatje's characters as "monsters" (59), Ondaatje's text is far more invested in ambiguity. Watson's preoccupation is with the use of photography in scientific investigations, but Ondaatje's project speaks back to these experiments and reveals the photograph as a tricky medium. *The Collected Works of Billy the Kid* opens, "I send you a picture of Billy made with the Perry shutter as quick as it can be worked" (5). These words sit under a "frame enframing nothing," as Smaro Kamboureli has called it (185), four black lines arranged in a square, not unlike a Polaroid yet to be developed. This photograph is attributed to open-range photographer L.A. Huffman, who applied his camera's shutter "*as quick as it could be worked*" to capture the elusive outlaw (Ondaatje 5). Later in the letter, he conjectures, "*I will send you proofs some time*," aligning photography with evidence and linking the single print taken during the printmaking process with the photograph as averment (5). The absent photograph documents Billy's equivocal nature, the impossibility of accurately depicting his character. Later in the text, Billy states, "I remember, when they took the picture of me there was a white block down the fountain road where somebody had come out of a building and got off the porch onto his horse and ridden away while I was waiting standing still for the acid in the camera to dry firm" (68). This direct reference to photographic emulsion reiterates photography's inability to document moving subjects. In this description we can also hear the echo of Watson's belief that the photograph is like a net, unable to ensnare the totality of its subject. Despite the overlaps in the analysis of these two thinkers, there are still important differences. Ondaatje's long poem offers readers an alternative interpretive framework through which to engage with photography. In showing the slippery nature of the medium, he resists the assumption that photographs hold any sort of truth status. For Ondaatje, the problem is not the photographic process, but rather the ways in which photographs are read as documents. His long poem finds a playful relationship to photography and encourages readers to see the photo as art, not science.

Watson, however, remains apprehensive, and the key to this apprehension is the way in which photography claims to see the world more clearly than the human eye. At the same time that Huffman was taking photos "*from the saddle*" (5), Muybridge was threading twenty-four cameras to trip wires, capturing the horse's gallop and settling the debate as to whether all four hooves are ever concurrently suspended (his photos prove that there is a moment mid-stride where all four limbs tuck upward).[6] His experiment proved the photographic process' ability to remedy a flaw in human perception by isolating movement into specific moments more efficiently than the naked eye. This both made the world alien from the ways in which we experience it and opened the door for an obsession with precision and efficiency.

Watson's investigation of photography preoccupied her for decades and eventually moved beyond her engagement with Lewis and McLuhan. For Watson, the function of art is not to explain the world but to encourage readers to embrace the mystic and myth-ical, to accept the world of shadows. Beyond being an aesthetic imperative, it is an ethical one. The net-like nature of photog-raphy allows the viewer to miss the "intensity of being" of the subject (HMMP, vol. 40, box 28). In this omission is the debut of the slippery slope that ends in the view that man is a machine, a dispensable object. This objectification of human gestures results in a lack of regard for the human spirit, which then enables the belief that human life is disposable. While her academic writing and correspondence demonstrates this consistent preoccupation, her creative work is notably devoid of photography and film, that is, until we get to her anomalous work, "The Rumble Seat" (1974).

The last story in Watson's mythic cycle, "The Rumble Seat" was written considerably later than the first three stories. Although "Brother Oedipus" (1954), "The Black Farm" (1956), and "Antigone" (1959), were published in the 1950s, "The Rumble Seat" was not published until the special Sheila Watson issue of the journal *Open Letter* in 1974. Read in the context of the mythic cycle, the story is a strange digression into foreign terri-tory, yet read in the context of Watson's larger oeuvre, the story is the culmination of Watson's theorization of technology.

In "The Rumble Seat" the uncle and the unnamed narrator sit in their living room, watching their television set as Oedipus is interviewed as a guest on *The Pierre Berton Show*. The story moves between the internal action of the talk show and the meta-commentary of the uncle, who hurls vitriolic frustration at the dialogue unfolding on screen. On set, there is something insidious about the technological apparatus that films the interview as "the cameras circle" (57) host and guest. The crooks of "mechanical arms" move the cameras "like vultures" (57) around their subjects; circumscribing their prey they bring "Pierre's face into full focus... [then pan] to include Oedipus" (65). In this description, the techno-logical apparatus has agency: it is the camera that frames its subject, acting devoid of human intervention. As "Pierre's deceptively small image dilate[s]" (57) on screen, the camera lens is linked with ocular expansion. Meanwhile, the viewer maintains a position of passive observance, noting that he must wait for the camera to adjust the focus on his behalf (60). In this world, the camera has supplanted the pupil. As the descriptions of the biological and the mechanical merge, Watson posits technology as an insidious inven-tion that has gained control over the very hands that made it.

Divisions between the biological and the mechanical begin to disintegrate: "Oedipus's voice had become a mere rumble. Then it rose suddenly as if some mechanism had adjusted efficiently" (59). The body is mechanized, just as the camera is anthropomor-phized. Dual hybridization confuses the distinction between the organic and the mechanical: the body as machine, machine as body. Just as Ondaatje's mechanized bodies fascinates Watson, the way the fingers of Billy's hand circle "like a train wheel" (Ondaatje qtd. in Watson, "Michael" 57), the characters on the set of *The Pierre Berton Show* are described as mechanized men. Their voices are disembodied, as their enunciations enter the program from offstage. As the camera's gaze pans away from the speaker, it severs voice from body (Watson, "Rumble" 64). At home, the viewer is subjected to the camera's line of sight, unable to witness an embodied voice. In contradistinction to McLuhan's argument that Graphic Man reunites the body and orality, Watson describes "bodiless voice[s]" (59) and a fractured graphic subject.

Watching these fractured subjects from his living room, the uncle rants at Oedipus and Pierre: "must we...live by the clock after the clock-maker has been sacked? Are we a mechanical sequence, an organized seriality? Has not Bergson proved beyond a doubt that we are snaky and submarine?" (63). Engaging with the concept of simultaneity expounded by Bergson in *Time and Free Will*, the uncle laments that the talk show progresses as if ignorant of modernist discourse. In spatialized time, moments are arrested into the artificial constructions of months, days, and minutes. Bergson proposes that although this notion of time as a structured constant is necessary for the organization of our daily lives, it is in opposition to pure time, which is time immaterial. Pure time "forms both the past and the present states into an organic whole, as happens when we recall the notes of a tune, melting, so to speak, into one another" (Bergson 60).

The uncle's question, are "we a mechanical sequence, an organized seriality?", could easily apply to Muybridge's photographic investigations. Caught in the tension between the mechanical and the biological, the uncle struggles with the changing world, with the unstable foundations of his universe, uttering, "we float, we flood, we flounder. Finally we are redundant" (Watson, "Rumble" 63). The uncle lives in a world post-Muybridge, whose photos were the debut of the slippery slope that ends in the view that man is a machine, a dispensable object. In this context, redundancy is the product of the mechanical lens, which allows for new ways of seeing. Watson argues that the function of art is not to explain the world, as Muybridge did, but to encourage readers to embrace the mystic and mythical, to accept the world of shadows. However, in the uncle's dystopic landscape, the oppression of technological development looms in the living room. Where is the space for the lithe movement of consciousness in the sterile environment of "uncompromising vertical" (63) blinds? The uncle is trapped; imprisoned by the seemingly innocuous décor, he remains seduced by "the gluey surface which solicit[s]...his attention (61–62).

This story is Watson's most biting condemnation of new technology and marks the culmination of decades of reflection on the ways in which photographs extend power and limit the body. As Watson's move out of her modernist milieu and into her contemporary moment, it broadens her theorization of technology with the introduction of film and television. This transition is not as random as it may first appear. Remember that Muybridge's invention of the zoopraxiscope is a precursor to film. At the time of its unveiling, the *Illustrated London News* described it as "a magic lantern run mad" (Wood 163). Its fear-inducing images were hauntingly familiar in their "illusion of life."[7] "The Rumble Seat" conjectures that the logical extension of photography's chemical reactions is a film camera that moves divorced from the cameraman. Technology has become so efficient that there is no longer a need for the artist. Just as the camera supplants the pupil, the artist is rendered redundant in a world of pure mechanization.

Notes

1   Both of these novels are published after this date, but their composition occurs before.

2   In reaction to the Nazi state, Benjamin linked mass communication technologies to social domination and the rise of fascism in Western Europe.

3   Simultaneously, the term "significant form" was popularized by Clive Bell in *Art* (1913), where he defined the relationship between lines and colour in visual art. Bell's definition solidified the role of the critic as important for educating the audience on the significance of formal composition. His assertion usurped the power of the spectator and championed the formally educated as the lone few capable of elucidating the significance of composition. In *Men Without Art*, Lewis discusses Bell's theory as an act of "domination" (Watson, *Wyndham Lewis* 51). Lewis's call for a vortex in *The Caliph's Design*—subtitled, *Architects, Where Is Your Vortex ?*—was the desire to reunite the "great Trinity of the plastic arts: Sculpture, Painting, and Architecture" (59), or what Lewis suggested was a fusion of the painter and the engineer. For Lewis, the cubists were halfway there: they had recognized the architecturally creative possibilities of their medium, but they had undercut these possibilities in "a flagrant exhibition of second-rate wit and in an exasperated interest in media within the studio itself" (59). The cubists failed to move out of the studio and into the city, which Lewis saw as the true manifestation of the human spirit. In focusing on self-promotion, the cubists privileged the interpretive over the creative imagination and failed to realize the true possibilities of their new style. Watson accuses Lewis of falling victim to a similar impulse, struggling to straddle the creative and interpretive modes. In Lewis's

analysis, the articulation of the formal principles of the movement jeopardizes the vitality of the form by ossifying it in the realm of the critic. Unlike Bell, who saw significant form as the critic's privilege, Lewis argued that the artist was stunted by the negative capabilities of analysis.

4   McLuhan was also deeply impacted by Giedion's thinking. Richard Cavell argues in *McLuhan in Space: A Cultural Geography* that McLuhan's thinking on the relationship between time and space fluctuated over his career. In 1949, McLuhan reviewed Sigfried Giedion's book *Mechanization Takes Command: A Contribution to Anonymous History*, in which Giedion "argues that the unifying element in the history of mechanization is the attempt to capture movement" (Cavell, *McLuhan in Space* 38). At this time, McLuhan was interested in the interfusion of space and time in the process of mechanization. By 1953, he became interested in the work of Harold Innis, which proposes that space and time are binaries that must be brought into balance in order to achieve a stable society. Only one year after assuming "a position characterizing space and time as oppositional (as Lewis and Innis had done), McLuhan reconfigured these notions dynamically and relationally," coining the term "spacetime" (Cavell, *McLuhan in Space* 35).

5   Giedeon contextualizes Marey's experiments inside a milieu that includes the photographic experiments of Muybridge; the paintings of Marcel Duchamp; the paintings of Wassily Kandinsky; and the philosophy of Bergson. In placing Marey's photos in this context, Giedion presents a unified representation of a movement that spanned the disciplines. Giedion's analysis employs an interdisciplinary approach, where he works to show the cross pollination between scientific experiment, political thought, and artistic practice. To this end, he implores his readers to consider the social implications of innovation and shows the way mechanization has affected different aspects of their world: the body, the soil, the professions, and the home.

6   Leland Stanford, the American industrialist, asked Muybridge to use his knowledge of photography to help him resolve a bet (Wood 161).

7   As discussed earlier, this is how Lewis described the writing of Gertrude Stein (Lewis qtd. in Watson, *Wyndham Lewis* 46).

PROLEPSIS

11

Marshall McLuhan as Vanishing Mediator

Darren Wershler

"Come into my parlor," said the computer to the specialist.
—Marshall McLuhan and Harley Parker, *Through the Vanishing Point*

"How liberating to be told your field is dying. You can
work in the gloaming, away from the glare. You are the
ghoul of academia."
—Mark Sample, channeling Don DeLillo on Twitter

I WOULDN'T BE THE FIRST to observe that there are
a great many different Marshall McLuhans in circulation at the
moment—perhaps even too many, by some influential accounts,
such as John Durham Peters's "McLuhan's Grammatical Theology."
Nor would it be much help to repeat, as so many others have,
that McLuhan's approach is inherently interdisciplinary (Peters
228), and that the scholars that are interested in it study his work
in interdisciplinary settings. What I'm curious about is why that
traffic rarely circulates back inside the academic fields in which
one might expect to find it—namely, the discipline in which
McLuhan was trained (English literary studies) and the one he
helped to found (communication studies), especially given the
professed interest that both disciplines have in interdisciplinarity. Instead of creating yet another mutant reading of McLuhan
and sending it shambling off into interdisciplinary space, I'd
like to spend some time considering the reasons for the qualified interest in McLuhan's work in Communications and English
departments. In the terms of McLuhan's own Laws of Media, I'm

also interested in the implications that the return of his previously obsolesced body of work might have for both fields, but for English departments in particular. The questions this chapter raises are as follows: What would it mean to "do media theory" with the literary text as the object of study? What do we call this work when it takes place in an English department, especially if there are people elsewhere on campus doing similar things? And what would it mean to pursue these questions "in McLuhan's name"?

These questions raise issues that range from the pragmatic to the bureaucratic, but I think that they're all important. It's one thing to get on with the business of research, but doing so within the context of any institution requires significant amounts of civility, collegiality, and respect, if we want the institution to continue to function. This requires the willingness to consider why there are so many conflicting accounts of "McLuhan" in contemporary discourse. What we might perceive as conflicts or distortions in the reception of his work are, as Jerry Aline Flieger puts it, "a sign of the world's inconsistency, of the unthinkable coexistence of perspectives that are irreconcilable with our own" (80). What's necessary at this juncture is to allow our questions about McLuhan's place in contemporary literary studies to be inflected (perhaps even infected) by those other perspectives, in order to recognize that the true answer will be probably not be what we desire, but an inverted version of it, or what McLuhan might deem a "flip" into something else. As Flieger notes, taking such a risk in our perceptions is an opportunity to move away from self-delusion "into a clear-sighted recognition of the limitations of our field" (80). For literary professors interested in media, the truth of an interest in McLuhan is that despite the fact that McLuhan himself worked inside English departments, his work pointed him relentlessly outside of them, and that, in response, the discipline, including his home department, largely ostracized him. The main reason for this is that McLuhan's constant exhortation to focus on the study of media themselves rather than their content poses a direct challenge to the basic activity of literary scholars for at least the last century:

the generation of interpretations of content. Thinking about books and other aesthetic objects in McLuhan's wake means moving away from the interpretive tradition toward considerations of the location of these objects in culture: their materiality and history; the political economy of their production, circulation, and reception; and the way that cultural policy and other networks of power position them, and us in relation to them. However, there are entire fields of scholars that already do these things—communication studies, media studies, film studies, cultural studies—and have been doing so for most of the last century. Many of these fields have historical roots in English departments, but most now make their homes in more-or-less independent departments, programs, or research centres. So the question for English scholars that are interested in such a move, have the support of their home institutions (and make no mistake, there are many that are actively hostile to such an idea), and are willing to reimagine their relationship to their primary object of study, is how to do so without reinventing the wheel.

For individuals, the only problem is diligence. Part of the answer lies in a willingness to begin a deep engagement with the scholarship that has been generated in these fields *after* McLuhan, and in response to him, because there's a lot of it. On the level of departments and institutions, the situation is more complex. Something like Alan Liu's notion of a "critical digital humanities" presents a way forward that, while perhaps unrecognizable to many conservative English scholars, is nevertheless particular to the way that people trained in literary studies think about media, rather than the way that communication studies approaches it. The disciplinary history of digital humanities is still being written, and, though its relative beginnings lie elsewhere than in McLuhan's work, it still takes him into account. But as Liu points out, if digital humanities is going to make a valuable contribution to the discussion of global-cultural issues, it needs to create "a methodological infrastructure in which culturally aware technology complements technologically aware cultural criticism" ("Where Is Cultural Criticism" n. pag.). This will require opening up ongoing and sometimes difficult conversations with scholars in traditional fields like English. McLuhan, for all his shortcomings—perhaps even because of them—might be a useful catalyst for such an encounter.

Personal Stakes

DARREN **Wershler**

I have a personal stake in these questions because of my own disciplinary formation. McLuhan's writing was largely absent from the discourse of literary studies in Canada at least for the last two decades—since I entered the field as an undergraduate in 1984. Over that period, in a program that was known for its intense focus on innovative theoretical approaches, the only time that I remember McLuhan's work ever being invoked by a professor or another student was in the context of Raymond Williams's critique of McLuhan.[1] After training in English literary studies during the late 1980s and early 1990s, I left the university to work as a consultant, writer (nonfiction and poetry), and editor, in all cases specializing in the emerging world of digital publishing. When I returned to the university, because of my professional experience, instead of going back into an English department, I went to work in several different communication studies departments, first as contract faculty, then as tenure-track. I forfeited my tenure in communication studies to take a job for the first time in an English department, and was almost immediately assigned a research chair in interdisciplinary work on media and contemporary literature. When I worked in communication studies, I spent a lot of time advocating for the importance of poetics for the study of media and communication. In English, I've spent a great deal of time talking about the necessity of focusing on material media, circulation, and cultural policy as part of the study of literature. As far as I can tell from studying and working in both English and communications departments in Canada over the last two and a half decades, each discipline has a McLuhan-sized blind spot.

Two Sides of McLuhan

In communication studies, McLuhan's early work (*The Mechanical Bride* to *Understanding Media*) is taken more seriously and receives more attention than at any other point in the discipline's history. However, with a few notable exceptions,[2] communications scholars largely abjure the poetic McLuhan, choosing to emphasize his focus on the importance of material media form. McLuhan's small body of literary criticism (most of which is collected in *The Interior Landscape*) and his interest in the modernist avant-gardes redeems him for literary scholars in some way, but this work isn't taught, and isn't what interests people when they think of McLuhan. When literary studies considers McLuhan (at all), it is the ludic, literary McLuhan it favours—this is the "McLuhan as avant-garde poet" position, best exemplified by Donald Theall's work. The present collection, in conjunction with special sections such as the Readers' Forum on "The Age of McLuhan, 100 Years On" in *ESC: English in Canada*, suggests that there is some degree of interest in the topic from literary scholars, if only on momentous occasions. Certainly Richard Cavell, one of Canada's preeminent contemporary McLuhan scholars, is housed in an English department, but as far as I can tell, the majority of researchers interested in McLuhan who are not in communication studies are in film studies, humanities and social sciences, or interdisciplinary programs (and this should come as no surprise, given the interdisciplinary nature of McLuhan's work). But Marco Adria and Catherine Adams conclude their Introduction to the *ESC* feature by noting the "nuanced irony" of dubbing the last century "the Age of McLuhan": "McLuhan has been with us a century, and we are still exploring the depth of his ideas and their potential meanings" (3–4). In other words, McLuhan's legacy in literary studies is the continual posing of the question of what, exactly, that legacy might be, without much in the way of curricular impact. The real irony is that this proliferation of interpretations and opinions is business as usual for the sort of hermeneutics that McLuhan eschewed with his exhortation to focus on medium rather than content.

When McLuhan's emphasis on material media form over content is ignored, it is usually because of the scandal such an approach presents for literary studies' ongoing vested interest in the production of readings and interpretations. Instead, the invocation of McLuhan outside of communication studies is frequently in the service of a call for the study of media without an accompanying study of communication. This happens for professional reasons having to do with institutional histories and institutional formations, and I'm not sure that it's enough.

Vanishing Mediator

In other words, English and communication studies each ignore a different aspect of McLuhan's work, focusing on the parts of his legacy that are the most familiar, rather than the parts that would be most challenging, and therefore most useful to them.

The problem that concerns me here is academic in the most literal sense, because it deals with the ways that knowledge is organized and policed in a university setting. It's a cliché of contemporary academic life that our introductions often begin with a phrase like, "I'm housed in the [X] department, but my research is really about [Y]." For many scholars, the sort of work we produce now has more to do with how able we are to add to the conversation on a given topic in a meaningful way than with what we studied in graduate school, what our transcripts and diplomas say we're qualified to do, or what we were initially hired to teach. While this sort of freedom can be a boon for scholars yearning to make a positive contribution to areas that excite them, it also presents some genuine difficulties. In "Genealogical Notes on 'The Field,'" John Durham Peters observes that "We can no longer assume a homogeneous audience that will understand how we frame questions; many scholars produce communication research without even being aware that they're participating in a larger field" (134). Because we don't read deeply in each others' fields (and that's the charitable take on the subject), we often miss entire bodies of research on subjects that seem fresh to us. My first conference paper as a communication studies scholar was on the way that McLuhan scholars have taken McLuhan's pronouncements on symbolism, Mallarmé, and the newspaper at face value and embedded them without apparently ever bothering to look at what Mallarmé actually wrote on the subject (TL; DNR: it flies in the face of what McLuhan claims) (Wershler "News"). Now that I'm back in an English department after spending eight years in communication studies, I'm curious about how the emergent interest among literary scholars in topics such as McLuhan, cultural policy, and material media studies will manifest itself in disciplinary terms, given that communication studies has had well-developed literatures on them for most of a century. Figuring out a way forward involves identifying and addressing such exclusions and omissions, and, unfortunately, dealing with the inevitable administrative headaches and departmental turf wars that will follow. As Peters notes, "The current arrangement of knowledge fits no grand philosophy of history, but it clearly is shaped by pressures from state, market, society, and professional fashion; this is particularly true for communication studies/research" ("Genealogical" 133). In order to make sense of what a renewed interest in McLuhan's work among literary scholars might mean, it's time to begin to inventory these pressures.

I've recently come to think of McLuhan as a "vanishing mediator." In Fredric Jameson's terms, this is "some central mediatory figure or institution which can account for the passage from one temporal and historical state to another one" ("Vanishing" 75). Once the presence of a vanishing mediator has brokered some sort of institutional reorganization, "it has no further reason for being and disappears from the historical scene. It is thus in the strictest sense of the word a catalytic agent which permits an exchange of energies between two otherwise mutually exclusive terms" (78). Of course, things rarely vanish completely; there is usually some sort of residue. Moreover, that residue is often the basis for the emergence of the New, in the form of a dialectical return of something that had previously vanished. As is often the case, the reality of such a return can be much less pleasant than the nostalgic memory of it. The question is, then, after it had helped to establish communication studies in Canada, did McLuhan's work ever actually vanish from the discourse of the discipline in any measurable way? What did his residual presence look like? Has there been a return, and, if so, how does the revived McLuhan differ from the first iteration?

Obsolescence and Retrieval (Communication Studies)

The answer to the first of these questions is an unqualified yes. McLuhan's production and reputation had both fallen off during the 1970s, the last decade of his life. Posthumously published works began to appear at the end of the 1980s, such as *Laws of Media* and a selected volume of letters. But the decline of interest in McLuhan's work within communication studies was one of the running themes of the 1989 special issue of the *Canadian Journal of Communication (CJC)* commemorating the twenty-fifth anniversary of the publication of *Understanding Media*. In his introductory remarks to the issue, guest editor and major McLuhan scholar Donald Theall wrote the following:

> The intervening period [between the *CJC*'s first McLuhan issue in 1969 and the 1989 issue Theall was editing], though, has seen McLuhan's reputation come under increasing criticism. While he probably contributed as much as any single person to making the public aware of communication as an issue of major importance, those professionally interested in communication research today do not as a rule take his work seriously. ("Guest" vii)

In the issue's lead article, Associate Editor Liss Jeffrey, who would shortly become the founding director of the McLuhan Global Research Network, echoes this sentiment: "McLuhan's influence persists in general cultural terms and his contribution is recognized in the work of a minority of serious communications scholars; yet simultaneously his academic reputation is in partial eclipse" (Jeffrey 4). In the issue's second article, Paul Heyer, a major Innis scholar, also uses the metaphor of "eclipse" to describe McLuhan's work, and goes on to state flatly that during the 1970s and early 1980s, McLuhan's work was "almost completely ignored" ("Probing" 31). Philip Marchand, McLuhan's biographer, describes how in McLuhan's last years, his reputation "continued to fade" ("Some Comments" 72). Such sentiments echo throughout later issues of the *CJC* as well; Paul Jones, for example, begins an article in 1998 with the sentence, "The immediate intellectual influence of the projects of Raymond Williams and Marshall McLuhan has long passed but their major works remain in print and each still warrants inclusion in textbooks of 'media theory'" (423).

Hot on the heels of the journal of record for Canadian communication scholars declaring that McLuhan's work was in decline, though, in the late 1980s and early 1990s, McLuhan's work was beginning to re-emerge in print, and to once again take a place on the stage of popular culture, in the context of the beginning of popular interest in networked home computing and the Internet. In 1989, McLuhan's pop collaborations with Jerome Agel and Quentin Fiore, *The Medium is the Massage* and *War and Peace in the Global Village*, both came back into print, and were reprinted again by *Wired* magazine's imprint HardWired, and yet again by Gingko Press in 2001. In the same year, MIT Press published Philip Marchand's biography of McLuhan; a new edition of *Understanding Media* followed in 1994. *Wired* (in)famously declared McLuhan its patron saint in the magazine's first issue in March/April 1993, and its editors continued to name-check "Saint Marshall" over the next few years (Wolf). This uptick of interest in McLuhan in west coast tech circles was prevalent enough that by 1995, Richard Barbrook and Andy Cameron noted it in *Mute* as a central feature of the stew of "right-wing neo-liberalism, counter-culture radicalism and tech-nological determinism" that they dubbed "The Californian Ideology." In the Introduction to their 2005 edited volume *The Legacy of McLuhan*, Lance Strate and Edward Wachtel provide a concise review of the entire literature around McLuhan's thinking, including the collections of McLuhan's minor works, reappraisals, new critical editions, and works by scholars with an interest in McLuhan that appeared in the later 1990s and early 2000s, especially among those working in digital media studies (8–11). From their perspective, five years into the new millennium, "The turn of the century has been accompanied by a kind of McLuhan revival or renaissance" (12). Since Strate and Wachtel's collection, we could add to their excellent literature review, at the very least, significant texts on McLuhan and his work by Coupland, Lamberti, Marchessault, Moss and Morra, Schnapp, and Watson and Blondheim. In addition, McLuhan's writing has been a constant touchstone for the German "Materialities of Communication" theorists,[3] whose work constitutes a major branch of contemporary media and communication theory.[4]

Despite this revival in popular culture and media studies at large, since the 1989 *CJC* special issue, McLuhan's ongoing presence in the discourse of Canadian communication studies itself could best be described as "residual" in the sense that Raymond Williams[5] and Charles Acland[6] use the term—a far from dominant but nevertheless stubbornly persistent element of the past that continues to play an active role in contemporary social processes (Williams 122). One of the more common recent approaches to the residual, particularly as enshrined in the subdisciplines of media archaeology and the study of imaginary media, is to treat it as having some sort of oppositional potential, because it not only provides alternatives to hegemonic discourse, but suggests that there always were other alternatives, even when it seems like there are none.[7] Acland, however, suggests that it's not that simple. An encounter with the residual should be the occasion to pose a variety of questions about it: "How do some things...become the background for the introduction of other forms? In what manner do the products of technological change reappear as environmental problems, as the 'new' elsewhere...? What are the qualities of our everyday engagement with the half-life of media forms and practices and with the formerly state of the art?" (Acland, Introduction xx). What characterizes the treatment of McLuhan's work in Canadian communication studies since 1989 is an ongoing interest in qualifying the significance of his thinking for the discipline, particularly in relation to that of Harold Innis.

Another special issue of the *CJC, Tracing Innis and McLuhan*, appeared in 2012, a year after the centenary of McLuhan's birth. This time, according to William Buxton, one of the issue's editors and, along with his colleague and frequent collaborator Paul Heyer, one of the leading authorities on Innis, part of the impetus was to "decouple" Innis and McLuhan, producing a "de-McLuhanized Innis" who is distinct from "the McLuhanist-centred Toronto School" (Buxton 577). Here, Buxton is reacting to a trend in the discipline's discourse that extends back to the early 1980s, in which a series of texts have linked McLuhan and Innis closely.[8] There are good reasons for this pairing. Supplementing McLuhan's media theory with Innis's work on empire, bureaucracy, and monopolies of knowledge provides an analysis of power that is largely absent from McLuhan's writing. What McLuhan provides in exchange, in addition to boiling Innis's ponderous volumes and gnomic prose down to a series of catchy and immediately memorable aphorisms, is to take Innis's interest in systems and mediation and transform it into a theory of media as material form. But Buxton's stance in 2012 is symptomatic of McLuhan's current cultural capital in Canadian communication studies; in comparison to the sober, scholarly work of Innis, dense with citations and the other furniture of serious scholarly writing, McLuhan's ludic, breezy prose and penchant for argument by assertion often come up short. The growing prefer-ence for Innis over McLuhan in Canada has much to do with Innis's roots in the legitimizing solidity of political economy and history.

In his Introduction to the 1964 edition of Innis's *The Bias of Communication* (first published in 1951), McLuhan claims, "I am pleased to think of my own book *The Gutenberg Galaxy* (University of Toronto Press, 1962) as a footnote to the observa-tions of Innis on the subject of the psychic and social consequences, first of writing then of printing" ("Introduction To" 8). Despite this high degree of praise from McLuhan himself, Innis spent the second half of the twentieth century in McLuhan's shadow. In 1998, McLuhan biographer Philip Marchand wrote, "If Innis is read in the future it will be as a footnote to McLuhan and not vice versa" (*Marshall McLuhan* 123). Marchand may have rushed to judgement, because in McLuhan's own terms, McLuhan and Innis are undergoing a figure-ground reversal. Due to the work of Innis scholars like Heyer, Buxton, and Acland, and Innis's biographer, Alexander John Watson, Innis's cultural capital in communication studies and media studies is waxing and McLuhan's is waning.

This ongoing qualification of McLuhan's legacy within Canadian communication studies occasionally finds its way into popular discourse as well. A few days before the McLuhan centenary, I was interviewed by Peggy Curran of the *Montreal Gazette*, along with my colleagues Charles Acland and Will Straw. Despite the fact that we all work together closely on a regular basis and are of like minds on most issues, including the foundational nature of McLuhan's thought for communication studies in Canada, the structure of the article positions me as the pro-McLuhan scholar ("[Wershler argues that McLuhan] was probably more familiar than anyone else in Canada at the time with what was happening among modernist writers and artists in Europe in the early part of the 20th century"), Acland as the critic ("[Acland] still has trouble with what he sees as McLuhan's shoddy scholarship—a bad habit of making blanket statements that weren't actually proven and didn't hold up under intense scrutiny"), and Straw as the synthesis of the two positions ("Straw said there has been a growing recognition of McLuhan's media musings as 'characteristically [if not uniquely] Canadian. That is, media help us to locate ourselves in the world and in relation to other people and places, and this has been a long-standing concern of other Canadian thinkers like the historian Harold Innis, now considered a key founder of media thinking'" [Curran]). Straw has the last word, once again asserting the growing interest in establishing Innis's reputation as a theorist of media and communications. Where Straw and Acland are diplomatic with their comparisons, John Durham Peters (citing Edmund Carpenter on McLuhan) is much more blunt: "Innis was a rock of integrity, while McLuhan was frankly irresponsible. Probes deserve probity" (Peters, "McLuhan's" 240). So within communication studies, a qualified interest in McLuhan's work certainly remains, but without the hagiographic aura that surrounds McLuhan in popular culture and technology journalism. But what about the growing interest in media studies broadly construed and McLuhan specifically among literary scholars?

Mediating Literature?

For Toby Miller, the difference between English departments on the one hand and communication studies and media studies on the other has everything to do with class politics. From Miller's perspective, English literary studies, with its cele-bration of the "life of the mind," is the provenance of elite institutions and the upper classes. Communication studies and media studies, however, are working-class disciplines, because of their perceived practicality (2, passim). Miller is clear that he is describing the situation in the United States, but his argu-ment also has a ring of truth for many Canadian institutions.[9]

There's another factor that complicates the situation: in the current tough economic climate, English literary studies spends an enormous amount of time defending itself from even the possibility that it might be perceived as anything less than relevant—Google "English degree" and "worthless" in the same search string to see for yourself. Alternatively, look at a classic example of the English-degree-disparaging genre, such as Thomas H. Benton's (a.k.a. William Pannapacker) "Graduate School in the Humanities: Just Don't Go," which jokes at the expense of English graduates that "No one is impressed by their knowledge of Jane Austen." The turn of English departments toward co-op programs and an interest in media reads, in part, like slumming: an attempt to capture some of communication studies' and media studies' perceived practi-cality and instrumentality for itself without sacrificing any of its remaining cultural capital. The counternarrative that asserts the ongoing value of an English degree in the workforce is part and parcel of the same attempt to reposition the discipline as instru-mental,[10] because, rather than resorting to the traditional narrative that the role of literary studies is to produce good citizens, not workers, it relies instead on a demonstration that literary studies

DARREN **Wershler**

is, above all, a form of training that will prove useful on the job.

Part of the reason that English literary studies is experiencing a crisis is that, after the so-called "failure" of theory[11] (also really more of a relegation to residual status), options other than a retreat into the canon are scarce. There will always be a central place in the academy for historical work; the chronicling and analysis of the history of literary studies as a discipline remains a large and daunting but necessary task as part of any next step. But in parallel to that project of historical reassessment, branching out into other media will prove to be more of a challenge for literary scholars in professional (if not practical) terms. If we consider literary studies and communication studies as fields of inquiry rather than disciplines, there is very little by way of a problem for established scholars. It's easy to imagine bringing a range of perspectives to bear on the same object of study, and, by virtue of the principle of academic freedom, it's easy to imagine established scholars in any field expanding what they do to include the study of media. Paul Heyer notes that before McLuhan, Innis was "an early proponent of interdisciplinarity. He did not, as some later devotees suggested, advocate the abolishment of conventional disciplinary parameters, but he did insist that there are ocasionally points of focal overlap, or common ground, between disciplines that can provide for cross-fertilization" (*Harold Innis* 18). Institutionalizing that study within an English department, though, in order to attract and retain faculty and students, is another matter. Philip Marchand has carefully documented the resistance to his work on media that McLuhan encountered from his colleagues in English during his lifetime (*Marshall McLuhan* 92–96). The subsequent history of the McLuhan Program in Culture and Technology is one of a constant struggle for resources and recognition. To this day, the University of Toronto lacks a communication studies program, though its iSchool, which has enfolded the McLuhan Program into its vast bulk, may develop to cover some of the same areas.

Part of the reason that literary scholars interested in media find themselves in a quandary is that many of the disciplines that literary scholars helped to found, which were often (and in some cases still are) housed inside English departments, such as communication studies, cultural studies, and film studies, have achieved enough legitimacy that they now exist as independent departments, schools, and programs in many universities. To some extent, these new disciplines have "eaten the lunch" of literary studies, growing their faculty and student populations as English departments shrink. So when English professors interested in media search for a vocabulary to describe what it is they are doing, the options are limited.

Less Poetics

"Media studies" might seem like an obvious solution, but as various disciplinary histories of the term demonstrate, it raises many difficulties. The term is much more common in the United States than in Canada, where communication studies departments predominate. Updating the classic mid-twentieth-century study of US media and communications research traditions by Paul Lazarsfeld, which instilled a surprisingly resilient binary between an "administrative" empirical tradition and a "critical" ideological tradition, Sheryl N. Hamilton's concise history of the disciplinary formation of communication studies in Canada points out that the dominant US tradition of communication and media studies was administrative until at least the 1980s (11), that is, much closer to what we would describe as public relations (helping private and public institutions communicate their messages to a range of audiences). In Canada, Hamilton writes, in response to both its marginalization by US histories and the specific conditions of the institutionalization of the discipline here, the signature quality of communication studies is to imagine itself as "always already critical" (17), whether justifiably or not. In the United States, histories that focus on the critical side of communication studies (see Peters's "Genealogical") often ignore the difference between Canadian and US traditions entirely, or overwrite (Hamilton 17) what would be termed "communication studies" in Canada with the label "media studies." The history of media studies in the UK

DARREN **Wershler**

is different again, as Tom O'Malley has begun to chart, following the work of Asa Briggs and Peter Burke. What all of these studies have in common is that they are attempts to establish claims for the legitimacy of a particular perspective against others. I think it's fair comment to observe that in Canada at least, the difference between "communication studies" and "media studies" has as much to do with *realpolitik* as anything else; "media studies" may be simply what academics interested in communication, mediation, and material media call what they do when they can't call it "communication studies" for fear of arousing the ire of another department at the same institution—or to block someone else from studying it. I know of at least one instance in the last decade where a department changed its name to include the terms "media" and "film" precisely to keep the English department at the same university from launching a media studies initiative. What Hamilton calls for instead of this sort of turf warfare is a delicate balancing act, "honouring our ghosts but only and always while encouraging more ferment in the field" (23). For Hamilton, McLuhan is explicitly one of those ghosts. But if the problem with his legacy in communication studies is a need for a more active critical imagination, in English, the obverse is true. Literary studies needs McLuhan to point to a less poetic and a more critical future.

Following the work of Theall's *The Virtual Marshall McLuhan*, I've argued elsewhere that, in the context of communication studies, it makes sense to think of McLuhan as adopting the tactics of the modernist avant-gardes (see Wershler, "News"). My reasoning was that even though "the analogy between a poem and a medium of communication was, according to McLuhan, extremely tight" (Marchand, *Marshall McLuhan* 129), poetics in general and McLuhan in particular is what communication studies has largely disavowed in the interest of establishing itself as a "serious" discipline rooted in the methods of social science and the gravitas of history. Any discipline consists of an assemblage of intersecting systems of production, circulation, and consumption that constantly compete (and occasionally co-operate) with each other in order to produce meaning (Wershler, "Marshall McLuhan"). For communication studies, poetics is one such system. Further, poetics is not something that can be purged from the discipline, but rather a constituitive element of it. Recent contributions that have pushed the discipline of communication studies in productive new directions, such as the rise of the discourse of research-creation (Chapman and Sawchuk), owe much to the ongoing residual influence of poetics.

However, now that I'm housed in an English department rather than a communication studies department, I'm beginning to wonder if a poetic McLuhan does what English literary studies *needs*, or merely what it *desires*. Media poetics is a heterogeneous practice without theory, or, as Charles Bernstein would claim, a "strategy of tactics" (164). As such, it is fully congruent with contemporary poetics and therefore not much of an irritant, and unlikely to push the discipline to do something other than the status quo. From some perspectives, such as Paul Bové's critique (38) of the Practical Criticism that McLuhan practiced and tried to emulate in his media work, it might even be actively deleterious. The assumption that the theoretical tools that have always been useful for the analysis of literature will continue to function when considering media doesn't necessarily hold.

Benjamin Peters gives voice to a common assumption among media scholars with a background in literary studies, namely, that "media behave a lot like words, or syntactical units identifiable to those fluent in the circumstances of their use" (22). I'd argue that that all depends on whose definition of words you happen to be using. I've already mentioned the significant role that the German "Materialities of Communication" scholars have played in contemporary communication studies; other than Friedrich Kittler, though, they aren't widely read in English departments. In both the Afterword to the eponymous *Materialities of Communication* collection (Gumbrecht and Pfeiffer 396), and its coda, "Materialities/ The Nonhermeneutic/Presence" (Gumbrecht 14), which appeared a decade later, Hans Ulrich Gumbrecht argued that the Saussurean definition of the sign, which many literary scholars still rely on heavily, should be abandoned. His reasoning is that the Saussurean sign abrogates all concern with materiality in favour of a transcendent meaning that is always located elsewhere; literary studies under the sign of Saussure is effectively a perpetual quest for the signified, endlessly generating interpretations of the same canonical texts from the perspective of every new theory that comes down the pike.

Instead, Gumbrecht advocates for an adoption of Louis Hjelmslev's schema, which imposes "substance" and "expression" on to form and content in order to form a matrix of four fields that would be components of each and every sign. For Gumbrecht, "substance of content" is the field of unstructured impressions, thoughts and memories—in short, the Imaginary; "form of content" would refer to something like Foucauldian discourse, that structures what is possible to say and not say in a given culture at a given historical moment. "Substance of expression" would consist of the physical aspects of signs—the material of media itself; and finally, "form of expression" would refer to organized materiality, or, what communication scholars including McLuhan refer to as media forms and formats. Gumbrecht's point is that none of these fields can produce meaning on its own, which solves the problem of the effacing of the material signifier in favour of the evanescent signified. The job of the critic working with this model becomes the reconstruction of the processes through which articulated meaning can emerge rather than hermeneutic interpretation (Gumbrecht and Pfeiffer 398). (Franco Moretti arrives at the same conclusions from another direction entirely, advocating "a clear preference for *explanation over interpretation*" ["Graphs...−3" 63].)

Gumbrecht's schema maps approximately onto Lisa Gitelman's influential definition of media as "socially realized structures of communication, where structures include both technological forms and their associated protocols, and where communication is a cultural practice, a ritualized collocation of different people on the same mental map, sharing or engaged with popular ontologies of representation" (7). Throughout her work, Gitelman demonstrates the power and efficacy of beginning from such a position. Gitelman literally occupies a space between English literary studies and communication, being cross-appointed to both departments. What she does in her own practice, though, bears little resemblance to what most literary scholars do. And this is the point: working with media cannot be business as usual for literary scholars. So what if, to use Elena Lamberti's formulation, "applying McLuhan" "to the critical evaluation of society" rather than "engaging with" McLuhan (*McLuhan's Mosaic* 231) should consist of not thinking about literary content poetically at all? In the best-case scenario, McLuhan's return from obsolescence might be the harbinger of another mediation, namely, one that could produce something distinct from an *arriviste* version of communication studies or media history, namely, what we have come to refer to as the digital humanities.

The history of digital humanities is distinct from the complex histories of communication studies and media studies, as field histories like Susan Hockey's "The History of Humanities Computing" delineate. As the title of Matthew Kirschenbaum's key essay "What Is Digital Humanities and What's It Doing in English Departments?" suggests, though digital humanities has now gained a foothold in many different disciplines, it is playing a particularly active role in determining the future of literary studies in English. This is due to the way that the term is deployed instrumentally, with what Kirschenbaum's prose suggests is a certain righteous zeal:

> Digital humanities has also, I would propose, lately been galvanized by a group of younger (or not so young) graduate students, faculty members (both tenure line and contingent), and other academic professionals who now wield the label "digital humanities" instrumentally amid an increasingly monstrous institutional terrain defined by declining public support for higher education, rising tuitions, shrinking endowments, the proliferation of distance education and the for-profit university, and underlying it all the conversion of full-time, tenure-track academic labor to a part-time adjunct workforce. ("What is Digital Humanities")

Digital humanities is still very much in an active and productive ferment, as collaborative volumes such as *Debates in the Digital Humanities* and *Digital_Humanities* indicate. It seems to me that digital humanities is even more misunderstood than media studies by many English professors. On the subject of several of the young digital humanities scholars that Kirschenbaum references, comments from my colleagues in English frequently include phrases like "They'd fit better in a communication studies department." These comments are telling, because they misunderstand the present of English departments and the history of communication studies alike. Communication studies has its own epistemology and its own problematics, even on the occasions when it and digital humanities share the same objects (and, sometimes, the same methods). One challenge digital humanities will have to face is finding a way to do what many communication studies have been doing now for decades without reduplicating efforts and erasing intellectual histories.

The core move of the digital humanities—namely, to incorporate techniques rarely used until now in the humanities to study the objects that humanities traditionally engages with—is McLuhanesque in spirit rather than letter. Rather than attempting to *write like* McLuhan, in a poetic style, it *acts like* McLuhan did, launching into a deep engagement with modes of intellectual investigation from outside of its home discipline, such as quantitative analysis, data visualization, and distant reading. As Franco Moretti notes of his own attempts to apply network theory to literature, such experiments are not always successful, and can fail entirely ("Network Theory"). But the point of Moretti's work is not to assert the superiority of quantitative analysis. Over and over, what his writing does is to reveal the blind spots in what literary studies knows about its objects, and about itself. For example, out of his engagement with graphs comes not the suggestion that English professors need to spend all of their time graphing the books that they read, but that between the traditional temporal categories of literary analysis, the event and the *longue durée*, there is a middle level, the cycle, that literary scholars rarely work with and don't fully understand ("Graphs...–1" 76). This is the payoff: an entire category of analysis that has been ignored for the entire history of the novel, a form we thought we knew well. There is a lot of work to be done here for scholars willing to take up the challenge.

Another intriguing aspect of the digital humanities is its investment in the notion of "critical making." McLuhan wrote in 1961 that "The humanities are moving out of their centuries-old consumer and appreciation phase into a depth phase of rigorous producer-orientation" ("The Humanities" 14). Critical making fully occupies this contention with a range of practices and accompanying manifestos whose basic contention is that scholars need to make things as well as write about them, and that making can also be a critical practice (see especially Garnet Herz's 352-page collection of 10 zine-like pamphlets, *Critical Making*[12] for a range of examples; for a different take on the same notion, see the "Carpentry" chapter of Ian Bogost's *Alien Phenomenology*.) For Matt Ratto, who coined the term in 2008 (and, like McLuhan, a professor at the University of Toronto), the goal of critical making is to reconnect aspects of the world that are often held separate...as was McLuhan's in 1961, attempting to think past the deadlock of C.P. Snow's two cultures ("The Humanities" 17).

This is, of course, the best-case scenario.

The Grim Stuff: Inoculations and Edupreneurianism

To his credit, McLuhan anticipated the necessity for a shift in what English professors do a long time ago. In 1951, in the only extant letter from McLuhan to Innis, McLuhan wrote that believed that the serious study of the "function and effect of communication on society" was the only thing that would keep English departments from the decline in perceived value that already afflicted the study of the classics in the mid-twentieth century: "As a teacher of literature it has long seemed to me that the *functions* of literature cannot be maintained in present circumstances without radical alteration of the procedures of teaching. Failure in this respect relegated Latin and Greek to the specialist; and

English literature has already become a category rather than an interest in school and college" (*Letters* 222). When the analysis of communication and material media forms in conjunction with literature is limited to a few individuals rather than departments or disciplines, though, it may exacerbate the situation.

In his essay "Operation Margarine," Roland Barthes uses the metaphor of inoculation to describe a strategy that dominant discourses can use to neutralize opposition from residual alternatives. Inoculation proceeds not by direct confrontation, but by allowing a little of its opposition to manifest itself, in the name of diversity and democracy. The net effect is to strengthen the existing system rather than challenging it: "revolt disappears all the more surely since, once at a distance and the object of a gaze, the Established Order is no longer anything but a Manichean compound and therefore inevitable, one which wins on both counts, and is therefore beneficial" (*Mythologies* 42). As Paul Bové pointed out several decades ago, many English departments maintained and continue to maintain a fantasy of equality rooted in professional pluralism. From such a stance, an ideal department would consist of scholars with as many different critical points of view as possible; a concentration in any one area—especially "contemporary" areas like media studies—threatens the notion of pluralism itself. For Bové, though, the implicit assumption that no critical stance can be more timely or desirable than any other is tantamount to the very consumerism it purports to stave off—a sort of boutique liberalism (27–28). So when they can be found at all inside English departments, academics interested in media studies in general and McLuhan in particular often serve as inoculations for their departments against anyone else having to learn anything about media or technology. The source of such resistance, even when significant numbers of literary scholars are seeking a way forward "after" high theory and should be willing to investigate any likely options, are external economic pressures on the university itself.[13]

As a consequence of the ongoing economic crisis and increases in university enrolment (T. Miller 8), the humanities are under attack (Turcato); organizations like 4Humanities (http://4humanities.org)

and scholars such as Toby Miller have made an analysis of the situation central to their current work. Miller describes how (as McLuhan anticipated) when the classics were unseated from their role as "a privileged entry point into civilization" (35), English departments assumed that mantle, and are now being challenged for it by competing discourses that advocate for the primacy of STEM (Science, Technology, Engineering, and Mathematics) fields. The re-emergence of interest in McLuhan's work is, I think, a harbinger of that shift. The issue is what form the humanities in general and literary studies in particular will take once the shift is complete.

Alan Liu uses the word "encounter" to describe the relationship between media scholarship (with McLuhan as its figurehead) and literary studies, because an encounter indicates "a thick, unpredictable zone of contact—more borderland than border line— where (mis)understandings of new media are negotiated along twisting, partial, and contradictory vectors" ("Imagining"). The fantasy is that the result of this encounter will be something like the "critical digital humanities" that Liu calls for elsewhere ("Where Is Cultural Criticism"): a marriage of the best of cultural criticism, book history, and materialist media studies. Presumably this would also mean a greater degree of intercourse between the academy and culture at large. In "McLuhan and the Humanities," Richard Cavell points out that McLuhan's championing of interdisciplinarity and process over the traditional model of knowledge production by specialists was in the interest of creating an "involved world" where research was a part of everyday life and even politicians have doctorates. But with the observation that "a process model of knowledge doesn't allow the certainties, or even the satisfactions, of traditional research" (17), Cavell implies that there is a price to be paid for a greater integration of the academy and public life as well.

The truth of this encounter could be quite depressing for the humanities in general and English literary studies in particular. Cavell's take is that "as Google and Wikipedia attest, research is now a full-time activity in which everyone is involved—research is corporate, in this sense, with students increasingly taking on the roles of 'edupreneurs'" ("McLuhan and the Humanities" 17). As

Liu's *The Laws of Cool* and edited collections such as Catherine McKercher and Vincent Mosco's *Knowledge Workers in the Information Society* anticipated, and, as the 2014 panic over the sudden rise and fall of rhetoric around MOOCs (Massive Open Online Courses) demonstrated all too well, there is a real and present desire to gain access to the academy as a new market, "disrupting" traditional structures like tenure, peer review, departments and faculty unions in the name of market efficiencies and profitability (Bogost, "Educational Hucksterism"). As Liu's "Where Is Cultural Criticism in the Digital Humanities?" and *The Laws of Cool* describe, knowledge work and digital humanities both have an uneasy relationship with the neoliberal and the instrumental. Whether housed in English departments or extradepartmental research centres (Mueller), a McLuhan-inspired approach to media studies brings with it no guarantee of criticality. John Durham Peters, for one, suggests that McLuhan lost his bet that it would be possible to "dispense with facts for the sake of truth" ("McLuhan's" 240). But this is precisely the mode of contemporary politics, from George W. Bush's faith-based presidency to Rob Ford's Toronto. McLuhan's iconoclasm and irreverence for academic institutions have value for those institutions, but play into the hands of their enemies all too easily, which is precisely why it's necessary to consider Hamilton's caveat. The best way to honour the spirit of our ghosts might be to betray the letter of their work.

McLuhan remains a significant figure not simply because of his own writing, but because he represents the truth of what an interdisciplinary approach means: its transformation into something that many professors will not recognize and do not want. Rather than wallpapering over that reality with a fantasy, we—and here I mean those of us that are housed in English departments regardless of our interdisciplinary commitments—need to begin by thinking about McLuhan in terms of his residuality: not just what his work meant in its precise social and historical context, but what has been able to appear because of his work that nevertheless questions and challenges it.

Notes

1   For a summary of Williams's position on McLuhan, see Paul Jones, "The Technology Is Not the Cultural Form?"

2   Exemplary contemporary Canadian communications scholars with a deep investment in an approach that might be called "poetic" include Kim Sawchuk, Peter C. van Wyck, Elena Lamberti, and the late Donald Theall.

3   See especially Hans Ulrich Gumbrecht and Karl Ludwig Pfeiffer, *Materialities of Communication*; Friedrich A. Kittler, *Gramophone, Film, Typewriter*; and Wolfgang Ernst, *Digital Memory and the Archive*.

4   Here again there are a number of oddities that merit further discussion. For example, Kittler's championing of both McLuhan and the mathematical communication theory of Shannon and Weaver, as the way that McLuhan describes the relationship between content and media channels is conflicts with Shannon and Weaver's approach.

5   See Williams, "Dominant, Residual, and Emergent" in *Marxism and Literature*.

6   See Acland's Introduction to *Residual Media*.

7   See especially Siegfreid Zielinski, "Modelling Media for Ignatius Loyola." Zeilinski writes, "the main purpose of this archaeological work is to counter current tendencies towards standardization and universalization in the interest of a uniform global market with the rich variety of variants offered by bygone eras" (54).

8   See Daniel J. Czitrom, *Media and the American Mind*; Arthur Kroker, *Technology and the Canadian Mind: Innis/Mcluhan/Grant*; Paul Heyer, *Communications and History*; James W. Carey, *Communication as Culture*; Graeme H. Patterson, *History and Communications*.

9   For example, the University of Toronto, home to both McLuhan and Innis as well as a world-class English department, still has no communication studies department, though it has recently sprouted a variety of units that conduct media studies. At my former home institution, Wilfrid Laurier University, the traditional role of the English department as the default home of arts undergraduates seeking a general BA has been supplanted by Communication Studies, which boasts a student complement that approaches a tenth of the entire university's student population in size.

10 For example, see Jordan Weismann, "The Best Argument for Studying English? The Employment Numbers."

11 See Paul A. Bové, *In the Wake of Theory*; and Judith Butler, John Guillory, and Kendall Thomas, eds., *What's Left of Theory?*

12 Garnet Herz, ed. *Critical Making*, 2012-11-14-1225 ed., 10 vols. (2012). See http://conceptlab.com/criticalmaking/.

13 For two accounts, see Bové, *In the Wake of Theory*, and John Guillory, *Cultural Capital*.

Works Cited

Acland, Charles R. Introduction. *Residual Media*. Ed. Charles Acland. Minneapolis: U of Minnesota P, 2007. xiii–xvii.

——, ed. *Residual Media*. Minneapolis: U of Minnesota P, 2007.

Adria, Marco, and Catherine Adams. "Readers' Forum Introduction: The Age of McLuhan, 100 Years On." ESC: *English Studies in Canada* 36.2/3 (2010): 1–4.

Armstrong, Isobel. "When Is a Victorian Poet Not a Victorian Poet? Poetry and the Politics of Subjectivity in the Long Nineteenth Century." *Victorian Studies* 43.2 (2001): 279–92.

Ash, Mitchell G. *Gestalt Psychology in German Culture, 1890–1967: Holism and the Quest for Objectivity*. Cambridge: Cambridge UP, 1995.

Barbrook, Richard, and Andy Cameron. "The Californian Ideology." *Mute* August 1995.

Barclay, Pat. "Close to the Truth." *Books in Canada* 21.6 (1992): 11–13.

Barthes, Roland. "Longtemps je me suis couché de bonne heure." *The Rustle of Language*. Trans. Richard Howard. Berkley: U of California P, 1989. 277–90.

——. *Mythologies*. 1957. Trans. Annette Lavers. London: Paladin, 1973.

——. "Myth Today." *Mythologies*. Trans. Annette Lavers. New York: Hill and Wang, 1972. 109–59.

Bell, Clive. *Art*. New York: Capricorn Books, 1958.

Benjamin, Walter. "The Work of Art in the Age of its Technological Reproduction. Third Version." *The Cultural Studies Reader*. 3rd ed. Ed. Simon During. New York: Routledge, 1993. 72–79.

Benton, Thomas H. [William Pannapacker]. "Graduate School in the Humanities: Just Don't Go." *Chronicle of Higher Education* 30 January 2009.

Bergson, Henri. *Key Writings*. Eds. Keith Ansell Pearson and John Mullarkey. Trans. Melissa McMahon. New York: Continuum, 2002.

Berner, Geoff, ed. *Astronauts of Inner-Space: An International Collection of Avant-Garde Activity*. San Francisco: Stolen Paper Review Editions, 1966.

Bernstein, Charles. "Optimism and Critical Excess." *A Poetics*. Cambridge, MA: Harvard UP, 1992. 150–78.

Berton, Pierre. *The Comfortable Pew: A Critical Look at Christianity and the Religious Establishment in the New Age*. Toronto: McClelland & Stewart, 1965.

Bessai, Diane. "Wilfred Watson." *Canadian Writers Since 1960: Second Series* (Volume 60 of *Dictionary of Literary Biography*). Ed. W.H. New. Detroit: Gale Research Company, 1987. 382–86.

Betts, Gregory. *Avant-Garde Canadian Literature: The Early Manifestations*. Toronto: U of Toronto P, 2013.

——. "Media, McLuhan, and the Dawn of the Electric Age in Sheila Watson's *Deep Hollow Creek* and *The Double Hook*." *Essays on Canadian Writing* 84 (Fall 2009): 254–82.

The Bible. Revised Standard Version. London: Fontana, 1952.

Bodolai, Joe. "Borderlines in Art and Experience." *artscanada* 188/189 (Spring 1974): 65–81.

Bogost, Ian. *Alien Phenomenology, or, What It's Like to Be a Thing*. Minneapolis: U of Minnesota P, 2012.

——. "Educational Hucksterism, or, MOOCs Are Not an Educational Technology." www.bogost.com, 5 January 2013. Blog.

Bonin, Vincent. "Documentary Protocols: 1967–1975." *Documentary Protocols (1967–1975)*. Ed. Vincent Bonin and Michèle Thériault. Montreal: Leonard and Bina Ellen Art Gallery, 2010. 17–62.

"Borderline Research Project Submissions." April 1972. Mr. Peanut Issue of *FILE* (vol. 1, no. 1). *FILE Megazine* Series, General Idea fonds. On loan to the Library and Archives, National Gallery of Canada. Courtesy AA Bronson.

Bowering, Angela. *Figures Cut in Sacred Ground: Illuminati in* The Double Hook. Edmonton: NeWest, 1988.

Bowering, George. "Narrative Valley." Rev. of *Deep Hollow Creek* by Sheila Watson. *Canadian Literature* 136 (1993): 132–34.

——. "Sheila Watson, Trickster." Afterword. G. Bowering, ed. 187–99.

——, ed. *Sheila Watson and The Double Hook*. Ottawa: Golden Dog, 1985.

Bové, Paul A. *In the Wake of Theory*. Middletown, CT: Wesleyan UP; Hanover: UP of New England, 1992.

Bradbury, Malcolm, and James McFarlane, eds. *Modernism: A Guide to European Literature 1890–1930*. London: Penguin Books, 1976.

Breton, André. "Second Manifesto of Surrealism." 1930. *Manifestoes of Surrealism*. Trans. Richard Seaver and Helen R. Lane. Ann Arbor: U of Michigan P, 1972. 117–94.

Briggs, Asa, and Peter Burke. *A Social History of the Media: From Gutenberg to the Internet*. Cambridge, UK and Malden, MA: Polity in association with Blackwell, 2002.

Bronson, AA. "Copyright, Cash and Crowd Control: Art and Economy in the Work of General Idea." *General Idea Editions: 1967–1995*. Ed. Barbara Fischer. Mississauga, ON: Blackwood Gallery, U of Toronto at Mississauga, 2003. 24–28.

——. "Myth as Parasite/Image as Virus: General Idea's Bookshelf 1967–1975." *The Search for the Spirit: General Idea 1968–1975*. Toronto: Art Gallery of Ontario, 1997. 17–20.

Bultmann, Rudolf. *Jesus Christ and Mythology*. New York: Scribner's, 1958.

Burroughs, William S. *Nova Express*. New York: Grove, 1992.

Butler, Judith, John Guillory, and Kendall Thomas, eds. *What's Left of Theory?: New Work on the Politics of Literary Theory*. New York: Routledge, 2000.

Buxton, William J. "The Rise of McLuhanism, the Loss of Innis-Sense: Rethinking the Origins of the Toronto School of Communication." *Canadian Journal of Communication* 37.4 (2012): 577–93.

Buxton, William J., and Thierry Bardini, eds. *Tracing Innis and McLuhan.* Spec. issue of *Canadian Journal of Communication* 37.4 (2012).

Cage, John. Introduction. *Marshall McLuhan: The Man and His Message.* Ed. George Sanderson and Frank MacDonald. Golden, CO: Fulcrum, 1989.

Calinescu, Matei. *Five Faces of Modernity: Modernism, Avant-Garde, Decadence, Kitsch, Postmodernism.* Durham: Duke UP, 1987.

Carey, James W. *Communication as Culture: Essays on Media and Society.* Boston: Unwin Hyman, 1989.

Carpenter, Edmund, and Marshall McLuhan, eds. *Explorations in Communication: An Anthology.* Boston: Beacon, 1960.

Carter, Thomas H. "Rationalist in Hell." *The Kenyon Review* 18.2 (Spring 1956): 326–36.

Cavell, Richard. "McLuhan and the Humanities." *ESC: English Studies in Canada* 36.2 (2010): 14–18.

——. "McLuhan in Space." *At the Speed of Light There is Only Illumination: A Reappraisal of Marshall McLuhan.* Ed. John Moss and Linda M. Morra. Ottawa: U of Ottawa P, 2005.

——. *McLuhan in Space: A Cultural Geography.* Toronto: U of Toronto P, 2002.

Chapman, Owen, and Kim Sawchuk. "Research-Creation: Intervention, Analysis and 'Family Resemblances.'" *Canadian Journal of Communication* 37.1 (2012): 5–26.

Chrystall, Andrew Brian. "The New American Vortex: Explorations of McLuhan." PhD thesis. Massey U, New Zealand, 2007.

Coupland, Douglas. *Marshall McLuhan.* Toronto: Penguin, 2009.

Cuddy-Keane, Melba. "Global Modernisms." *A Companion to Modernist Literature and Culture.* Ed. David Bradshaw and Kevin J.H. Dettmar. Oxford: Blackwell, 2006. 558–64.

Curran, Peggy. "McLuhan's Legacy Is Alive and Tweeting." *Montreal Gazette* 17 July 2011.

Czitrom, Daniel J. *Media and the American Mind: From Morse to McLuhan.* Chapel Hill: U of North Carolina P, 1982.

Danzker, Jo-Anne Birnie. "Vancouver: Land- and Culture-Scape." *Vancouver Art and Artists: 1931–1983.* Vancouver: Vancouver Art Gallery, 1983. 208–25.

Dasenbrock, Reed Way. *The Literary Vorticism of Ezra Pound and Wyndham Lewis.* Baltimore and London: Johns Hopkins UP, 1985.

Davey, Frank, ed. *Sheila Watson: A Collection.* Spec. issue of *Open Letter* 3rd series, 1 (1974–75).

Davis, Warren, dir. *The Summer Way.* Perf. Warren Davis, Marshall McLuhan, and Norman Mailer. CBC. 26 November 1967. Television.

Deer, Glenn. "Miracle, Mystery, and Authority: Re-Reading *The Double Hook*." *Open Letter* 6th series, 8 (1987): 25–43.

Dilworth, Thomas. "Out of Canada: Wyndham Lewis's North American Writings." Mastin, Stacey, and Dilworth 157–65.

Donald, Merlin. *Origins of the Modern Mind: Three Stages in the Evolution of Culture and Cognition.* Cambridge, MA: Harvard UP, 1993.

———. "Précis of Origins of the Modern Mind: Three Stages in the Evolution of Culture and Cognition." *Behavioural and Brain Sciences* 16 (1994): 737–91.

Donne, John. "The Relic." *John Donne: The Complete English Poems*. Ed. A.J. Smith. Markham, ON: Penguin, 1971. 76–77.

Downton, Dawn Rae. "Messages and Messengers in *The Double Hook*." *Studies in Canadian Literature* 4 (Summer 1979): 137–46.

Dragland, Stan. "Apocrypha: An Alphabetical Sampler." *The New Quarterly* 19.3 (1999): 5–39.

Dudek, Louis, and Michael Gnarowski. *The Making Of Modern Poetry in Canada*. Toronto: Ryerson, 1970.

Edwards, Paul. Afterword. *The Vulgar Streak*, by Wyndham Lewis. Santa Barbara, CA: Black Sparrow, 1985.

Eliot, T.S. *The Use of Poetry and the Use of Criticism*. London: Faber & Faber 1955.

Elliott, Robert C. *The Power of Satire: Magic, Ritual, Art*. Princeton: Princeton UP, 1960.

Ernst, Wolfgang. *Digital Memory and the Archive*. Minneapolis: U of Minnesota P, 2013.

Fischer, Barbara. Introduction. *General Idea: Editions 1967–1995*. Ed. Barbara Fischer. Mississauga, ON: Blackwood Gallery, U of Toronto at Mississauga, 2003. 20–23.

———, ed. *General Idea: Editions 1967–1995*. Mississauga, ON: Blackwood Gallery, U of Toronto at Mississauga, 2003.

Flahiff, F.T. Afterword. *The Double Hook*. By Sheila Watson. Toronto: McClelland & Stewart, 1989. 119–30.

———. *Always Someone to Kill the Doves: A Life of Sheila Watson*. Edmonton: NeWest, 2005.

———. Preface. *Wyndham Lewis and Expressionism*. By Sheila Watson. Ed. Paul Tiessen. Waterloo: MLR Editions Canada, 2003. n. pag.

Flieger, Jerry Aline. *Is Oedipus Online? Siting Freud after Freud*. Cambridge, MA: MIT P, 2005.

Foran, Charles. "End of Story." *The Walrus* March 2013.

Foucault, Michel. *Madness and Civilization: A History of Insanity in the Age of Reason*. 1961. Abr. ed. Trans. Richard Howard. New York: Random House, 1971.

Fox, C.J. "The Wild Land: A Celebration of Globalism." *Wyndham Lewis in Canada*. Ed. George Woodcock. Vancouver: U of British Columbia Publications Centre, 1971. 41–48.

Frank, Josef. "Spatial Form in Modern Literature: An Essay in Three Parts." *Sewanee Review* 53.4 (Autumn 1945): 643–53.

General Idea. "Are You Truly Invisible?" *IFEL/FILE* 2.3 (September 1973): 34–35.

———. "Borderline Research." *FILE Megazine* 1.1 (April 1972): 31.

———. "General Idea's Borderline Cases." *IFEL/FILE* 2.3 (September 1973): 12–31.

———. "General Idea's Framing Devices," *FILE* 4.1 (Summer 1978): 12.

———. "Glamour." *FILE* 3.1 (Autumn 1975): n. pag.

———. "Pablum for the Pablum Eaters." *FILE* 2.1/2 (May 1973): 16–31.

——. "Some Malicious and Juicy Gossip." *FILE* 1.1 (April 1972): 3.

Giedion, Sigfried. *Mechanization Takes Command: A Contribution to Anonymous History*. New York: Oxford UP, 1948.

——. *Space, Time and Architecture: The Growth of a New Tradition*. 1941. Cambridge, MA: Harvard UP, 2003.

Gitelman, Lisa. *Always Already New: Media, History and the Data of Culture*. Cambridge, MA: MIT P, 2006.

Godard, Barbara. "'Between One Cliché and Another': Language in *The Double Hook*." *Studies in Canadian Literature* 3.2 (1978): 149–65. Rpt. in G. Bowering, ed. 159–76.

Gold, Matthew K., ed. *Debates in the Digital Humanities*. Minneapolis: U of Minnesota P, 2012.

Gombrich, E.H. *Art and Illusion: A Study of the Psychology of Pictorial Representation*. 1960. Princeton: Princeton UP, 2000.

Goody, Jack. Introduction. *Literacy in Traditional Societies*. Ed. Jack Goody. Cambridge: Cambridge UP, 1968. 1–26.

Goody, Jack, and Ian Watt. "The Consequences of Literacy." *Comparative Studies in Literature* 5 (April 1963): 304–45.

Gordon, W. Terrance. *Marshall McLuhan: Escape into Understanding*. Toronto: Stoddart, 1997.

——. *McLuhan: A Guide for the Perplexed*. New York: Continuum International, 2010.

Grace, Sherrill E. *Regression and Apocalypse: Studies in North American Literary Expressionism*. Toronto: U of Toronto P, 1989.

Grosswiler, Paul. "Introduction: Transforming McLuhan." *Transforming McLuhan: Cultural, Critical, and Postmodern Perspectives*. Ed. Paul Grosswiler. New York: Peter Lang, 2010.

Grube, John. Introduction. *The Double Hook*. By Sheila Watson. 1959. Toronto: McClelland & Stewart, 1969.

Guillory, John. *Cultural Capital: The Problem of Literary Canon Formation*. Chicago: U of Chicago P, 1993.

Gumbrecht, Hans Ulrich. *Production of Presence: What Meaning Cannot Convey*. Stanford, CA: Stanford UP, 2004.

Gumbrecht, Hans Ulrich, and Karl Ludwig Pfeiffer. *Materialities of Communication*. Stanford, CA: Stanford UP, 1994.

H. Marshall McLuhan Papers. MG 31, D 156. Library and Archives Canada.

Hamilton, Sheryl N. "Considering Critical Communication Studies in Canada." *Mediascapes: New Patterns in Canadian Communication*. Ed. Leslie Regan Shade. Toronto: Nelson Education, 2010. 9–26.

Hammond, Adam. "Self Condemned: Wyndham Lewis Hated His Native Canada, but His Ideas Helped Shape the Nation." *The Walrus* October 2010, 78–81.

Havelock, Eric A. *Preface to Plato*. Cambridge, MA: Harvard UP, 1963.

Heise, Ursula K. "Unnatural Ecologies: The Metaphor of the Environment in Media Theory." *Configurations* 10.1 (2002): 149–68.

Herz, Garnet, ed. *Critical Making*. 2012-11-14-1225 ed. 10 vols., 2012.

Heyer, Paul. *Communications and History: Theories of Media, Knowledge, and Civilization*. New York: Greenwood, 1988.

——. *Harold Innis*. Lanham, MD: Rowman & Littlefield, 2003.

——. "Probing a Legacy: McLuhan's Communications/History 25 Years After." *Canadian Journal of Communication* 14.4/5 (1989): 30–45.

Highmore, Ben. "Home Furnishings: Richard Hamilton, Domesticity, and 'Post-Avant-Gardism.'" *Neo-Avant-Garde*. Ed. David Hopkins and Anna Katharina Schafnner. New York: Rodopi, 2006. 243–62.

Hjartarson, Paul, and Shirley Neuman. *The Thinking Heart: The Literary Archive of Wilfred Watson*. Exhibition catalogue. Edmonton: University of Alberta Libraries, 2014.

Hockey, Susan. "The History of Humanities Computing." *A Companion to Digital Humanities*. Ed. Susan Schreibman, Ray Siemens, and John Unsworth. Oxford: Blackwell, 2004. http://www.digitalhumanities.org/companion/.

Hutcheon, Linda. *A Poetic of Postmodernism: History, Theory, Fiction*. New York: Routlegde, 1988.

Hyde, Lewis. *The Gift: Creativity and the Artist in the Modern World*. New York: Vintage Books, 2007.

Jacobs, Jane. "Making a Movie with McLuhan." *Marshall McLuhan: The Man and His Message*. Ed. George Sanderson and Frank Macdonald. Golden, CO: Fulcrum, 1989. 121–23.

Jameson, Fredric. *Fables of Aggression: Wyndham Lewis, the Modernist as Fascist*. Berkeley and London: U of California P, 1979.

——. *Marxism and Form*. Princeton: Princeton UP, 1971.

——. "The Vanishing Mediator: Narrative Structure in Max Weber." *New German Critique*, no. 1 (1973): 52–89.

Jean, Marie-Josée. "The Conceptual Works of Bill Vazan." *Bill Vazan: Walking into the Vanishing Point, Conceptual Art*. Ed. Marie-Josée Jean and Bill Vazan. Montreal: VOX Centre de l'image contemporaine, 2009. 54–60.

Jeffrey, Liss. "The Heat and the Light: Towards a Reassessment of the Contribution of H. Marshall McLuhan." *Canadian Journal of Communication* 14.4/5 (1989): 1–29.

Ji, Yinglin. "Transitivity, Indirection, and Redemption in Sheila Watson's *The Double Hook*." *Style* 39.3 (2005): 348–62.

Jones, Paul. "The Technology Is Not the Cultural Form?: Raymond Williams's Sociological Critique of Marshall McLuhan." *Canadian Journal of Communication* 23.4 (1998): 423–54.

Kamboureli, Smaro. *On the Edge of Genre: The Contemporary Canadian Long Poem*. Toronto: U of Toronto P, 1991.

Kandinsky, Wassily. "Inner Necessity." Trans. Edward Wadsworth. *Blast: Review of the Great English Vortex* 1 (1914): 119–25.

Kanizsa, Gaetano. *Organization in Vision: Essays on Gestalt Perception*. New York: Praeger, 1979.

Kennedy, Paul. "The Enemy in Exile." *Anthology*. CBC Radio. Toronto. 6 March 1982. Radio.

——. "Marshall McLuhan and the Modernist Writers' Legacy." *At the Speed of Light There is Only Illumination: A Reappraisal of Marshall McLuhan*. Ed. John Moss and Linda M. Morra. Ottawa: U of Ottawa P, 2004. 63–83.

Kenner, Hugh. *Wyndham Lewis*. London: Methuen & Co., 1954.

Keziere, Russell. "Cdn Art Mags: Implications and Consequences of the Proliferation of Art Periodicals in Canada." *Criteria* 3 (1977): 9–13.

Kirschenbaum, Matthew G. "What Is Digital Humanities and What's It Doing in English Departments?" *Debates in the Digital Humanities*. Gold. http://dhdebates.gc.cuny.edu/debates/part/2.

Kittler, Friedrich A. *Gramophone, Film, Typewriter*. 1986. Trans. Geoffrey Winthrop-Young and Michael Wutz. Stanford, CA: Stanford UP, 1999.

Kostelanetz, Richard. "ABC of Contemporary Reading." *Poetics Today* 3.3 (1982): 5–46.

Kroetsch, Robert, with Diane Bessai. "Death Is a Happy Ending: A Dialogue in Thirteen Parts." *Figures in a Ground: Canadian Essays on Modern Literature Collected in Honour of Sheila Watson*. Ed. Diane Bessai and David Jackel. Saskatoon: Western Producer Prairie Books, 1978. 206–15.

Kroker, Arthur. *Technology and the Canadian Mind: Innis/McLuhan/Grant*. Montreal: New World Perspectives, 1984.

Kuester, Martin. "Myth and the Postmodernist Turn in Canadian Short Fiction: Sheila Watson, 'Antigone.'" *The Canadian Short Story: Interpretations*. Ed. Reingard M. Nischik. Rochester, NY: Camden House, 2007. 163–73.

——. "(Post-)modern Bricolage: Classical Mythology in Sheila Watson's Short Stories." *Zeitschrift für Aglistik and Americanistik* 42.3 (1994): 225–34.

Lamberti, Elena. "Ezra Pound's *Guide to Kulchur*: la citazione tra sperimentazione modernista e costruzione del 'Nuovo Sapere'!" *Leitmotiv* 2 (2002): 165–79.

——. "Marshall McLuhan and the Modernist Writers' Legacy." *At the Speed of Light There Is Only Illumination: A Reappraisal of Marshall McLuhan*. Ed. John Moss and Linda M. Morra. Ottawa: U of Ottawa P, 2004. 63–83.

——. *Marshall McLuhan's Mosaic: Probing the Literary Origins of Media Studies*. Toronto: U of Toronto P, 2012.

——. "Wyndham Lewis: Blasting Time, Blessing Space." *Marshall McLuhan's Mosaic. Probing the Literary Origins of Media Studies*. Toronto: U of Toronto P, 2012. 213–27.

Lazarsfeld, Paul. "Remarks on Administrative and Critical Research." *Studies in Philosophy and Social Sciences* 9.1 (1941): 2–16.

Legge, Valerie. "Sheila Watson's 'Antigone': Anguished Rituals and Public Disturbances." *Studies in Canadian Literature* 17.2 (1992): 28–46.

Lewis, Wyndham. *America and Cosmic Man*. London: Nicholson and Watson, 1948.

——. *America, I Presume*. New York: Howell, Soskin, 1940.

——. "American Melting Pot." *Contact* 2 (Oct. 1946): 57–60.

——. *Anglosaxony: A League That Works*. Toronto: Ryerson, 1941.

———. *The Art of Being Ruled*. 1926. Ed. Reed Way Dasenbrock. Santa Rosa: Black Sparrow, 1989.

———. ed. *Blast: Review of the Great English Vortex* 1 (1914). Santa Rosa: Black Sparrow, 2000.

———. ed. *Blast: Review of the Great English Vortex* 2 (1915). Santa Rosa: Black Sparrow, 2000.

———. "Canadian Nature and Its Painters." *The Listener* 36.920 (1946): 267–68.

———. *The Childermass*. 1928. London: Calder, 2000.

———. "The Cosmic Uniform of Peace." *The Sewanee Review* 53.4 (Autumn 1945): 507–531.

———. *Hitler*. London: Chatto and Windus, 1931.

———. *The Hitler Cult*. London: Dent, 1939.

———. "Lecture at Institute of Arts, Nov. 30, 1934 [*sic*: 1943] 'The Frontiers of Art,' or, 'The Cultural Melting Pot.'" "America" Folder. C.J. Fox Collection. U of Victoria. Victoria, BC.

———. *Letters of Wyndham Lewis*. Ed. W.K. Rose. Norfolk: New Directions, 1963.

———. *Malign Fiesta*. 1955. London: Calder, 1965.

———. "Manifesto." *Blast: Review of the Great English Vortex* 1 (1914). Santa Rosa: Black Sparrow, 1982. 9–28.

———. *Men Without Art*. London: Cassell, 1934.

———. *The Mind of the Artist, About to Make a Picture*. 1941. Private collection. Mastin, Stacey, and Dilworth 47.

———. *Monstre Gai*. 1955. London: Calder, 1965.

———. "Mr. Lewis's plans." Letter. 1943. "America" Folder. C.J. Fox Collection. U of Victoria. Victoria, BC.

———. "On Canada." *Canadian Literature* 35 (1968): 20–25.

———. "A Review of Contemporary Art." *Blast: Review of the Great English Vortex* 2 (1915): 38–47.

———. *Rude Assignment*. 1954. Ed. Toby Foshay. Santa Rosa: Black Sparrow, 1984.

———. *Self Condemned*. London: Methuen, 1954.

———. *Tarr*. London: Chatto and Windus, 1918. Rpt. London: Calder and Boyars, 1968.

———. *Time and Western Man*. London: Chatto and Windus, 1927. Rpt. Ed. Paul Edwards. Santa Rosa: Black Sparrow, 1993.

———. "Towards an Earth Culture or the Eclectic Culture of the Transition." *The Pavilion: A Contemporary Collection of British Art & Architecture*. Ed. Myfanwy Evans. London: I.T., 1946. 3–11.

———. *The Vulgar Streak*. London: R. Hale, 1941.

Liu, Alan. "Imagining the New Media Encounter." *A Companion to Digital Literary Studies*. Ed. Ray Siemens and Susan Schreibman Oxford: Blackwell, 2008. http://www.digitalhumanities.org/companionDLS/.

———. *The Laws of Cool: Knowledge Work and the Culture of Information*. Chicago: U of Chicago P, 2004.

———. "Where Is Cultural Criticism in the Digital Humanities?" *Debates in the Digital Humanities*. Gold. http://dhdebates.gc.cuny.edu/debates/text/20.

"Long Live the Vortex!" *Blast: Review of the Great English Vortex* 1 (1914): 7–8.

Lukács, Georg. "Expressionism: Its Significance and Decline." 1934. *Essays on Realism*. Trans. Rodney Livingstone. Cambridge, MA: MIT P, 1980. 77–113.

Lunenfeld, Peter, Anne Burdick, Johanna Drucker, Todd Presner, and Jeffrey T. Schnapp. *Digital_Humanities*. Cambridge, MA: MIT P, 2012.

Marchand, Philip. *Marshall McLuhan: The Medium and the Messenger*. Toronto: Random House, 1989.

——. *Marshall McLuhan: The Medium and the Messenger*. 1989. Cambridge: MIT P, 1998.

——. "Reflections on the Canadian Canon." *Open Book* blog. *The National Post* 7 Nov. 2009. Web.

——. "Some Comments on the McLuhan Papers in the National Archives of Canada." *Canadian Journal of Communication* 14.4/5 (1989): 69–72.

Marchessault, Janine. *Marshall McLuhan: Cosmic Media*. London: Sage, 2005.

Marinetti, F.T. "The Pope's Monoplane." *Selected Poems and Related Prose*. Trans. Elizabeth Napier and Barbara R. Studhomle. New Haven: Yale UP, 2002. 43–54.

Mastin, Catharine M. "'The Talented Intruder.'" Mastin, Stacey, and Dilworth. 24–106.

Mastin, Catharine M., Robert Stacey, and Thomas Dilworth, eds. *"The Talented Intruder": Wyndham Lewis in Canada*. Windsor, ON: Art Gallery of Windsor, 1992.

Mbembe, Achille. "What is Postcolonialist Thought?" *Esprit*. 1 September 2008. PDF.

McKercher, Catherine, and Vincent Mosco, eds. *Knowledge Workers in the Information Society*. Lanham, MD: Lexington Books, 2007.

McLuhan, Marshall. "14." *Essential McLuhan*. Ed. Eric McLuhan and Frank Zingrone. Toronto: Anansi, 1995. 197–218.

——. "Art as Anti-Environment." *Art News Annual* 31 (1966): 55–57.

——. "Canada: The Borderline Case." *The Canadian Imagination: Dimensions of a Literary Culture*. Ed. David Staines. Cambridge, MA: Harvard UP, 1977. 226–48.

——. "Canada, the Borderline Case." 1967. McLuhan and Staines 105–23.

——. *Counterblast*. Designed by Harley Parker. Toronto: Self-published, 1954.

——. *Counterblast*. Designed by Harley Parker. 1954. Berlin: Transmediale, 2011.

——. *Counterblast*. Designed by Harley Parker. Toronto: McClelland & Stewart, 1969.

——. "Culture and Technology." *Astronauts of Inner Space: An International Collection of Avant-Garde Activity*. Ed. Geoff Berner. San Francisco: Stolen Paper Review Editions, 1966. 18–19.

——. *Culture Is Our Business*. New York: McGraw-Hill, 1970.

——. "Defrosting Canadian Culture." *American Mercury* March 1952: 91–97.

——. "A Dialogue." Interview with Gerald E. Stearn. *McLuhan: Hot and Cool*. New York: Dial, 1967. 266–302

——. "The Future of Man in the Electric Age." 1965. McLuhan and Staines 56–75.

——. *The Gutenberg Galaxy: The Making of Typographic Man*. 1962. Toronto: U of Toronto P, 2011.

——. "The Humanities in the Electronic Age." *Marshall McLuhan Unbound*. Ed. Eric McLuhan and W. Terrence Gordon. Corte Madera, CA: Ginko, 2005.

———. *The Interior Landscape: The Literary Criticism of Marshall McLuhan (1943–1962)*. Selected, compiled, and edited by Eugene McNamara. New York: McGraw-Hill, 1969.

———. "Introduction To: The Bias of Communication." 1951. *Marshall McLuhan Unbound* Ed. Eric McLuhan and W. Terrence Gordon. Corte Madera, CA: Gingko, 2005.

———. Letter to Sheila Watson, n.d. [Fall 1961]. Sheila Watson fonds, John M. Kelly Library, Special Collections, U of St. Michael's College, box 21, file 2006-01-352.

———. Letter to Sheila Watson, 6 August 1974. Sheila Watson fonds, John M. Kelly Library, Special Collections, U of St. Michael's College, box 21, file 2006-01-352.

———. *Letters of Marshall McLuhan*. Selected and edited by Matie Molinaro, Corinne McLuhan, and William Toye. Toronto: Oxford UP, 1987.

———. "Lewis's Prose Style." *Wyndham Lewis: A Revaluation*. Ed. Jeffrey Meyers. Montreal: McGill-Queen's UP, 1980. 64–67.

———. "The Marfleet Lectures (1967): Part I: Canada, the Borderline Case." McLuhan and Staines 104–22.

———. *The Mechanical Bride: Folklore of Industrial Man*. New York: Vanguard, 1951.

———. *The New American Vortex*. 1948. Unpublished typescript manuscript. Library and Archives Canada, 63.24

———. "Notes on Burroughs." *The Nation* 28 December 1964. 517–19.

———. *Report on Project in Understanding New Media*. Washington: U.S. Office of Education, 1960.

———. "Technology and Environment." *artscanada* 105 (February 1967): 5–7.

———. *Understanding Media: The Extensions of Man*. New York: Signet, 1964.

———. "Wyndham Lewis: His Theory of Art and Communication." *Shenandoah* 4.2/3 (1953): 77–88.

———. "Wyndham Lewis: Lemuel in Lilliput." *Studies in Honour of St. Thomas Aquinas: Key Thinkers and Modern Thought* 2 (1944): 58–72. Rpt. in *The Medium and the Light: Reflections on Religion*. Ed. Eric McLuhan and Jacek Szklarek, 1999. 178–97.

———. "Wyndham Lewis Recalled." *artscanada*. The Society for Art Publications. 1967. LP.

McLuhan, Marshall, and David Carson. *The Book of Probes*. Corte Madera, CA: Gingko, 2003.

McLuhan, Marshall, and Eric McLuhan. *Laws of Media: The New Science*. Toronto: U of Toronto P, 1988.

McLuhan, Marshall, and Harley Parker. *Through the Vanishing Point: Space in Poetry and Painting*. New York: Harper & Row, 1968.

McLuhan, Marshall, and Bruce R. Powers. "The United States and Canada: The Border as a Resonating Interval." *The Global Village: Transformations in World Life and Media in the 21st Century*. New York: Oxford UP, 1989. 145–66.

McLuhan, Marshall with Quentin Fiore and Jerome Agel. *The Medium is the Massage: An Inventory of Effects*. New York: Bantam, 1967.

———. *War and Peace in the Global Village: An Inventory of Some of the Current Spastic Situations That Could Be Eliminated by More Feedforward*. New York: Bantam, 1968.

McLuhan, Marshall with Wilfred Watson. *From Cliché to Archetype*. New York: Viking, 1970.

McLuhan, Stephanie, and David Staines, ed. *Understanding Me: Lectures and Interviews*. By Marshall McLuhan. Toronto: McClelland & Stewart, 2003.

Miller, Judith. "Rummaging in the Sewing Basket of the Gods: Sheila Watson's 'Antigone.'" *Studies in Canadian Literature* 12.2 (1987): 212–21.

Miller, Toby. *Blow up the Humanities*. Philadelphia: Temple UP, 2012.

Molinaro, Matie, Corinne McLuhan, and William Toye, eds. *Letters of Marshall McLuhan*. Toronto: Oxford UP Canada, 1987.

Monk, Philip. *Glamour Is Theft: A User's Guide to General Idea*. Toronto: Art Gallery of York University, 2012.

Monkman, Leslie. "Coyote as Trickster in *The Double Hook*." G. Bowering, ed. 63–69.

Moretti, Franco. "Graphs, Maps, Trees: Abstract Models for Literary History—1." *New Left Review* 24 (November/December 2003): 67–93.

———. "Graphs, Maps, Trees: Abstract Models for Literary History—3." *New Left Review* 28 (July/August 2004): 43–63.

———. "Network Theory, Plot Analysis." Stanford U: Literary Lab, 2011.

Morra, Linda. "The Anti-Trickster in the Work of Sheila Watson, Mordecai Richler, and Gail Anderson-Dargatz." *Troubling Tricksters: Revisioning Critical Conversations*. Ed. Linda Morra and Deanna Reder. Waterloo, ON: Wilfrid Laurier UP, 2010. 77–91.

Morris, Michael. "The Artist as Curator of the Imagination." *artscanada* 220/221 (May 1978): 41.

Morriss, Margaret. "'No Short Cuts': The Evolution of *The Double Hook*." *Canadian Literature* 173 (2002): 54–70.

Moss, John George, and Linda M. Morra. *At the Speed of Light There Is Only Illumination: A Reappraisal of Marshall McLuhan*. Ottawa: U of Ottawa P, 2004.

Mueller, Benjamin. "Hiring That Crosses Disciplines Can Create New Tensions." *The Chronicle of Higher Education* 24 February 2014.

Mumford, Lewis. *Technics and Civilization*. 1934. New York: Harcourt, Brace & World, 1962.

Murphy, J. Stanley. "Wyndham Lewis at Windsor." *Canadian Literature* 35 (Winter 1968): 9–19.

Nesbitt, Bruce. "Displacement in Patrick White and Sheila Watson: Musical and Mythics." *Australian/Canadian Literatures in English: Comparative Perspectives*. Ed. Russell McDougall and Gillian Whitlock. Melbourne: Methuen, 1987. 151–69.

Neuman, Shirley. Introduction. *Figures Cut in Sacred Ground: Illuminati in The Double Hook*. Edmonton: NeWest, 1988. [iii-iv].

Newfield, Jack. "Hippies and New Frontier on 'Desolation Row.'" *The Village Voice* 6 July 1967.

Norris, Ken. "The Beginning of Canadian Modernism." *Canadian Poetry: Studies/ Documents/Reviews* 11 (Fall/Winter): 1982. Canadian Poetry, UWO.ca, Web, 25 March 2011.

O'Keefe, Paul. *Some Sort of Genius: A Life of Wyndham Lewis*. London: Jonathan Cape, 2000.

O'Malley, Tom. "Media History and Media Studies: Aspects of the Development of the Study of Media History in the UK 1945–2000." *Media History* 8.2 (2002): 155–73.

Ondaatje, Michael. *The Collected Works of Billy the Kid: Left-Handed Poems*. Toronto: Anansi, 1970.

Orr, Leonard. "Modernism and the Issue of Periodization." *CLCWeb: Comparative Literature and Culture* 7.1 (2005).

Orwell, George. "The English People." 1942. *In Front of Your Nose: The Collected Essays, Journalism, and Letters of George Orwell*. Vol. 4. Ed. Sonia Orwell and Ian Angus. New York: Harcourt Brace and World, 1968. 1–37.

Patterson, Graeme H. *History and Communications: Harold Innis, Marshall McLuhan, the Interpretation of History*. Toronto: U of Toronto P, 1990.

Peacock, Gordon. "Wilfred Watson and the Modern Canadian Theatre." *Plays at the Iron Bridge, or, The Autobiography of Tom Horror*. Ed. Shirley Neuman. Edmonton: Longspoon and NeWest, 1989. [9]–11.

Pennee, Donna Palmateer. "Canadian Letters, Dead Referents: Reconsidering the Critical Construction of *The Double Hook*." *Essays on Canadian Writing* 51/52 (Winter 1993/Spring 1994): 233–57.

Peters, Benjamin. "And Lead Us Not into Thinking the New Is New: A Bibliographic Case for New Media History." *New Media & Society* 11.1/2 (2009): 13–30.

Peters, John Durham. "Genealogical Notes on 'the Field.'" *Journal of Communication* 43.4 (1993): 132–39.

——. "McLuhan's Grammatical Theology." *Canadian Journal of Communication* 36.2 (2011): 227–42.

Poggioli, Renato. *The Theory of the Avant-Garde*. 1962. Trans. Gerald Fitzgerald. Cambridge: Harvard UP, 1968.

Pound, Ezra. "Come My Cantilations." *Blast: Review of the Great English Vortex* 1 (1914): 45.

——. *Guide to Kulchur*. New York: New Direction Book, 1970.

——. "Vortex." *Blast: Review of the Great English Vortex* 1 (1914): 153–54.

Puchner, Martin. *Poetry of the Revolution: Marx, Manifestos, and the Avant-Gardes*. Princeton: Princeton UP, 2006.

Radu, Anca Raluca. "'More Like a Devil': Coyote in Sheila Watson's *The Double Hook* and Gail Anderson-Dargatz's *The Cure for Death by Lightning*. Open Letter 13th series, 2 (2007): 120–33.

Ratto, Matt. "Critical Making: Conceptual and Material Studies in Technology and Social Life." *The Information Society: An International Journal* 27.4 (2011): 252–60.

Richards, I.A. "The Niceties of Salvation." *Wyndham Lewis and I.A. Richards: A Friendship Documented, 1928–57.* Cambridge: Skate, 1989. 60–64.

Riesman, Paul. "De l'homme typographique à l'homme électronique." *Critique* 225 (Feb. 1966): 172–82.

Rooke, Constance. "Women of The Double Hook." *Fear of the Open Heart: Essays on Contemporary Canadian Writing.* Toronto: Coach House, 1989. 82–92.

Rosenberg, Harold. "Philosophy in a Pop Key." *The New Yorker* 27 February 1965.

Russell, Charles. *The Avant-Garde Today.* Chicago: U Illinois P, 1981.

Sample, Mark. "How liberating to be told your field is dying. You can work in the gloaming, away from the glare. You are the ghoul of academia." 7 April 2014. Tweet.

Schnapp, Jeffrey T. *The Electric Information Age Book: McLuhan/Agel/Fiore and the Experimental Paperback.* 1st ed. New York: Princeton Architectural, 2012.

Scobie, Stephen. *Sheila Watson and Her Works.* Toronto: ECW, 1984.

Selz, Peter. *German Expressionist Painting.* Berkeley: U of California P, 1957.

Sheila Watson fonds. St. Michael's College, U of Toronto.

Sinclair, Upton. *The Jungle.* 1906. London: Penguin, 2006.

Sloan, Johanne. "Bill Vazan's Urban Coordinates." *Bill Vazan: Walking into the Vanishing Point, Conceptual Art.* Ed. Marie-Josée Jean and Bill Vazan. Montreal: VOX Centre de l'image contemporaine, 2009. 86–89.

Stamps, Judith. *Unthinking Modernity: Innis, McLuhan, and the Frankfurt School.* Montreal and Kingston: McGill-Queen's UP, 1995.

Stevens, Peter. *The McGill Movement.* Toronto: Ryerson, 1969.

Stimson, Blake. "For the Love of Abstraction." *Third Text* 22.5 (2008): 639–50.

Strate, Lance, and Edward Wachtel. Introduction. *The Legacy of McLuhan.* Ed. Lance Strate and Edward Wachtel. Creskill, NJ: Hampton, 2005. 1–21.

Test, George A. *Satire: Spirit and Art.* Tampa: U of South Florida P, 1991.

Theall, Donald F. Guest Editor's Introductory Remarks. *Canadian Journal of Communication* 14.4/5 (1989): vii–ix.

——. *The Virtual Marshall McLuhan.* Montreal and Kingston: McGill-Queen's UP, 2001.

Tiessen, Paul. "From Literary Modernism to the Tantramar Marshes: Anticipating McLuhan in British and Canadian Media Theory and Practice." *Canadian Journal of Communication* 18.4 (Fall 1993): 451–67.

——. "'I Want My Story Told': The Sheila Watson Archive, the Reader, and the Search for Voice." *Basements and Attics, Closets and Cyberspace: Explorations in Canadian Women's Archives.* Ed. Linda Morra and Jessica Schagerl. Waterloo, ON: Wilfrid Laurier UP, 2012. 263–80.

——. "'Shall I Say, It Is Necessary to Restore the Dialogue?': Wilfred Watson's Encounter with Marshall McLuhan, 1957–1988." *At the Speed of Light There Is Only Illumination: A Reappraisal of Marshall McLuhan.* Ed. Linda Morra and John Moss. Ottawa: U of Ottawa P, 2004. 95–145.

Toye, William. Annotations and commentary. *Letters of Marshall McLuhan.* Selected and edited by Matie Molinaro, Corinne McLuhan, and William Toye. Toronto: Oxford UP, 1987.

Toupin, Gilles. "La Géographie De Bill Vazan / The Geography of Bill Vazan."
  Vie Des Arts 69 (Winter 1972/73): 60–63, 98–99.

Turcato, Mark. "Confronting the Criticisms: A Survey of Attacks on the Humanities."
  4Humanities.org, 9 October 2012.

Turner, Margaret E. "Fiction, Break, Silence: Language in Sheila Watson's *The Double
  Hook.*" *Ariel* 18.2 (1987): 65–78.

Vanderbilt, Tom. "Affirmative Action." *Artforum* 43.6 (2005): 55–56.

Vazan, Bill. Interview by Adam Welch. 9 March 2012.

Vazan, William. *Worldline 1969–71 / Ligne Mondiale / Eine Linie Die Um Die Welt
  Geht / Una Linea Che Cirola Il Mondo / Una Linea Que Circula El Mundo.*
  Montreal: W. Vazan, 1971.

Veblen, Thorstein. *The Theory of the Middle Class: An Economic Study in the
  Evolution of Institutions.* New York: Macmillan, 1899. Rpt. as *The Theory of the
  Middle Class.* Intro. by C. Wright Mills. New Brunswick, NJ: Transaction, 1992.

Video McLuhan 6. "York University Lecture, 1979." *The Video McLuhan.* Written and
  narrated by Tom Wolfe. McLuhan Productions, 1996. Set of six VHS videotapes.

Wallace, Keith, ed. *Whispered Art History: Twenty Years at the Western Front.*
  Vancouver: Arsenal Pulp, 1993.

Watson, A. John. *Marginal Man: The Dark Vision of Harold Innis.* Toronto:
  U of Toronto P, 2006.

Watson, Rita, and Menahem Blondheim. *The Toronto School of Communication
  Theory: Interpretations, Extensions, Applications.* Toronto: U of Toronto P;
  Jerusalem: Hebrew U Magnes P, 2007.

Watson, Sheila. "And the Four Animals." Toronto: Coach House, 1980. Rpt. in
  Five Stories 71–76.

——. "Antigone." Davey 26–32. Rpt. in *Five Stories* 41–54.

——. "Artist-Ape as Crowd-Master." Davey 115–18.

——. "The Black Farm." Davey 16–25. Rpt. in *Five Stories* 16–25.

——. "Brother Oedipus." Davey 9–15. Rpt. in *Five Stories* 7–20.

——. "Canada and Wyndham Lewis the Artist." Davey 80–96.

——. *Deep Hollow Creek.* Toronto: McClelland & Stewart, 1992.

——. *The Double Hook.* 1959. Toronto: McClelland & Stewart, 2008.

——. *Four Stories.* Toronto Coach House, 1979.

——. *Five Stories.* Toronto: Coach House, 1984.

——. "Gertrude Stein: The Style is the Machine." *White Pelican* 3.4 (Autumn 1973):
  6–14.

——. "The Great War: Wyndham Lewis and the Underground Press." *artscanada*
  24.11 (November 1967).

——. "Interview/Sheila Watson." With Daphne Marlatt, Pierre Coupey, and
  Roy Kiyooka. *Capilano Review* 8/9 (1976): 351–60.

——. Letter to Marshall McLuhan. 20 July 1962. 7593-1-3-E, box 40, file 28, Marshall
  McLuhan fonds. Library and Archives Canada.

——. "Michael Ondaatje: The Mechanization of Death." *White Pelican* 2.4 (Fall 1972):
  56–64.

——. "Myth and Counter-Myth." Davey 119–36.

——. "Power: Nude or Naked." Davey 151–57.

——. "A Question of Portraiture." Rev. of *The Letters of Wyndham Lewis*, edited by W.K. Rose. Davey 43–49.

—— [Doherty, Sheila]. "Rough Answer." *Canadian Forum* 18.212 (1938): 178–80. Rpt. in *A Father's Kingdom. The Complete Short Fiction*. Toronto: McClelland & Stewart, 2004. 10.

——. "The Rumble Seat." Davey 33–40. Rpt. *Five Stories*. Toronto: Coach House, 1984.

——. "Sheila Watson: 'It's What You Say.'" *In Their Words: Interviews with Fourteen Canadian Writers*. By Bruce Meyer and Brian O'Riordon. Toronto: Anansi, 1984. 156–67.

——. "Swift and Ovid: The Development of Metasatire." 1967. Davey 151–57.

——. "Unaccommodated Man." 1973. Davey 97–114.

——. "What I'm Going to Do." 1973. Davey 181–83.

——. "Wyndham Lewis and Expressionism." PhD thesis. U of Toronto, 1965. Rpt. as *Wyndham Lewis and Expressionism*. Waterloo, ON: MLR Editions Canada, 2003. Web. 29 April 2013.

——, ed. *Wyndham Lewis and the Underground Press*. Spec. issue of *artscanada* 114 (November 1967).

Watson, Wilfred. "Education in the Tribal/Global Village." *Twentieth Century Literature* 16.3 (1970): 207–16.

——. *Friday's Child: Poems by Wilfred Watson*. London: Faber and Faber, 1955.

——. *Gramsci x 3*. Edmonton: Longspoon, 1983.

——. "Marshall McLuhan and Multi-Consciousness: The Place Marie Dialogues," *Boundary* 2.3 (Fall 1974): 197–211.

——. *Mass on Cowback*. Edmonton: Longspoon, 1982.

——. "McLuhan's collective wordplay." Typescript draft, 10 pages.

——. "McLuhan's Wordplay." *Canadian Forum* 61.709 (1981): 10–12.

——. *Plays at the Iron Bridge, or, The Autobiography of Tom Horror*. Ed. Shirley Neuman. Edmonton: Longspoon and NeWest, 1989.

——. "The Preface: On Radical Absurdity." *Canadian Literature* 30 (Autumn 1966): 36–44.

——. "Wail for Two Pedestals: A Farce in Three Acts." *The Humanities Association Bulletin* 16.2 (1965): 61–92.

Wees, William C. *Vorticism and the English Avant-Garde*. Toronto: U of Toronto P, 1972.

Weightman, John. *Poets, Prophets, and Revolutionaries: The Literary Avant-Garde from Rimbaud through Postmodernism*. Oxford: Oxford UP, 1985.

Weismann, Jordan. "The Best Argument for Studying English? The Employment Numbers." *The Atlantic* 25 June 2013.

Weisstein, Ulrich, ed. *Expressionism as an International Literary Phenomenon: 21 Essays and a Bibliography*. Paris and Budapest: Didier and Akademai Kiado, 1973.

——. "'Vorticism: Expressionism English Style." *Yearbook of Comparative and General Literature* 13 (1964): 28–40. Rpt. in Weisstein 167–76.

Wershler, Darren. "Marshall McLuhan and the Economies of Knowledge." *Canadian Journal of Communication* 37.4 (2012): 625–36.

——. "News That Stays News: Marshall McLuhan and Media Poetics." *The Journal of Electronic Publishing* 14.2 (2011).

Westgate, Barry. Review of *O holy ghost dip your finger in the blood of Canada and write, I Love You*. By Wilfred Watson. *Edmonton Journal* 24 November 1967.

Willmott, Glenn. Afterword. *A Father's Kingdom: The Complete Short Fiction*. By Sheila Watson. Toronto: McClelland & Stewart, 2004. 87–98.

——. *McLuhan, or Modernism in Reverse*. Toronto: U of Toronto P, 1996.

——. "The Nature of Modernism in *Deep Hollow Creek*." *Canadian Literature* 146 (1995): 30–48.

——. "Sheila Watson, Aboriginal Discourse, and Cosmopolitan Modernism." *The Canadian Modernists Meet*. Ed. Dean Irvine. Ottawa: U of Ottawa P, 2005. 101–16.

Whittaker, Robin C., ed. *Hot Thespian Action! Ten Premiere Plays from Walterdale Playhouse*. Edmonton: Athabasca UP, 2008.

Williams, Raymond. "Dominant, Residual, and Emergent." *Marxism and Literature*. Oxford: Oxford UP, 1977. 121–27.

Wolf, Gary. "The Wisdom of Saint Marshall, the Holy Fool." *Wired* 1 January 1996.

Wood, Gaby. *Living Dolls: A Magical History of the Quest for Mechanical Life*. London: Faber and Faber, 2002.

Woodcock, George, ed. *Wyndham Lewis in Canada*. Vancouver: U of British Columbia Publications Centre, 1971.

——, ed. *Wyndham Lewis in Canada*. Spec. issue of *Canadian Literature* 35 (Winter 1968).

Wong, Paul. "Void Space: New Media (Out of Context)." *Vancouver Art and Artists: 1931–1983*. Vancouver: Vancouver Art Gallery, 1983. 306–11.

Worringer, Wilhelm. *Abstraction and Empathy: A Contribution to the Psychology of Style*. 1908. Trans. Michael Bullock. London: Routledge and Kegan Paul, 1953.

Zielinski, Siegfried. "Modelling Media for Ignatius Loyola: A Case Study on Athanasius Kircher's World Apparatus between the Imaginary and the Real." Trans. Nicholas Grindell. *Book of Imaginary Media: Excavating the Dream of the Ultimate Communication Medium*. Ed. Eric Kluitenberg. Rotterdam and London: NAi/Art Data, 2006. 28–55.

Contributors

Gregory Betts is the Chancellor's Chair for Research Excellence at Brock University, where he is also the director of the Centre for Canadian Studies, and an associate professor in the Department of English Language and Literature. He is the author of *Avant-Garde Canadian Literature: The Early Manifestations* (University of Toronto Press, 2013), editor of six critical editions of experimental Canadian literature, and currently serves as the curator of the bpNichol.ca digital archive.

Adam Hammond is assistant professor in the Department of English and Comparative Literature at San Diego State University, where his work focuses on British modernism and digital humanities. He is author of *Literature in the Digital Age: A Critical Introduction* (Cambridge University Press, 2016) and co-author of *Modernism: Keywords* (Wiley-Blackwell, 2014).

Paul Hjartarson is professor emeritus in English and Film Studies at the University of Alberta. His scholarly work is on life writing, Canadian literature, modernism, print culture, and the digital humanities. His most recent book, co-authored with Shirley Neuman, is *The Thinking Heart: The Literary Archive of Wilfred Watson* (University of Alberta Press, 2014).

Dean Irvine is an associate professor in the Department of English at Dalhousie University. Author and editor of books on Canadian modernism, he is also the director of Editing Modernism in Canada, Agile Humanities Agency, and the University of Ottawa Press's Canadian Literature Collection.

Elena Lamberti teaches North American literature and media studies at the University of Bologna, Italy. Her areas of research include Anglo-American modernism, literature and technology, cultural memory, and war literature. Her volume *Marshall McLuhan's Mosaic: Probing the Literary Origins of Media Studies* (University of Toronto Press) was a finalist for the 2013 Canada Prizes.

Philip Monk is director of the Art Gallery of York University in Toronto. He has written eleven books, the most recent being *Glamour Is Theft: A User's Guide to General Idea* (2012) and *Is Toronto Burning?: Three Years in the Making (and Unmaking) of the Toronto Art Scene* (2015). As well, he has written dozens of catalogues on international and Canadian artists.

Linda M. Morra is full professor in the Department of English at Bishop's University. Her publications include *Unarrested Archives: Case Studies in Twentieth-Century Authorship* (2014), which was a finalist for the Gabrielle Roy Prize in 2015, and a co-edited collection of essays called *Basements and Attics, Closets and Cyberspace: Explorations in Canadian Women's Archives* (2012).

Kristine Smitka teaches in the Department of English and Film Studies at the University of Alberta. To better understand the relationship between print and digital forms of publishing, her research focuses on the paperback book as a medium that defies the old vs. new media binary.

Leon Surette taught at the University of British Columbia (1962–1964), the University of Guelph (1966–1970), Queen's University in Kingston, ON (1979–1980), and Western University until mandatory retirement in July 2004. He has published seven books, five of which are currently available. The latest is *Art in the Age of the Machine* (self-published e-book, Amazon, 2013).

Paul Tiessen is professor emeritus, English and Film Studies, Wilfrid Laurier University. He has published essays on Wyndham Lewis, Sheila Watson, Marshall McLuhan, and Wilfred Watson. Currently, he is an editorial collaborator on a trilogy of novels by Malcolm Lowry, while also working on a study of McLuhan and spectatorship.

Adam Welch is an associate curator, Canadian Art at the National Gallery of Canada. He is currently working toward his doctorate in art history at the University of Toronto, with a dissertation titled "'Borderline Research': Art between Canada and the United States, 1965–1975."

Darren Wershler is an associate professor at Concordia University, the University Research Chair in Media and Contemporary Literature, the Provost's Fellow for Interdisciplinarity, and, with Charles Acland, the co-founder and co-coordinator of the Concordia Media History Research Centre. He is the editor of over thirty-five books and the author or co-author of twelve books, including *The Iron Whim: A Fragmented History of Typewriting*, and Guy Maddin's *My Winnipeg*.

Index

MacDonald, W. L., 208n9
Mailer, Norman, 30–31
Marchand, Philip
  on McLuhan as professor, 15, 20
  on McLuhan-Innis, 261–62
  on McLuhan's reputation, 259
  on S. Watson, 80
  on W. Watson-McLuhan friendship,
    109, 113, 130, 131, 133
Marey, Étienne-Jules, 239–40, 246n5
Massey Report, 74, 88
Mass on Cowback (Watson), 141
Mbembe, Achille, 82
McLuhan, Eric, 104n11, 129, 130, 134,
    135, 136
McLuhan, Marshall
  as avant-garde writer, 26–29, 32,
    34–35, 36–37, 255
  and belief in interdisciplinarity,
    273–74
  belief that sensory balance is altered
    by mode of communication, 5–6, 7,
    8–10, 11, 14
  brain tumour of, 127
  on Canada's position in avant-garde,
    24–25, 30
  collaboration with W. Watson on
    From Cliché to Archetype, 117, 120,
    123, 124–27, 128, 129–30, 131–32,
    133–36, 143
  communication theories in *The
    Gutenberg Galaxy*, 5–14
  correspondence with C. Bissell,
    89–90
  correspondence with E. Pound, 27,
    28, 37n2, 72
  correspondence with W. Watson on
    theatre, 115–16, 117–19, 120–23,
    124, 129
  and cosmopolis idea, 36
  criticism of Canada, 46–48, 51–52
  and DEW Line, 90, 91, 97–98, 104n11
  dialogue with S. Watson on
    photography, 233–37

and digital humanities, 270
disorientation produced by writing of,
    30–31, 32–33
and distant early warning system,
    xxvii–xxviii, 89, 90, 91, 97–98
fame of, 114–15, 133
founding of Centre for Culture and
    Technology, xix–xx, 20, 31, 35, 129
friendship with W. Watson, xviii,
    108–09, 110, 111–13, 129, 144–46
on gestalt, 236
and globalization, 48
and global village, 47, 71–72
and The Gutenberg Galaxy, 3, 5–14,
    72, 238
and H. Innis, 15n1, 15n2, 260–62
idea of Canada as artist figure, 36, 87,
    88–91, 98, 103
and image of sleepwalking public,
    25–26, 41, 90
influence of E. A. Poe on, 26
influence of L. Mumford on, 7–8
influence of S. Giedion on, 8, 246n4
influence of W. Lewis on, 21–23, 27,
    32, 70, 71–72, 74, 177
influence on General Idea, 149–52,
    154–55, 163
influence on S. Watson, 214, 227n5
influence on W. Watson, 107, 108
interest in puns, 145
on language, 33–34, 223
legacy in communication studies,
    251, 255, 258–63
legacy in literary studies, 251, 254,
    255–56
legacy of, xx–xxii
legacy of his communication theories,
    13–14
as literary critic, 255
on making communication, 34,
    211–13, 227n6
meaning of 'cool' to, 26, 37n5
modernism and, 41–45, 48, 56

Other Titles from The University of Alberta Press

Landscapes of War and Memory
The Two World Wars in Canadian Literature and the Arts, 1977–2007

SHERRILL GRACE

636 pages | 30 B&W photographs, notes, bibliography, index
978–1–77212–000–4 | $49.95 (T) paper
War and Cultural Memory | Literature, Visual Arts & Film

Magazines, Travel, and Middlebrow Culture
Canadian Periodicals in English and French, 1925–1960

FAYE HAMMILL & MICHELLE SMITH

256 pages | 32 colour photographs, notes, bibliography, index
Copublished with Liverpool University Press
978–1–77212–083–7 | $49.95 (T) paper
Cultural Studies | Travel

The Thinking Heart
The Literary Archive of Wilfred Watson

PAUL HJARTARSON & SHIRLEY NEUMAN

160 pages | Over 100 colour illustrations
Published by the Bruce Peel Special Collections Library
978–1–55195–339–7 | $34.95 (T) paper
Biography | Archives | Literature